DIASPORIC COMMUNICATION IN THE DIGITAL AGE

Abiodun Adeniyi

Published by New Generation Publishing in 2021

Copyright © Abiodun Adeniyi 2021

First Edition

Paperback ISBN: 978-1-80031-157-2
Hardback ISBN: 978-1-80031-156-5

www.newgeneration-publishing.com

New Generation Publishing

Contents

ACKNOWLEDGEMENTS

This work is essentially a product of a Ph.D. research in the university of Leeds, somewhat updated to capture contemporary essences. I conceive it (for further ease of access), as an offline variant of the wide online presence it has since enjoyed, courtesy of the White Rose E-theses Online, and more; and aside from the patches of expositions it has received in peer-reviewed journals.

That said, God deserves praises for seeing me through the anxieties of the research programme. To my parents, the late Mr. Lawrence Adeniyi Okoh and Mrs. Lucy Adeniyi Okoh. I am thankful for bequeathing an education legacy. To the Foreign and Commonwealth Office (FCO), which in 2003 awarded me the British Chevening Scholarship that eventually revived this old dream, I doff my hats. For my siblings, Mrs. Mary Ogunleye (nee Adeniyi) (1959-2005) and Raphael Adeniyi, (1968-2004), who died while this project was on, your absences these times are sorrowful. To my elder sister, Mrs. Elizabeth Oloruntobi (nee Adeniyi) my brother, Pastor Michael Adeniyi and younger sister, Mrs. Christiana Obafemi (nee Adeniyi) (now also late), accept my thanks for the tabs in the distance. Then for my immediate family, Doyinsola, Oyindamola, Oyinkansola and mum, Cleopatra, the breathers through an endless radiation of innocence, and a can-do spirit are profoundly appreciated.

For my supervisors, Drs. Myria Georgiou (lead) and Stephen Lax, many credits for the intellectual directions. The diligence, patience and criticisms of Professor Georgiou is noteworthy for sustaining the zeal through the trying research years. Loads of thanks, Myria! Thanks also to Dr. Robin Brown, who as Head of School offered a last-minute Master's Degree place that preceded this project. Professor Stephen Coleman's interest in this work was also gratifying, just as Professor Katharine Sarikakis was not only inspiring but also marvelous as an academic guiding light. The Institute of Communication Studies'(ICS) fund was easing.

I need also appreciate many more persons for one form of support or the other. Beyond the limitations of space, memory would hamper a comprehensive collection. However, a representative list would suffice. To Dr. and Mrs. Felix Oloniyon Akande, I thank you for those encouraging calls. And thank you Barrister Olugbenga Ajayi for administering my Nigerian affairs in my absence. For my pal, Chief Henry Ugbolue, thanks for reminding me of the success dream. Then for Mr. Waziri Adio, Dr. Ambrose Akor, Mr. Olusegun Adeniyi, Professors Ebenezer Obadare, Wale Adebanwi, Ahmed Balogun, Mercy Ette, Gbenga Oduntan, Ola Ogunyemi, Adeolu Durotoye, Tayo Olakanmi, and Akin Adesokan, I am grateful. Dr. Wunmi Bewaji, Kabiyesi Oba Adedokun Abolarin, Mr. Olugbenga

Odugbesan, Commissioner of Police, Idowu Owohunwa, Pastor Olamide Asiwaju, your reminders on the worth of letters are memorable. Professor Adesina Azeez deserves special praises for valuable last-minute suggestions and for his search for undotted tees and uncrossed ies.

Thanks also to my colleagues, Fabro Steibel for initial helps with MS word, and to Stephen McDermott for those suggestions on expressions. Fred also deserves praises for his useful expertise on MS word. So, does Jacob Udo Jacob, May Jacob and Qian Gong and my other colleagues for collegiality. To former Rivers State Governor, Dr. Peter Odili, Senator Tokunbo Afikuyomi and House of Representative Member, Chief Chudi Offodile, I am honoured by your concerns despite state duties. I need also thank Dr. Halilu Hamman, whose son's christening ceremony in Holborn Terrace, Leeds, became a venue to arrange interviews with some participants, and Mr. Dupe Ashama that helped in snowballing in London and other interviewees and survey questions respondents for their time. Many thanks to Professors Ken Amaechi (University of Edinburgh), Kole Ade-Odutola (Florida State University), who provided useful advice on publishing, and to Channels TV Chairman, Dr. John Momoh, OON, for his paternal roles. If you expect a mention here, accept my thanks as well.

*To my daughters, Doyinsola, Oyindamola
and Oyinkansola, and mum, Cleopatra*

List of Abbreviations

AIT: African Independent Television
ANA: Association of Nigerians Abroad
AOL: America On line
AU: African Union
AUK: Arewa United Kingdom
BBC: British Broadcasting Corporation
BEI: Bureau for External Aid
BEN: Bright Entertainment Network
C&S: Cherubim and Seraphim
CAC: Christ Apostolic Church
CCDI: Community Conservation and Development Initiative
CE: Christ Embassy
CNN: Cable Network News
DHL: Dalsey, Hillblom and Lynn
DLBC: Deeper Life Bible Church
DVD: Digital Versatile Disc or Digital Video Disc
EC: Eko Club
EPA: Egba People's Association
EU: European Union
FEPA: Federal Environmental Protection Agency
GDP: Gross Domestic Product
GNP: Gross National Product
HIV/AIDS: Human Immunodeficiency Virus/Acquired Immune Deficiency syndrome
ICAN: Igbo Community Association of Nigeria
ICC: International Call Cards
ICT: Information and Communications Technology
IFU: Ife Descendants Union
IJA: Ijaw People's Association
IMF: International Monetary Fund
IND: Immigration and Nationality Directorate
INGO: International Non-Governmental Organisation
IPA: Igbomina People's Association
IPA: Itsekiri People's Association

IT: Information Technology
IU: Ilaje Union
KICC: Kingsway International Christian Centre
KU: Kwara Union
MFM: Mountain of Fire and Miracles
MOSOP: Movement for the Survival of Ogoni People
NADECO: National Democratic Coalition
NCL: Nigeria Community Leeds
NDI: National Democratic Institute
NGO: Non-governmental Organisation
NIDO: Nigerian in Diaspora Organisation
NIDOE: Nigerian in Diaspora Organisation Europe
NITPA: Nigerian Information Technology Professionals in America
NTA: Nigeria Television Authority
OBJ: Olusegun Obasanjo
ODU: Ogidi Development Union
ODU: Owo Descendants Union
OHO: Oduduwa Heritage Organisation
OIA: Ose Indigenes Association
ONS: Office of National Statistics
PC: Personal Computers
RCCG: Redeemed Christian Church of God
SMS: Short Messaging Service
TNC: Transnational Corporations
UAE: United Arab Emirate
UK: United Kingdom
UN: United Nations
URLS: Uniform Resource Identifiers
USA: United States of America
UU: Urhobo Union
VOIP: Voice over Internet Protocol
WB: World Bank
WWW: World Wide Web

List of Figures

INTRODUCTION

This work is about Internet uses and potentials for transnational connections; for the development of a sense of nationalism; and for the construction of identity. Its focal point is on the case of the Nigerian diaspora. Though focussing mainly on the Internet, the role of other media are also highlighted in order to understand the complexities of long distance communication and the meanings of mediated connection, within the broader context of international communications. The work analyses migrants' media and communication technologies' uses and appropriations in a triangular framework of many possibilities for longing and belonging, involving communication practices that connect migrants with Nigeria, the hostland and with each other. The project employs qualitative and quantitative research methods, which include interviews, participant observation and survey in an attempt to locate the practices and the meanings of Internet connection and online media activities.

Though the work explains communication practices through the people's use of the Internet, the uses are still not all pervasive. While identifying limitations in access and appropriations of the Internet, the project notes the significant role of online communication (and exchange) in the construction of Nigerian migrants' identities. It also demonstrates how the online space becomes a hospitable location for constructing a complex sense of belonging that includes, at the same time, a sense of Nigerian nationalism and a transnational attachment to a community of fellow diasporic subjects, living and participating in dispersed hostlands. The research shows that even though the Internet is yet to permeate all dimensions of communication, it still plays an increasingly significant role for many, particularly for migrants and diasporas. Such creative appropriations might include the construction of consistent and sometimes conflicting narratives. While focusing on diasporic and migrant communication practices, the thesis argues that advanced possibilities for creativity, connectivity and imaginings of belonging emerge in new media environments. At the same time, the Internet – like all individual media – comes with limitations in access, in relevance and in its potential for combating experiences of exclusion and deterritorialisation, and thus the celebration of its liberating effect is yet to become a reality.

OVERVIEW

Communication technologies are changing fast with direct and indirect consequences for human interaction, knowledge and understanding of each other and of the world. The Internet sits on a pedestal as the latest, widely celebrated, full of potentials technology that can arguably bridge gaps between time and space (Giddens, 1990; Harvey, 1990) and bring people closer into meaningful relations (Rheingold, 1993) and to sustain transnational imagined communities (Karim, 2003; Tsaliki, 2003; Georgiou, 2006). Are these claims valid and if so, what is the degree of separation and the degree of connection that Internet communication allows? Who benefits from online connectivity and who losses? Is the Internet really this medium, which can offer individuals and groups so much more than the other media? And more importantly, is this ultimately transnational medium changing the experience of the world, distance, mobility and belonging for people who are mostly on the move, but not in control of globalisation (Massey, 1995): the migrants and diasporas? Are there hierarchies within transnational groups and their communication practices, inclusion, exclusion and different priorities or restrictions? With these questions in mind, I develop this specific study focusing on one of the least studied within the context of communication, migration and diaspora studies: the Nigerian diaspora[1] and its communication practices online.

The research examines whether Nigerian migrants' connection with the *homeland*[2] is advanced through Internet communication. The study focuses more particularly on the ways Nigerian migrants engage with the Internet and the medium's role in the processes of identity construction and their sense of nationalism and experience of transnationalism. Furthermore, it explores what is unique about the Internet and how it can function as a connection medium across dispersed groups. Is the Internet more or less important than other media, such as television, radio, and the press, in negotiating belonging and identity in transnational contexts? Or does it complement other media?

---

[1] Can Nigerian migrants be a diaspora just yet? It may be to the extent that they fit into the new group of voluntary economic migrants increasingly regarded as diasporas. They may not, however, be if strictly analysed from the viewpoint of the traditional Jewish archetype. The debate on how the term has become dynamic provides ample room for choice of use. This is, however, not an excuse for uncritical use (Braziel and Mannur, eds, 2003). While this work proposes that a Nigerian diaspora is emerging, their characteristics somewhat resembling Turks in Europe (Robins and Aksoy, 2003) are also evident. It means, therefore, that while they are an emerging diaspora, they are nevertheless migrants in the first instance. This allows discretionary use to describe their otherness in hostland, or their search for a temporary or permanent home in hostland.

[2] *Homeland* is not necessarily a fixed location, but could be a place for possible imagination and belonging. In this work, it appears in italics because its construction process is subjective and relates more to emotional affiliation rather than a real location.

EXAMINING INTERNATIONAL COMMUNICATION

International communications is advancing our insights into dispersed and distant peoples cultures and societies (Castells, 1996, 2001; Thussu, 2001, 2007) through interactions facilitated by different forms of communication. The processes of media production and consumption in different places, physical and virtual crossings of space lead to complex interactions with the "absent other" (Giddens, 1990:18-21). These complexities are, however, not receiving the attention they deserve in international communications' literature. Other than this is that representations of some distant people are skewed. The skewed representations are ironically understood through the consumption and appropriation of modern media. The unequal involvement in the dominant activities in the new age of "complex connectivity" (Tomlinson, 1999), further confirms the uneven representations. Analyses of these global activities include the transnational movement of people and capital (Glick Schiller, et al, 1992; Portes, 1996, 1997; Vertovec, 1999) and diasporic experiences (Gilroy, 1993, 1997, 2000; Cohen, 1997; Brah, 1996). The rise and decline of nation, and the question of nationalism (Gellner, 1983; Anderson, 1983, 1998; Smith, 1995, 1999) are also important in our bid to analyse global trends. Conceptualisation and experience of individual and collective subjectivities are as well changing in the context of globalisation (Giddens, 1990, 1991; Castells, 1996, 2000; Hall, 1990, 1996; Gilroy, 1993, 1997). Yet most analyses of these changes are situated in the Western world. However, in order to understand both international communications and global change, we need to expand our analyses to cover the experiences of those at the margin of development.

More particularly, the study of migrants and diasporic experiences are important in the context of both globalisation and international communications. On one hand, this study can help us understand the connections between human mobility and the challenges to nation-states and ideologies of nationalism. On the other hand, the study helps us understand subjectivity and identity in the context of transnationalism. Diaspora and migration give us access to experiences of groups otherwise marginal and inaccessible and further advance our understanding of community and communication in global context. This study consequently focuses on Nigerian migrants, and investigates meanings of engagement with a new medium like the Internet. These meanings are most importantly in relation to connections, nationalism, transnationalism and identity. However, the complexity of these areas cannot be exhaustively covered here. But I focus on these areas as they connect social life that the media partly facilitates. The research notes that Nigerian migrants, like all migrants, are, of course, not located in the *homeland.* Their emotional, mediated and physical mobility between the country of origin, the country of settlement and other location, creates a context for imagining and belonging. On one hand, the *homeland* is constantly constructed through mediation and everyday imaginings of a community. On the other hand, experience in the hostland[3], and struggle for economic emancipation and social integration interrupt what could be a continuous link with the *homeland*. The mediation of relationships between the *homeland* and hostland, between themselves and with the host country, could create emotional stability. The stability is often achieved through the media, sometimes the Internet in particular, which is the focus of this work. Of what purpose therefore, is the framework and focal point of the study?

This work argues that the Nigerian diaspora is an important case study, as a global, highly mediated community, originating in the global periphery and currently residing in the global core (Galtung, 1971:83, cited in Thussu, 2001:65). International communications studies focus on the activities of states and corporations that essentially emanate from the centre. This work comes as an important endeavour in the process of determining the composition of mediation not between and within the metropolis, but partly between the metropolis and the marginal societies, while exploring the human experiences, interpersonal and community communication. The case study allows us to explore the potentials of new technologies for economic and social development, and for groups with limited financial resources. In addition, for many diasporic and migrant groups, the Internet is the only medium that connects them to news and current affairs in the *homeland*, as there is limited and costly access to other media, such as television, radio, and the press. Besides, the Internet enables real time interaction, networking, storage, sharing and retrieving of data. For these reasons, the research aims to expand the understanding of the processes of online mediation of distance. Taking that Nigerians are not alone in a position of relative disadvantage, I shall now explain why this case is chosen over others.

WHY THE NIGERIAN CASE

The Nigerian case is significant primarily because of its huge migrant population. A nation of about 140 million people (accessed at www.prb.org on 13/04/2007), Nigeria is reputedly "Africa's equivalent to Brazil, India

---

[3] Hostland refers to the base of the migrant. In most cases, they are Western counties. In the particular case of this work, it refers to Britain, which is used as a case for mapping the migrants' agencies. The research also notes attempts to replace the word host society with "settlement society" (AHRB Papers, 2004). The argument is that the word host makes diasporas look like "parasites". Therefore, changing it to settlement society seems more considerate. While diasporas may not essentially be parasites, the continual challenges of integration make them troubled people. This uneasy experience does not, therefore, qualify them simply as settlers, but as people differentiated from natives, which is why I favour the idea of their being hosted.

and Indonesia" (Maier, 2000, xix-xx). The largest country in West Africa, its landmass covers an area of about 923,768 sq.km. Nigeria's population, Castells writes, accounts for "one-fifth of the total population of sub-Saharan Africa" (2000: 101). The United Nations (UN) notes the country as the ninth most densely populated country in the world. Besides, one of every four Africans is likely to be a Nigerian (accessed at www.un.org on 25/09/07). These facts make the country notable in the entire African continent, with its government voice having substantial weight in the continents' affairs. Nigeria's fate, according to Castells again, "is likely to condition the future" (2000: 101) of the continent. The country has however being in a long period of political and economic crises. Military dictatorships have been a major obstacle to its growth.

Nigeria gained political independence from Britain in 1960. The military was in charge for 30 out of its 46 post-independent years. Nigerians, Castells argues further "were poorer in 1995 than at independence, their per capita income having declined by 22 percent between 1973 (date of increase in world oil prices) and 1987 (date of economic adjustment programme" (2000: 104). The world Bank 2001 report puts Nigeria amongst the "20 poorest countries in the world with the GDP of US$41.2 billion and a GNP per capita of about US$260" (cited in CCDI, 2003: 5). Partly responsible for the poor state is poor leadership (Achebe, 1983). The outcome of this has been a prevailing widespread corruption, high rate of crime, poor infrastructure, dearth of utilities, frequent assassinations and increasing fraud in public life (Ajibewa and Akinrinade, 2003). The ills have incidentally being associated with both the military rulers and the shorter period of civilian rule. Many frustrated citizens fed up with failures of successive governments opt for migration as a solution. Maier notes:

> Millions of Nigerians, including much of the cream of the educated and business elite, have fled their country to escape impoverishments and political repression. Most live in the United States and Europe, although almost every country has a Nigerian community (2000: xxiii).

Many of the migrants are indeed moving in search of better economic life, partly belonging therefore to the population of the world poor who "migrate to seek security" (Seabrook, 2003:91). Over the years as a result, large numbers of this migrant population have resettled in many Western countries. Many are still moving, in what they conceive as an immediate and long-term solution to a life of high quality. This is expected through good healthcare, qualitative education, regular power supply, security of lives and properties, good roads, and drinkable water. These migrants are however not attracting much attention in the academia. Contributions like this work will no doubt expand the understanding of globalisation, through the perspective of communication, as a key element of global connectivity, economy and culture.

Significant again is the political state of the country. Nigerian governments have alternated between military regimes and civil administration. As earlier said, the military has ruled for more than half of Nigeria's post independent years. The military influence reigns in the brief period of civil rule. This is either through a return of past military rulers as civil leaders, like in the case of Olusegun Obasanjo (who ruled between 1976 and 1979, as military head of state, and 1999 and 2007 as civilian president); or through influencing the emergence of civil heads. Obasanjo, who was himself favoured to take over power by the outgoing military elite in 1999, subsequently supported the emergence of a civilian successor in 2007, who is Alhaji Umar Yar'adua. The country has been under civil democratic rule since 1999. In effect, military repression has always hindered not only a free press, but also freedom of expression. In the thick of military rule, many newspaper houses were shut. Journalists were jailed, often without trial. Killings of reporters were as well frequent. Many publishers left business, escaped or towed military governments' line[4]. Often, some elected governments harass the press. These hindrances mix with limitations of the economy and a relatively traditional social structure to restrict the freedom of the Nigerian press (Faringer, 1991; Jong-Elliot, 1997). The result of this situation is a covert or overt yearning amongst practitioners and the citizenry for freedom-a freedom to disseminate information and one to exercise the right to be heard, as enshrined in the Universal Declaration of Human Rights[5]. Organising traditional means of communication from outside the country is always difficult as well. That is why the Internet has become an alternative for the exercise of freedom of expression. It is an option not only because of its capacity to connect users in distant places, other than the *homeland* location, but also because of the difficulty to regulate and censor. The Internet has become important to them because it eliminates fears of dangerous consequences often experienced by the critical mainstream media practitioners in the *homeland*. Its relative low cost of use is an additional advantage, as it reduces the economic strains that

---

[4] Some newspapers shut down at one time or the other in the lethal days of military rule were *The Guardian* (of Nigeria); *The Punch*; and the *National Concord*. Some journalists detained without trial included Mohammed Adamu, Godwin Akproko, Osa Director, Akin Adesokan, and Austin Uganwa. Those jailed for alleged participation in a military coup, as "accessory after the fact of treason", were Chris Anyanwu, Kunle Ajibade, George Mba, Ben Charles Obi, and Niran Malaoulu. Amongst tens that were briefly detained or questioned for publishing "unsuitable" stories included this researcher, Henry Ugbolue, Femi Adeoti, and Wahab Gbadamosi. On the escaping list at one time or the other were Nduka Obaigbena, Bayo Onanuga, Dapo Olorunyomi, Dele Momodu, and Alex Kabba. Bagauda Kaltho was not that lucky: he was killed.

[5] The rights states: "Everyone has the right to freedom of opinion and expression: this right includes freedom to hold opinions without interference, and impart information and ideas through any media regardless of frontiers". (Accessed at http://www.article19.org on 19/04/2008).

persistently hinder smooth operations of *homeland* media (Faringer, 1991).

This case is important for a number of other reasons as well. Analyses of Nigerian migrants have not been studied like other dispersal cases in history. Nigerians have not been given attention like, for instance, the Jewish, the Greeks, the Armenians, the Chinese in South-East Asia, the Cubans in America, the Turks in Germany, the Maghrebs in France or the Pakistanis in Britain. This is a migration case, which is rather too large to be a simple element of the African diaspora. The Nigerian diaspora case is important because it is coming from a massive movement of people, easily classified amongst new diasporas, or migrant groups. These new diasporas arise not through extreme occurrences that are life threatening, but because of economic crises in their countries of origin. Modern literature on diasporas emphasises the question of life being at risk to account for dislocation, with classic cases like the Jewish as archetypes (Safran, 1991; Cohen, 1997; Gilroy, 1993, 1997). It is reasonable to argue that the economic pains of some migrant groups like the Nigerians are no less threatening to life than the traumas of exile and prosecution shared by the archetypical diasporas. This can be so because economic deprivation prevents good quality of life. The emerging diasporic condition arising from economic problems as in the case of the Nigerians therefore demands further attention.

The new experiences of upsetting dislocation need proper contextualisation. With a growing population, plagued by poverty, Nigeria migrants are notable in studies of modern migration. The prominence they have is principally in literature on African migration to the West (Castles and Miller, 1993; Stalker, 2001; Sheffer, 2003). In addition, if the number of its migrants are many (Maier, 2000) and vibrant, would it not be appropriate as a case for the examination of hostland versus *homeland* communication relationships? The mediation potential of the Internet becomes important as a focus. This is because the technology is new, non-linear, non-hierarchical, convergent, cheaper, and ultimately transnational. The Internet is, therefore, more accessible to the migrants than some other more costly technologies. It also guarantees communication between many people, across diverse geographies, even with time differences (Jones, 1997; Castells, 2001). It is important to investigate whether migrants who engage with the Internet are able to effectively network with the *homeland*. As a people that suffer from a representation of being crime-prone in many Western societies (Peel, 2006; Adebanwi, 2001), how essentialist can this image be in a world where new technological potentials and opportunities create many more diverse possibilities for representation?

Communication keeps expanding over space and time and the Internet is not the only transnational medium. The telegraph was a key discovery that began long distance, speed of light communication (Winston, 1998; Lax, 2001). Invented in 1832 by Samuel Morse, it was popular in use amongst merchants, corporations and governments. The coming of the telegraph reduced the previous role of postal services for long distance communication. An old form of international communications, the telegraph led the way for exchange of information amongst nations through the written word. The dissemination of messages across long distances began through sound with the invention of the telephone in 1876. An initiative of Alexander Graham Bell, the telephone largely guarantees one on one communication. It thus ensures a minimum level of privacy during use. The growth of the television from the mid-20th century introduced the visual element in long distance communication. Initially under state boundaries' controls, it grew across transnational territories with the advent of satellite broadcasting and a new campaign for global neoliberalism (Herman and McChesney, 1997; Mohammadi, 1997; Chalaby, 2005a, b). A medium between one (or a few) to many, transnational television has been instrumental to the rise of globalisation. It also benefits moving peoples, including migrants, diasporas, and expatriates who for one reason or the other seek a connection with their countries of origin. Thussu (2001:207) agues that traditional means of communication, including books, newspapers, magazines and letters, formerly dominated diasporas quest for links with the *homeland*. While the press and letters still remain useful as means for the shaping and communicative imagination of origin, videos, audiotapes, (Thussu, 2001) mobile phone texts and images, telephone, fax, satellite television and the Internet (Gillespie, 1995; Dayan, 1999: 22; Karim, 2003: 1; Robins and Aksoy, 2003, 2005) have become additional means for the likely rekindling of memories. This research focuses on the Internet and the possibility of migrants' utilisation of it to communicate with the *homeland*, not simply because it is relatively new, but also because it often provides greater participation amongst users. It uses the Nigerian migrants' case because it represents a case among many minorities in western nation-states and transnational groups across the world that seeks representation and spaces of expression, which are accessible, cheap and democratic.

METHOD

The work combines qualitative and quantitative methods in a process of triangulation, by the use of interviews, participant observation and survey. It uses interviews to record the voices of Nigerian migrants in two cities-London and Leeds. The interviews took place in these cities, which represent two distinct urban locations of migrant concentration in the context of globalisation. The choice of the cities was also the result of limited funds that did not allow me to cross the British borders. Data from casual conversations, probably serving as leads and/or pointers in some instances, was important as well, as it was an invaluable source of information in the location of my residence, Leeds. The study also uses participant observation to explore Internet activities among the group being studied. Participant observation took place both online and offline, with the former predominating. Then, survey helps to understand categories, main trends and behaviours across a purposive nonprobability sample of Nigerian migrants in London and Leeds[6]. Eventually, triangulation features as a tool for analyses in the crossroads of the findings collected with different methods.

OUTLINE

The project is presented in eight chapters. Chapter one discusses theories on key issues and concepts that relate to the research. These include communication and the troubled concepts of diaspora, migration, nationalism, transnationalism, home and *homeland*. The chapter explores the arguments in defining these subject matters from the normative paradigms to the anti-essentialist. Chapter Two focuses on Nigeria as the real and imagined *homeland* of migrants. It describes the country and its history. It also explains the socio-economic and political challenges causing migration from the past to the present and the likely state of the exodus in the future. Chapter Three identifies the methodology for the study, the reasons behind this selection and the strengths and weaknesses of the methods. Chapter Four marks the beginning of analyses. It reveals the overriding communication element of the research, through a critical account of findings on the migrants' ability to connect, the possibility to disconnect and to engage in alternative communication practices. Chapter Five explores the relevance of the migrants' communication activities to our understanding of transnationalism. This takes place in the light of multiple interactions of dispersed people. In this situation, actors, including people, corporations and nation-states, unite absences and presences (Sreberny, 1991) across distances. Chapter Six focuses on the possible emergence of

---

[6] The purposive nonprobability sampling allows less restriction in the representation of object of study. It is based on a researchers' judgement, and is often a result of considerations for cost and convenience. Unlike probability sampling, where the researcher decides the sample size after a pre-planned representation, nonprobability sampling enables the researcher to draw samples based on an adjudged fair choice of sample categories (Smith, 1993:394-5). It is often used where subjects are huge and probably difficult to represent through a probability sample, because a representation for such sampling is either not available, or difficult to obtain. In that case, nonprobability can be used to make inferences. In this research, therefore, the method was helpful in the choice of cities to represent the diverse locations of Nigerian migrants and in the process of selecting those interviewed. It was also useful in the course of choosing those to whom questionnaires were administered; and sometimes, in the selection of online functions to analyse. Further details shall be discussed in Chapter three.

nationalism in the course of transnational mediation. It discusses the chances of expressing nationalism from afar through a medium like the Internet. The section uses illustrations, while the analysis demonstrates likely attachments (or their absence) to a nation despite physical distance. Chapter Seven examines some processes of the construction of identity in using the Internet. It asserts that some changes take place in the migrants' appreciation of themselves as individuals and as a collective, while taking advantage of the new freedom offered in Internet spaces. Chapter Eight is the concluding chapter. This chapter argues that the Internet's role is still limited in use as an everyday communication tool among Nigerian migrants. It also demonstrates that the limitation is two-fold. On the one hand, the Internet is yet to become a routine, day-to-day medium and still exists as a distant and *detached* alternative medium for some, particularly the elites. On the other hand, its use is essentially for information sourcing, and sharing (and related matters like entertainment and education). Even in this regard, it remains a medium benefiting primarily the privileged or fascinated few. At the same time, and very importantly, there is evidence that many online activities and exchanges advance ideologies of nationalism, sustain transnational belonging, and allow the formation of identities. The conclusions also examine the limitations of the investigation, while noting its implications for policy and future research.

CHAPTER ONE:

COMMUNICATION, DIASPORA, AND INTERRELATING CONCEPTS: THEORIES, TENSIONS AND CONTENTIONS

The meanings of some key concepts, which intersect current discourse of communication, are experiencing stimulating and "even polemical debates" (Özkirimlii, 2000). Some of these concepts are, for instance, diaspora, nationalism, identity, home, the *homeland* and transnationalism. A few definitions of these concepts challenge essentialist and normative approaches. Some examples are those of Cohen (1997) on diaspora; Giddens (1991), Gilroy (1993), Hall (1996), and Ang (2000) on identity; Anderson (1983), Gellner (1983), Smith (1994) on nationalism; Glick Schiller, et al (1992), Portes (1996, 1997), Robins and Aksoy (2003, 2005) on transnationalism; and Brah (1996), Naficy (1999), Connor (2001), and Hammer (2007) on home and the *homeland*. Some other works situate definitions within an otherwise restrictive analytical framework. Examples of these are Safran (1991), Marienstras (1999) on diasporas; Kedourie, (1960), Deutsch (1969), Nairn, (1997), on nationalism; and Rapport and Dawson, (1998) on home and the *homeland*. In attempting to discuss the concepts, including media and Internet, therefore, I shall emphasis "how they should be theorised", rather than "what they are". This is because of emerging new meanings in a world of constant global changes, such that the productions and reproductions of meanings require regular reviews.

I shall begin with the problematic concept of diaspora. I will discuss its past and present framework as has been done by seminal theorists. The section will also examine the definitions of the concept in ideal types by Safran (1991), Cohen (1997) and Marienstras (1999. I will explain along with them the theories of those who are partly anti-essentialists, partly anti-normative through their opposition to the development of ideal types. Thereafter, the chapter will discuss the central issue of mediation of distance amongst migrants and diasporas. I will do this with a focus on the Internet, because of its present popularity. Then the chapter will engage with debates on nationalism. For a better structuring of arguments on nationalism, the focus will be on the post-1980 theorists (Zuelow, 2006). The multiple construction process of identity, its temporal and spatial specificity, its reflexivity and the certainty of conflicts in what it is, and what it is not, will afterwards be focussed on. Home and the *homeland* come next in this analytical process, and their relevance to place, placelessness, memories, or symbolic imagination will be discussed. Lastly, I shall examine transnationalism as a concept relevant to international communications in an age of increasing migration. In addition, the manner in which its course intersects nationalism, through "borderlessness", and how it is apparent in migrants' mediation of distance will become clear. Media and communication, which is the framework of the research, will be central to the discussions.

THEORIES OF DIASPORA

The concept of diaspora has a long history. Its interdisciplinarity as related to sociology, political science, cultural studies, geography, anthropology, history, philosophy, literature, communication, religion, cinema, music, theatre, (Vertovec, 2000:2; Karim, 2003:1; Brubaker, 2005:4), qualifies it as one of the few terms helpful to theorising human mobility in present times. Originally Greek, diaspora in its recent definition compares with other socio-cultural and economic terms like globalisation, transnationalism, identity, nationalism, nations and nations-state, amongst other expressions that define global changes. The concept became more popular since the 1980s (Cunningham and Sinclair, 2001:9), into the 1990s, when global economies began witnessing a boom, with increase in human mobility. Issues around movement and settlement often lead to discourses on diaspora. It also involves notions on "travelling and dwelling" (Morley, 2000). Besides, displacements across borders, dislocations and relocations, integrations and disintegrations, "outsiders" and "insiders", *sameness* and difference (Gilroy, 1993, 2000; Hall, 1996), frequently relate to the concept. Diaspora is also used to address issues like cosmopolitanism and multiculturalism (Georgiou, 2006c); nation and nationalism (Anderson, 1998); transnationalism and migration (Cohen, 1997; Vertovec and Cohen, 1999; Vertovec, 2004, 2005). Other than these are ideas on "strangeness", and identity (Gilroy, 1997; Georgiou, 2006a), while "notions of ethnicity, immigration, settlement and race are all found to intersect and dissect conceptualisation of diaspora" (Kalra, et al, 2005: 9), just as it "shares an overlapping semantic field (Tololyan, 1991, 1996)", with these subject matters (Brubaker, 2005:10). Diaspora is additionally a culturalist approach to the contextualisation of resettlement amongst a people, as it emphasises boundedness, (amongst themselves) and possible integration (in hostland), as against individualism (Robins and Aksoy, 2003).

The concept refers to the sowing or the scattering of seeds in Greek. It implies forceful dispersal of people from an original location, or the *homeland,* to different other places, or nations, when it is about humans. A people who voluntarily live in a place outside an original home, with strong collective identity can be a diaspora (Cohen, 1997: ix). This sense of the word is increasingly becoming common. However, the term "sometimes defined as *galut*-exile or bondage-and as *golah*-a relatively stable community in exile[7]" (Skinner, 1993:11), is yet a subject of intense and inconclusive theoretical debate. This is because of the ever-shifting variables and contexts that it covers. For instance, while some writers (Safran, 1991; Cohen, 1997; Marienstras, 1999) define it in ideal terms, others (Brah, 1996; Clifford, 1997; Georgiou, 2000) argue against it.

To start with, Safran's (1991:83-84) ideal types were particularly pioneering in the development of criteria for defining diasporas. Additions, modifications, or sometimes, absolute disagreements with thoughts of finding a model, follow his suggestions, because of the interweaving character of diasporic experience and consciousness. Safran's conditions for identifying diasporas are that:

> People or their ancestors have been dispersed from an original centre; They retain a collective memory, vision or myth of their *homeland*; They believe they are not fully accepted in the host society; The ancestral home is idealised and there is a myth of return; They believe that all members of the diaspora should be committed to the maintenance, safety and prosperity of the original *homeland* (and they); continue in different ways to keep links with *homeland* – ethno communal consciousness and solidarity (Safran, 1991: 83-84).

Representative as it appears, modern realities of diasporas expose the ideals to criticisms. For instance, the first criterion does not consider the nature of dispersal, whether voluntary or involuntary. The case of the former seems now more common with modern economic migrants (Brah, 1996; Sheffer, 2003; Kalra, et al, 2005; Portes, 1997, 1999) like Nigerians. The remainder is largely presuming. It undermines the fact of continuous attachment to the *homeland*, forgetting that these sometimes normalise over time (Clifford, 1997:255). The attachment it assumes could evolve to nothingness, through "assimilation and distancing" (Clifford, ibid.). The exilic (Bhabha, 1994:xii; Naficy, 1999) migrant, or the activist fleeing dictatorships, like the Nigerian activists escaping military repression, often may not "keep links with *homeland*" (Safran, 1991:83-84), for fear of detection and harming. Cohen (1997:26) expanded these ideals in his own suggestions. He put forward nine criteria as follows:

---

[7] *Galut* and *Golah* are Hebrew words. The first often refers to exiles, while the second means diaspora (accessed at www.zionistyoungster.blogspot.com/2007/04/out-of-galut.html-45- on 18/02/2008).

Dispersal from an original *homeland*, often traumatically, to two or more foreign regions; Alternatively, the expansion from a *homeland* in search of work, in pursuit of trade or to further colonial ambitions; A collective memory and myth about the *homeland*, including its location, history and achievements; An idealisation of the putative ancestral home and a collective commitment to its maintenance, restoration, safety and prosperity, even to its creation; The development of a return movement that gains collective approbation; A strong ethnic group consciousness sustained over a long time and based on a sense of distinctiveness, a common history and the belief in a common fate; A troubled relationship with host societies, suggesting a lack of acceptance at the least or the possibility that another calamity might befall the group; A sense of empathy and solidarity with co-ethnic members in other countries of settlement; The possibility of a distinctive creative, enriching life in host countries with a tolerance for pluralism (Cohen, 1997: 26).

Thoughtful as these ideals are, the danger of overgeneralisations limits their credibility. For instance, the question of return movements gaining "collective approbation" is yet inapplicable to the Nigerian experience. There is also yet to be a "strong ethnic group consciousness over a long time and based on a sense of distinctiveness, a common history and the belief in a common fate" (Cohen, 1997). Nigerian migrants are products of a multi-ethnic society. The often antagonistic groups hardly find permanent bond abroad. Marienstras' (1999) also overgeneralises in his own classification, as he limits explanations to three elements, namely, time; possibility of movement between home and the *homeland*; and networking amongst diasporic members. He argues:

(i.) diaspora is a population, which is dispersed from a *homeland* to two or more territories; (ii.) the presence abroad is enduring, though exile is not necessarily permanent and it might include movements between *homeland* and host country; (iii.) there is some kind of exchange: social, economic, political, cultural between the dispersed populations in the diaspora (Marienstras, 1999:357-8).

Marienstras' hint of connections of diaspora people and the multi-sectoral framework is important in his description of the different sides to diasporic experiences. Examining the ideas, therefore, Georgiou (2002:15-6) suggests twelve criteria, which highlight transnationalism; the changing nature of diaspora and the influential role of new media in the shaping of diasporic experiences. However, like preceding definitions, her approach is rather too general, as it shrugs off details of groups testing dispersal, but seen only via regional or more global classifications. The experiences of these groups are temporally and spatially useful for the understanding of the general picture. The beginning of identification from a broad description always overwhelms these neglected groups. As an example, the idea of the

African diaspora will always take precedence over the Nigerian, or the Ghanaian case. Nevertheless, respective African countries presently bear diasporic narratives relevant to the consideration of the age more than the more general African diaspora notion.

Indicatively, the term is experiencing an evolution in meanings in terms of "semantic, conceptual and disciplinary space" (Brubaker, 2005:1). It can therefore at once be too essentialising or too exclusionary, when one, two, or a few ideas define it. This often amounts to reductionism. The assumptions, like Safran's (and others), will always include and exclude. Hardly can a people also "qualify on all counts, throughout its history" (Clifford, 1996, 306; 1997: 250), apart from the descriptive tendency of the ideal definitions (Kalra, et al, 2005). The models also undermine the mediation impact of modern media like the Internet (Gilroy, 1997; Georgiou, 2002-2003; Kalra, et al, 2005:19) in diasporic processes of seeking integration, and in the likely idealisation of the *homeland*. The thought of "homogeneity and a historically fixed identity" (Vertovec, 2005:2) is constantly in contest following these definitions of diaspora. It is why Gilroy (1993) and Clifford (1997) depart and regard diaspora as a process. To some others, it is an ideology; a type of consciousness; and a mode of cultural production (Vertovec and Cohen, 1999: xvii-xix; Benesch and Genevieve, 2004; Kalra, et al, 2005: 13).

Common features of diasporas, however, include dispersal; memories and commemoration; myth and imagination (Georgiou, 2006a: 40); nostalgia, or *homing* (Brah, 1996: 180); idealisation or a practicalisation of return; and sometimes, a strong communal sensitivity. These, to a degree, make diaspora matters to revolve around the *"homeland, displacement and settlement"* (Sayyid, 2004). It all makes the concept different from other forms of movements like tourism, migration[8], and excursion (Braziel and Mannur, eds, 2003). This is in spite of Tolayan's argument that:

The term that once described Jewish, Greek and Armenian dispersion now shares meanings with a larger semantic domain that includes words like immigrant, expatriate, refugee, guest worker, exile community, overseas community, ethnic community (Tololyan, 1991:4, cited in Brubaker, 2005:3).

---

[8] Though migration is different from diaspora, the definition of diaspora begins from migration experience. Every diaspora person was once a migrant, or could also become one, in a case of re-migration. As said earlier, the word migrant is used in this work sometimes as a synonym for the diaspora person. It is not necessarily as an effective replacement, but as a description of their otherness.

Tourists and migrants may turn into diaspora people, but diaspora people are not continually tourists or migrants. Diaspora may not also be equivalent to exiles or refugees, but exiles and refugees can turn out to be diaspora people after a considerable passage of time. The crisscrossing character of the concepts can however be regular. Imperatively, long period of domicile in host societies characterises diaspora people. A period long enough to challenge the mere reproduction of an original culture. These alongside the position of diaspora vis-à-vis exiles, refugees, tourism, migrants, alongside other evolving concepts[9] are still subject of intense academic disagreements.

Many groups have fallen into the description of being a diaspora over the years. The biblical connection of diaspora with the exile of the Jews to Babylon following the 586 BC demolition of Jerusalem temple somewhat stands as a scriptural antecedent of the term as a synonym for travails, dislocation, insecurity, and homelessness (Cohen, 1997; Sheffer, 2003; Kalra, et al, 2005). While they later went back to Jerusalem, they spread across Babylon, Rome, Syria, Greece, and Egypt. The Jewish dispersal, first out of Jerusalem and then out of Babylon, Eastern Europe and the Mediterranean, has the foremost diasporic description. The Armenian dispersal experience from the 18th to the 19th century, which rose further after the 1915 murder of their leaders, qualifies them (like the Jewish), as victim diasporas (Cohen, 1997: 42). The Greek migration to Asia Minor in 800 to 600 BC for reasons of overpopulation and poverty disconnects with the first two experiences to give the term an encouraging colour (Cohen, ibid.: 2). That prepared the grounds for present day use of the word for non-traumatic migrancy occurrences (Georgiou, 2002: 15). The Nigerian case may belong to this non-traumatic category, as dispersal is not, in most cases, necessarily a result of ordeal, as was the case of the Jewish for instance, but largely a result of a search for a better economic life. Notably though, the initial experiences of the Jewish, the Armenians and the Greeks, which today confirm them as traditional diasporas, is a prototype of sorts, for the Latter-Day description of dispersing peoples as diasporas (Kalra, et al, 2005:9).

---

[9] The study of diaspora has produced a motley crowd of related concepts including diasporism, diasporology, diasporists, diasporan, diasporific, diaspornography, diasportfolio, diaspersion, diasporapathy, diasporactivists and diasperanto (Brubaker, 2005). There are also diasporic, diasporisation (Braziel and Mannur, eds, 2003: 4; Brah, 1996: 179), diasporist, diasporism (Clifford, 1999: 332), diasporicity (Dudrah, 2004), re-diasporisation (Clifford, 1997:305; Brubaker, 2005), de-diasporisation (Kalra, et al, 2005:7; Brubaker, 2005). *Diasporic* is sometimes used in this work as a verb to describe a diaspora or migrant process.

Seen as a "category of practice, project, claim and stance, rather than as a bounded group" (Brubaker, 2005:13), the concept also depicts "the migration of borders over people, and not simply from that of people over borders". Other than this, it defines:

> a very large residual set of putative ethno-cultural or country defined diasporas (like) Belarusian, Brazilian (and) Cambodian…and then there are putative diasporas of other sorts: the dixie diaspora, the yankee diaspora, the white diaspora, the liberal diaspora, the conservative diaspora, the gay diaspora, the deaf diaspora, the redneck diaspora, (and) the digital diaspora…(Brubaker,2005:3)

Early diasporas like those of the Jewish, the Armenians and the Greeks, have been extensively studied. Some Latter-Day diaspora, like the Cubans and Mexicans in the US, the Chinese in South-East Asia, the Blacks in the Caribbean and in North America, the Magrebs in France, the Turks in Germany (Safran, 1999: 83) and the Lebanese in West Africa (Cohen, 1997:98) are common in investigations. The more familiar African diaspora context subsumes the Nigerian case, as with many new sets of migrants, often at the margin of analyses. In a few "beneficial" instances, analyses are part of the processes of globalisation and the fact of an inevitable minimal participation (Castles, et al, 1993; Stalker, 2001; Vertovec, 2006). This research, therefore, aims at giving a full view to the Nigerian case.

Emerging diasporas belong to recent classifications that include populations not necessarily moving because of violence, but voluntarily migrating to improve their living standards. With global changes resulting from the compression of time and space (Giddens, 1990), which new technologies of communication help, economic reasons play an important role in determining present day migrations. Many modern migrants move in search of economic wellbeing, mainly from the developing South to the industrial North, where the "natural end point" (Braziel and Mannur, 2003: 285) appears to be. Recent stories of diaspora are resulting from the usual shattering source to economic, educational, and cultural reasons (Cohen, 1997:1; Appiah, 2005).

Characteristically, diaspora people make at least one major journey, and interact with a minimum of two cultures (Georgiou, 2001: 68), which arises in a progression (Gilroy, 1987: 161). Within the sequence is loneliness, as a common feature. The Jewish experience in Babylon as in Psalm 137, where they "sat and wept…by the rivers of Babylon", again gives a scriptural beginning to this experience of diaspora people. It illustrates the usual loneliness of many diasporas. In another land, the Jews were lamenting, remembering their origin with nostalgia. They regretted their helplessness when Nebuchadnezzar, the king of Babylon, humiliated them in different ways. That experience is largely the lot of diaspora people, as in the traumatic tales of dispersing Jews, Greeks, Irish and Blacks.

To diasporas, the *homeland* could evoke deep emotions, illustrating the link to a source, usually described with different tags. Some are motherland, fatherland, ancestral land, native land, home (Connor, 2001: 1), land of birth, or origin. Literary enthusiasts including Petrarch (1946), Mehmed Emin (1977), besides Walter Scott, and Joseph Plunkett (all cited in Connor, 2001: 54-55), poetically document the *homeland* feelings, in what further demonstrates the diversity of its appeal, particularly at the level of emotions. A shaping of the appeals may, however, arise in host society through an engagement with modern media like the television (Robins and Aksoy, 2003), and in the case of this research, the Internet.

Diaspora usage sometimes relates only to people that are not Caucasian (Karim, 2003:2; Kalra, 2005:106). That is probably because of little references to "white" movements as diasporas. For instance, the Poles in Canada, the Germans in Argentina and the Australians in Earl's Court, London, are different from the Cubans in America or the blacks in the Caribbean in terms of diasporic experience. Kalra argues that "the USA, for instance, is often cited as a 'nation of immigrants', yet the conflation of European migrants that constitute part of its population are never termed diasporic or hybrid in the same way" (2005: 106). This provokes arguments that diaspora is more often used to describe the have-nots, rather than the haves inhabiting the main destination of migrants, which is the West.

Nevertheless, diaspora and migration discourse needs to consider specifics that represent shapes of movements. This means, for instance, that there should be a proper classification of the expatriate who leaves her/his domain in the "North" for the rich oil fields, or promising colleges/universities in the "South", and again the thousands of the over 50,000 transnational corporations' (Webster, 2002: 69) personnel that are mainly Western, who are spread across the globe. Are they less diasporic, and more transnational, or less transnational and more migrant international workers or experts? That is besides the old Western Christian priests on missionary work in the "South" that eventually take up homes in those countries, and the Caucasian spouses of migrants from the South to the North, who eventually return to the South with their spouses, with the former resolving on a "Southern" home.

From another perspective, there is sometimes a problem when economic reason causes migration. This is because it would imply all classes of labour. However, it may not easily be applicable to the investing entrepreneur or industrialist (Brah, 1996: 178), who is exploring markets in the North from the South. The investing entrepreneur, like the Rothchilds and Hinduja group (Karim, 2003:5), is likely seeking further economic prosperity in the North instead of some insignificant breakthroughs. The eighteenth century banking business successes of the Rothchilds and the Hinduja diasporic group (Karim, ibid.) in global business, which thrives mainly in the West, where 37,000 of the world largest companies (Schiller, 1996: 94) operate from, testifies to the investment mission of some new diasporas (Van Hear, 1998).[10]

This leads to the thinking that security could be a key cause of migration, but which lack attention in literature. Insecurity can be destabilising both emotionally and physically. Insecurity limits the potentials of a being, sometimes leading therefore to a search for ontological security (Giddens, 1991; Bilton, et al, 1996: 665). Ontological security is a form of security resulting from mental stability through an ability to predict events (Bilton, et al, ibid.: 665), or the regularisation of a person's experience and the possibility of sourcing meanings from there (Giddens, 1991). Arguments speculate that anxiety, depression, disturbances and crises, which are more common in migration source countries, are obstacles to ontological security. On the other hand, orderliness, predictability and stability of the social process that features more in dominant global migrants' and diasporic destinations are grounds for ontological security. A likely human desire for ontological security drives the need to reject ontological insecurity, and, therefore, leading to movements. This is because of people's preference for stability as against instability, comfort as against discomfort, and peace as against crises. The condition that takes priority influences ontology in contradiction to the other situation.

The absence of, and search for security, has another biblical reference (Deuteronomy, 28: 58-68; Cohen, 1997:1) in diasporic elements of place, placelessness, and the search for a soothing permanence. Weighed down or not, the moving person who partly desires safety is longing for security, simply as the investing entrepreneur that Brah identifies above. S/he is, for instance, from the South but investing in the North, in the course of seeking security of her/his capital in the more vibrant economies of the North. Again, the individual labour migrant in pursuit of better working condition elsewhere is also looking for some form of financial security. From the biblical, teleological viewpoint, insecurity is a curse following disobedience. Logically, if there were security in the *homeland*, dispersion that come with its own physical and emotional inconveniences (Portes, 1996) will likely not be an option. The Nigerian case is within this

---

[10] The economic pull to the more prosperous West is in fact that (the rich) for instance "pay only 4% on debt compared with the 17% paid by poor nations. The gap between the 'haves' and 'have nots' widens daily", (Mohammadi, ed, 1997: 10). In addition, of the United Nations estimated 6 billion world population, 25% have, while the remainder 75% have not. Halloran (1997:45) agues that $50 billion was paid by developing countries to the developed as interest in 1990 alone. Moreover "from 1960-91" he stresses, "the share of the world's poorest population fell from 7.35 to 1.7%, while the share of the richest 20% increased from 70-85%" (Halloran, ibid.: 45), indicating an increase in inequality between nations in half a century.

framework-that is the search for security, economic security, as a main cause of migration.

Largely, however, diasporas do evolve. Their experiences are not only an evidence of a changing same (Gilroy, 1993, 2000)[11], but evolve across borders. The borders are unequal, discontinuous and are complete with regulations. The differences in the wealth of nations explain this inequality. The discontinuity is in the limits to the reception of moving groups, while regulation is about the expression of the limitations. "Citizenship, passports, visas, surveillance, integrated databases and biometric mediums" (Brubaker, 2005:9), are some of the ways of regulation. Others are deportation, designation as asylum seeker and periodisation of residency time. These processes imply categorisations in terms of citizens or non-citizens and natives or non-natives. They are psychological reminders of "strangeness" to the stranger, or "otherness" to the other.

To Nigerian migrants, I am proposing that the rigid interest in migration has become a way in which they understand personal or collective progress. Travelling and re-settlement is not essentially a matter of pleasure, or an epistemological engagement, but one to add to the self, in ontological terms. It should even up to an improvement of living standards, especially in the face of persisting economic crises, political instability, high crime rates, insecurity of lives and properties, poor health facilities, better educational facilities and qualitative provision of social amenities. This way of life is partly a product of historical experiences of colonialism, post-colonialism, and a product of frustrating attempts for development in Nigeria. It results in a disillusioned citizenry preferring an external alternative to better life, instead of hoping for an elusive solution from Nigeria. In the furtherance of these migration ways, the media becomes relevant, as it enhances the ways, through the sustenance of contacts in the distance. The Internet, as a new medium, can be particularly useful both in the manner it helps in shaping their character in migration and as medium of mediation. How therefore do we situate the Internet as a new and important medium? I shall examine this in the section that follows.

INTERNET AND COMMUNICATION

The growth of Internet influence is unparalleled (Castells, 1996, 2001; Thussu, 2007), and has a historically special feature relative to preceding media (Slevein, 2000; Thussu, 2001). Its uniqueness partly comes through its multi-million record of users few years after the invention (Tehranian and Tehranian, 1997: 160). Its notable convergence quality is of no less

---

[11] The concept "the changing same" describes "something endlessly hybridized and in process, but persistently there", (Clifford, 1994: 320, cited in Brubaker, 2005:7). A further explanation is in the section on identity.

importance. Celebrations of the Internet probably cannot compare with the telegraph, radio, and television, despite their equally unrivalled receptions. Many writers (Tehranian and Tehranian, 1997; Naughton, 1999; Slevein, 2000: 40; Castells, 2000: 3; Thussu, 2001: 225) attempt a demonstration of the Internet record in statistical terms. Naughton records, for instance, that the radio did not reach its first 50 million people until after 40 years. He adds that the television reached that record number 25 years less than the radio did. Nevertheless, the Internet beat those records by attaining the landmark in only three years. Slevein (2000: 40) notes that between 150 and 180 million Internet users were recorded in 1999. By 2000, the figure had risen to 320 million in Thussu's (2001:225) own estimate. A year after, Castells (2001: 3) notes 400 million, adding that the number of users was one billion in 2005, "and we could be approaching the 2 billion mark by 2010". Tehranian and Tehranian (1997: 160) says, "a million new users are estimated to be joining the network each month". As at May 2007, an estimated 1.1 billion people were users (accessed at www.Internetworldstats.com on 21/05/2007). Even then, the medium is still at an early stage of development, as an AOL Chairman, Steve Case (Waters, 2000, cited in Thussu, 2001:232) once attested. Beyond the statistical interpretations, is the question of spread: how even is the so-called widespread use of the Internet?

A network of networks, the Internet is a worldwide system of communicating computers. Exclusion from it is damaging to economies and cultures (Castells, 2001:3), as it also signifies underdevelopment. This is because the medium combines with other technologies of our times to define and advance social, economic and political relations, amongst peoples, societies, communities and countries (Jones, 1998; Baym, 1998). It does this through a dense flow of data, capital, information, sounds, images, and symbols (Castells, 2000:442). These activities may serve different purposes. First, they offer new grounds for the re-imagination of communities (Rheingold, 1993). Second, the re-configuration of groups and societies may result (Gillespie, 1995: 7; Karim, 2003). Third, the construction and re-construction of identities (Appadurai, 1996; Vertovec and Cohen, 1999), "by a culture of simulation" (Gilroy, 2000: 108), could as well come into view. Then new grounds for the understanding of social life may emerge. The consequences of the Internet arrival lead to a network society where societal relationships take place through nodes and networks, with the media as a facilitator (Castells, 1996; van Dijk, 1999; Barney, 2004). In the Internet age, information takes over from steam power of the old industrial society (Webster, 2002: 3). Some others analyse the evolving trends, as *mediascapes* (Appadurai, 1990) or *rhizomes* (Silverstone and Georgiou, 2005: 438). Human activities are interconnected in this understanding following the "death of distance" (Caincross, 2001). The changes add up to compress time and space (Giddens, 1999), or eclipse distance (Brubaker,

2005:9). These lead possibly to boom in economies following an increase in the pace of communication over geographies (Giddens, 1999).

Combining the audio-visual functions of television, the audio effect of radio, and the textual details of print, Internet offers users multiple opportunities for interaction, across space, in chosen time and with at a great speed. In basic terms, the Internet allows users to send and receive e-mails, and e-mail attachments. They are also able to chat with others (known or unknown), and to participate in discussions at newsgroups, listservs, and usenets, amongst peoples in different geographies. Besides, they are able to source and/or circulate personal or group information; to do audio or video teleconferencing; to transact business or businesses; to fall in and out of relationships; and to process, share, store and retrieve images, signs and symbols (Lax, 1997; Thussu, 2001; Karim, 2003). These partly leads to the description of the network as one that facilitates the "freedom of intimacy" (Chalaby, 2000: 19 &20), implying the inherent and evolving new rights available in the internet's space. There are the roles of the fax machine, the production of the celluloid and its ability to play the CD and the DVD. The tasks are doable at the individual level, as a group or collective, and importantly between many to many-another important feature of the Internet (Taylor, 1997; Winston, 1998; Slevein, 2000: 2; Castells, 2001:2). The Internet is not only a communication medium, but also a tool of interaction between many (Licklidier, et al, 1978; Harasim, 1993, cited in Smith and Kollock, 1999: 4). These possibilities and opportunities open up new social spaces, as they enable the remaking of previously existing ones. New meanings emerge in social interactions on a global scale in an incomparable scale. The changes in social, power and political relations (Adebanwi, 2001), which the network causes, continue in a sensational mode. It, therefore, constantly necessitates degrees of theoretical and empirical investigations.

Several analyses restate the significance of the Internet in the imagination and reconstitution of groups and societies. The technology is not only one for simple communication, but also one with the added benefit of integrating and re-integrating peoples, no matter the distance (Rheingold, 1993, 2000; Jones, 1997; Jordan, 1999). Rather than people relating to machines, the machines now relate people-to-people (Wellman, et al, 1996). The Internet fosters a new logic of unity and sometimes disunity (in the face of flaming[12]) when users are brought together. Through it, there is "a consensual hallucination experienced daily by billions of legitimate operators in every nation" (Gibson, 1984:51). The operators and users engage the space behind the computer screen, which is out-of-sight but real, effective and unifying (Gibson, ibid.; Elmer-Dewitt, 1996). The virtual

---

[12] Flaming implies abuses and heated disagreements in online discussions (Buckley and Clark, 2004: 218).

integration of people through its space is an introduction to a different sense of place. The previously leading place had been the physical and traditional offline life. The new life online provides an alternative or a complementary space for social interactions. The interface has most times being a forerunner of mutual, communal, and societal understanding, knowledge and ideas sharing, which gives participants a sense of companionship, even if virtual. This sense develops further, in manners that have either turned strangers into friends or acquaintances, aside the option of withholding ones' identity, or remaining anonymous in the process (Taylor, 1997:26). Therefore, human lives are affected by the technology, as the technology is also transformed (Castells, 2001: 5). The dialectical process challenges an essentially technologically deterministic course, given the mutual shaping between society and technology (Castells, ibid.; Ward, 2005). A medium that initiates and stabilises communities, Rheingold regards this trait of the technology as a "lifeline" (2001:171). In further celebratory terms, he notes:

> The net is the world's greatest source of information; misinformation and disinformation, community and character assassination, and you have very little but your wits to help you sort out the valid from the bogus (Rheingold, 2000: 174).

Evolving online communities leads to the imaginations of associations, which bridge gaps and close divides. Fundamental changes emerge from these circumstances, which again initiates thoughts on modes of communal relations (Woolgar, ed, 2002: 1-2). These could be within cultures and between cultures (Bhabha, 1994), on a micro, mezzo, or macro scale. A developing multiple approaches to the understanding of groups is not only a sign of something new, but is a refreshing occurrence to society. The place of the computer screen as a new, optional gateway to associating and relating extends the self-potentials through the power of technology. However, like Castells (2001) notes above, the exchange is not one-sided. It crops up in a dialectics as peoples' engagements with it also affect it.

The changing self in "being digital" (Negroponte, 1995) happens through disappearing "boundaries between the real and the virtual, the animate and the inanimate, the unitary and the multiple self, which is occurring both in advanced fields of scientific research and in the patterns of everyday life" (Turkle, 1995: 10). To Shields (1996:7), these disappearing boundaries become a crisis that exists between not only the concept of the real and the virtual, but between time zones and spaces. The crisis occurs again:

> Between bodies and technologies, between our sense of self and our sense of our changing roles: the personae we may play or the 'hats we wear' in different situations are altered (Shields, 1996:7).

Though seen as utopian by some writers, particularly in postmodern times (Robins and Webster, 1999; Hine, 2000:6), online interactions do affect individuals. The construction of the self, for instance, takes place in a process. First, it is possible to reflexively review the self through individual engagements with online facilities. Second, it comes through a group or social definition of what the self is. Again resulting from the setting is not only a new sense of self, but also an inabsolute being, whose identity is a mixture of being and becoming (Hall, et al, eds, 1996), which is also not a fixed or absolute construction (Gilroy, 1993). Donath (1999: 29) argues that the body in the virtual world is not like that in the physical world. On the Internet, he stresses, information instead of biological structure prevails. Additionally, the information is free, and available, with little regulation. "The inhabitants of this impalpable space are also diffuse, free from the body's unifying anchor. One can have, some claim, as many electronic personae as one has time and energy to create" (Donath, 1999:29). These possibilities leave room for deception or fake identities and then a possible "capacity to concentrate political power, to create new forms of social obfuscation and domination" (Theodore Roszak, 1986: xii, cited in Smith and Kollock, 1999: 4).

The Internet can also enable people to resolve the crisis of a problematic self-a self earlier lacking confidence regains composure in its interactive space. The confident self also has opportunities for reviews, through the Internet's space. From there "we at least partially reconstruct the self and its world, creating new opportunities for reflection, perception, and social experience" (Burnett and Marshall, 2003: 61). The constant sense of co-presence through engagement with the Internet features chances of simultaneity in interaction course (Preece, 2000: 161-2). Self-alterations go on in many ways. Though the self ironically manifests in modern society where identity is an important source of meaning, it yet occurs in "bipolar opposition between the net and the self" (Castells, 1996: 3), representing the new world setting. The setting is between not only the net and the self, but also involves the nation, as I will now discuss.

The Internet's operational space is wide ranging. It compresses distant territories into a unified virtual whole, despite time difference. The course of this challenges nations, given the questions it asks about their sovereignty. Images, sounds and texts flow freely in webpages, between and across boundaries, raising further questions on the continued existence of the nation-state. Because of a concern for this occurrence, some nation-states like Singapore, Bahrain, Turkey, Yemen, China, Malaysia, and Saudi Arabia have tried in different ways to regulate the flow of data into their territories (Chalaby, 2000: 23-4; Thussu, 2001). Others like North Korea discourage its spread in its territory. Everard (1999) argues that the Internet is an easier way to international relations, as it represents the exchange of electronic bytes rather than the bits of explosives. He notes that the Internet will change the context of national and international borders and boundaries instead of an outright erasure. International links grow through it, thereby reducing the rigidity of borders. Everard's proposition follows a classic poser on "w (h) ither the state?" regarding whether the nation was going to "whither" or "wither". The first implies the extent to which the deterritorialisation, which the internet brings, reduces the impacts of borders and the second, whether or not the borders were simply going to disappear. Everard concludes that the state would do neither, but simply change. Engel (2007) sounds like the so-called doomsayers who Everard tries to argue against (White, 2000: 1). He is less concerned about the relationship between the Internet and state, largely noting that the network affects sovereignty. This, he writes, comes through information dissemination, currency exchange, values, a developing prohibitive cost of autonomy, change in conventional structure of statehood, and the possibility of new international conflicts" (p. 244). Against the trend of international discourse, Clancy (2002) offers the national dimension via an analysis of Americans new life online. Rather than a network of nation-states, in agreement or disagreement, it is a network of people, organisations, and institutions within a nation-state. The scopes bring out the character of the Internet as not only one with convergent character, but also one that unites institutions. The manner in which migrants affect and are affected by the Internet is discussed in the next section.

DIASPORAS AND MIGRANTS' CONSUMPTION OF MEDIA PARTICULARLY THE INTERNET

Dayan (1999:22) argues that interdiasporic media are not only limited to the conventional media but also includes a reconstruction of the traditional, which is "neotraditional". These include:

> (1) production and circulation of news letters, audio and video cassettes, holy icons and small media in general…(2) Exchange of letters, photographs, home videos and travellers…(3) constitution of religious communities or cultural associations…(and) (4) creation of interdiasporic networks (and circulation of directives, slogans, sermons, preaching, (etc) by religious or political organisations, with specific agendas…(Dayan, 1999:22-3).

These experiences of diasporas occur in the process of global movements, symbolising networks (Castells, 1996, 2001; van Djik, 1999; Barney, 2004), or *mediascapes* (Appadurai, 1996), in unprecedented ways that reflect the complexities of the new age. In the process, it enhances migrants' ability to negotiate meanings (Fiske, 1987), as the control over the space between then and now becomes easier. Their identity is then positioned in an age of globalisation, of "planetary reconstruction" (Gilroy, 2000: 107), despite the contradictory role of the media in the shaping and shifting of identities (Scholte, 1996: 597; Ang, 2001).

To Ignacio (2003: 161; 2005), the media, particularly the Internet, helps dispersed peoples' sense of positioning, and in the case of Filipinos, assists them in setting aside "differences", and to "form a strong community" across distances (p.161). Other studies with similar themes as Ignacios', seek to explore the relevance of the Internet to particular groups at different points in time. (See for instance Kadend-Kaiser (2000) on Haitian diasporic group; Georgiou (2001) on the Greek Cypriot community; Miller and Slatter, (2001) on Trinidadian diaspora; Ang (2001) on the Chinese diaspora; Tsaliki (2003) on the Greek community; and Schulz and Hammer (2003) on the Palestinians). Karim (2003: 3) notes that the new media helps diasporic "nostalgic reminiscences". He agues further that the technologies facilitate the avoidance "of the hierarchical structures of traditional broadcast media" (p.13). By this, the linearity of the old media, their hierarchical and capital intensive nature are lost to the non-linearity, the minimised or non-existent hierarchy and the relatively low cost of engaging with Internet resources, like e-mails, e-mail attachments, usenets, newsgroups, blogs, listservs, and/or in using social networking spaces like Facebook, Myspace, *Orkut, Bebo*, and the all-embracing "Second Life".

The new diasporic communication experience is possible because in late modernity, the media connect distant people, given the redefinition of a sense of place (Moores, 1993). It indicates a "connection of presence and absence" (Sreberny, 1991: 94). Gillespie describes this as the dissolution of distances and the suspension of time, which "create new and unpredictable forms of connection, identification and cultural affinity" (2000:169). Besides, this takes place in everyday life (De Certeau, 1998; Silverstone, 2005:1; Georgiou, 2002, 2003), where "acceptance of, or resistance to new communication and information technologies" (Silverstone, 2005:1) occurs. Also taken for granted in literature is that dispersions are central to global changes. Many times, moving groups lead us to think of people in need of a temporary or permanent alternative home. The way the old home is thought about becomes subsequently important. The frameworks of changes in communication technologies, which are a part of global transformations, are equally significant. With migrants and diasporic networks (Hanafi, 2005: 583) rising almost in pace with phases of communication technologies, trends in new interaction processes (Siapera, 2005: 501), which dislocation experiences bring out, require critical monitoring, to understand their full implications.

The Internet provides an important location where migrants and diasporic spaces are re-negotiated. With the Internet deterritorialising space, diasporas re-construct the *homeland* in imagination processes (Karim, 1998; Georgiou, 2002; Ignacio, 2003). They, therefore, possibly increase our understanding of transnational online communication. The understanding is better appreciated when migrants witness the features of anonymity, informality and immediacy (Franklin, 2001: 400), through interactivity, that gives rise to new publics. While anonymity and informality may allow for greater freedom of expression, immediacy guarantees a higher pace in the display of the new liberty. Apart from anonymity, the internet brings the familiar closer, like friends and family members in distant places. Besides, online activities limit hierarchical relationships between the centre and the periphery from the conclusion of some studies (See for instance Hanafi's, 2002, analysis on Palestinian Scientists and Technologists Abroad, accessed at www.palesta.gov.ps on 20/08/2005, and Georgiou, 2002, discourse of Hellenic Resources Network, HR-NET).

It is noteworthy that communication has gone through shades of revolution in history. The way they vary in forms and concentrations (Winston, 1998; McQuail, 2000) reveal the creative potentials of peoples in different economic systems, especially capitalism. Before this technology came, however, diasporas and migrants already had communication systems in place (Thussu, 2001; 2007). Newspapers, first published in England in 1665, were of some relevance for communication. In addition, photography invented in 1827 reproduced images in the *homelands*, and the 1837 invention of the telegraph was of importance to imperial diasporic communities (Winston, 1998; Thussu, 2001). The postal services, which came in 1840, played its mediation role as well, besides the first radio airing of the human voice in 1902 and the coming of telephone about twenty-six years before. The television as a medium has been of importance to diasporas from its coming in the early 1930s (Goldberg, 2006). However, how does the internet challenge these preceding media for migrants?

Karim (2004) again notes that diasporas use the Internet for the production of different cultural resources. Furthermore:

A primary motivation on the part of immigrant communities seems to be survival in the face of the overwhelming output of the dominant culture and the limitations of their access to the cultural industries in the country of settlement (Karim, 2004:56)

Beyond that, the need to lessen the pains of distance, pains that can be reduced through virtual relations, which Rheingold (1993) claims, implies doing "just about everything people do in real life" (ibid.: 3), and in this case, in the *homeland,* encourage the cyber activities of people in dislocation. Regardless, it is logical to check aspects of these relations, especially with a focus on course and effect. The investigation is again necessary given assumptions that the Internet is a leader in the mediation process of moving people. For instance, one claim is that the Internet helps migrants to "feel at home", as Mallapragada (2000:185) argues of the Indians in the United States. Alternatively, it helps the recreation of pre-dispersal relationships (Karim, 2004: 27). However, how do we contextualise and conceptualise these?

The media equally helps other migrants' groups and diasporas to reinforce communal feelings. Examples of these are the Filipino diasporas; the Kurdish; the Iranians in the US; the Indians and Pakistanis in Britain; the Armenians; the Jewish; and the Palestinians (Dayan, 1999: 18; Ang, 2001; Ignacio, 2003: 2005). The reinforcement happens through interactions with variants of media like radio, television and the Internet. Dayan notes that the media remain a major instrument of unity for dying out cultures or fragile communities, which diasporas are (Dayan, 1999:22). In empirical terms, how then do we understand this unity and possible disunity? Robins and Aksoy (2001, 2003) have shifted the emphasis from the diaspora framework in the understanding of migrants' mediation of distance. They argue that instead of integration in hostland, or a hold on the departed culture, something else emerges in between (ibid., 2005:26). This emanates from their study of Turkish migrants in London. Can this "new thing" emerge in Nigerian migrants' engagement with the Internet?

It is significant to note that transnational television and film industries strengthen globalisation. It also makes them important to reflections on present times (Gillespie, 1995:2). The industries facilitate the distanciation of time and space (Giddens, 1990), or their compression (Harvey, 1990). Transnational network screens suspend the sense of distance, simply as they add to the "remapping [of] media spaces and involving new media practices, flows and products" (Chalaby, 2005a:30). Alongside the rise of the Internet and mobile telephony, transnational television and film industries broaden ways of visualising distant places. They provoke thoughts on the coming of global communication. The consumption of transnational television and film products again reshapes the space of interaction, such that "it is no longer dependent on simultaneous spatial co-presence" (Gillespie, 1995:3). Interactions with a close person or group can be virtually similar with persons and groups in distant places. Television screens have become virtual spaces for the production and reproduction of images in remote places. This makes it relevant to transitory or resettling peoples and groups, like migrants, trans-migrants and diasporas. As actors in transnational flows, they are central to the understanding of transnational networks. Now between locations, they negotiate relationships between places. It could be in search for belonging; to live between places; or to mitigate longing. Modern technologies of transnational communication become handy therefore for the mediation of multiple interactions.

The industries, Robins and Aksoy (2005) discuss, enable the realisation of "long distance 'bonding'" (Page 20), as it helps the advancement of what they term "transcultural disposition" (Page 14). These prevent the dissolution of minority cultures into those of the majorities in distant places of residence. The transnational expansion which extends televisions' scope of operation beyond the "national territory" (Chalaby, 2005a:1), permits the virtual integration of global spaces. Isolated events become closer, simply as nation-states expect a reproduction of remarkable actions in remote places. Webster (2002:60), for instance, argues that transnational television exposes the underbellies of nation-states. He writes "The whole world watched as the Berlin Wall came down, when Boris Yeltsin resisted a coup attempt in Moscow, and when the former Yugoslavia was torn apart" (2002:60). Migrants and diasporas use of the rapidly expanding transnational networks of origins go on alongside the rising operations of leading transnational networks, like the CNN, BBC, *Aljazeera* (English), and Sky News. The networks combine with the Internet to offer dispersing people a wider space for the expansion and contraction of imagination.

For Nigeria and many other African diasporas, the internet is being embraced as a medium of information about origin. The reason is that satellite broadcasting from the *homeland* is still limited. In few cases of availability, subscription rates are rather expensive for the typical economic migrant, while there is still a restricted time for broadcasting. These factors lead to less dependence on satellite broadcasting and a relative higher preference for the cheaper, timeless and easier access to websites that report events on country of origin.

This research is therefore about how Nigerian migrants form newsgroups, send and receive e-mails, between them and with those at home; shares information on the World Wide Web, apart from live chats on current events in the *homeland*. In doing this, "consequences of both connections and disconnections" (Castells, 2001:269) shall be part of investigations. It can be theoretically assumed that Nigerian migrants are in a relationship with their nation, the departed nation-state, and the inhabited nation-state. The relationships could be real or imaginary. Nevertheless, in what context shall we situate the nation and nation-state? Moreover, how does this implicate nationalism? In terms of a sense of belonging, are they like "Janus, the figure from the Greek Pantheon whose gaze is simultaneously directed both forward and backward, (which) suggests a certain temporality; the figure at once looks to the future and the past" (Braziel and Mannur, eds, 2003:9). I shall now therefore turn to the question of nationalism.

THE TROUBLED CONCEPTS OF NATION AND NATIONALISM

Analyses of nation and nationalism, which are figuratively about "'belonging', 'bordering', and 'commitment'" (Brennan, 1995:128), have come in various ways. While some scholars evaluate it from 1980 upwards (Zuelow, 2006), others concentrate on ideas around it across time (Smith, 1994; Brubaker, 1996; Özkirimlii, 2000). Many others try to group theories of nationalism into typologies, for easier understanding (Smith, 1994; Greenfeld, 1995; Hechter, 2000). There are also various theories on its manner of emergence (Anderson, 1983; Handler, 1988; Gellner, 1983; Hroch, 1996; Renan, 1996). While a grouping of the arguments can be elusive, relationships between the individual and the collective to the state are in the centre of most analyses. Issues are also around ways of considering the relation between the self and the nation

The discussion of nationalism can be from other points of view, including ethnic nationalism (Hastings, 1997; Brass, 1991; Guibarnau, 1999), where association with an ethnic group is central. Then, there is romantic or organic nationalism, which emphasises the link between the nation, race or tribe (Grosby, 2005: 14-5). On the other hand, there is cultural nationalism, where a common culture binds a nation (Hroch, 1996; Hechter, 2000). Civic nationalism, implying the dominance of the state over all, as determined by the people is also another (Greenfeld, 1995). Liberal nationalism considers nationalism without extremist tendencies as common with xenophobes (Guibarnau, 1999; Hechter, 2000). Besides, religious nationalism, which means links with a nation, with faith as its basis (Grosby, 2005: 8) also matters. Then pan-nationalism, meaning a mixture of similar ethnic or cultural groups over a territorial space (Kedourie, 1960; Gellner, 1983; Smith, 1991, 1995, 1999; Özkirimlii, 2000) is another analytical approach.

In late modernity, nationalism can be evident in meanings made out of interactions with technologies, in the process of longing and the negotiation of belonging (Pattie, 2001). Nationalism, as Grosby (2005) argues, can partly be through shared beliefs and structures like through the Jerusalem temple for ancient Israel, through the parliament for England, and through the Ise for Japan. It can also be through shared ways like wears, anthems, religion and language. With these, therefore, can it not also be through gatherings around Internet resources like newsgroups that are common to them because of origin or shared interests? The possible trace of nationalism or the absence of it through these technologies is part of this research.

Furthermore, Foucault's discussion of nations and nationalism as a discursive and as an evolving process (cited in Brennan, 1995: 128) was in two significant works on nationalism in 1983 (those of Anderson and Gellner). His discussion highlights its growth as constructive. This takes place through differences and similarities, and through consensus and dissenting. It develops in the consciousness to reveal what is sometimes referred to as nationalism. Anderson and Gellner unite on the importance of industrialisation in the definition of nationalism. However, they depart on the question of what nationalism is, in the age of technology which industrialisation guarantees. First, Anderson (1983) argues that the nation is imagined. This imagination is limited, sovereign and communal. It comes when "members of even the smallest nation will never know most of their fellow members, meet them, or even hear of them, yet in the minds of each lives the image of their communion" (ibid.: 6). An influential discourse on nationalism, the theory regards boundedness as a psychological construct. It comes through a people's interaction with the print media like the newspaper. The coming of the printed word through industrial capitalism, in Anderson's conception, conditions the visualisation of the "absent other" (Giddens, 1990; Gillespie, 2000: 167). It yet leaves behind a memory of a "relationship" with multiple others, indicating an imagined collectivity. Besides, this "may be as important culturally as any information conveyed" (Gillespie, ibid.).

Gellner (1983) argues that the principle of nationalism could be obvious if there is an agreement between the political and the national unit. In this context, he implies that nationalism is a necessity, which arose in an industrial society and a resulting need for continuous growth. There should, therefore, be an integration of culture and the state for the realisation of progress. Before industrialisation (agro-literate period), heterogeneity of culture could be possible given the absence of technologies which reduced the need for the classification of culture. In modern times, however, industrialisation leads states to enhance technical progress via a meeting of culture and political boundaries (Gellner and Smith, 1996: 367-8). Hobsbawn (1990) extends Gellner's idea, arguing that the principles of nation could sometimes override those of political units. Nations are insignificant except as they relate to territories in a changing sense. He further departs from Gellner by arguing that nation and nationalism cannot only be from above, but from below through the expression of the wishes and aspirations of the constituting people. Handler's (1998) analysis then proceeds from the perspective of "below", through the individual:

> Nationalism is an ideology about individuated being. It is an ideology concerned with boundedness, continuity, and homogeneity, encompassing diversity. It is an ideology in which social reality, conceived in terms of nationhood is endowed with the reality of natural things (p. 6).

While Breuilly (1985:11) concerns himself with "political movement, principally of opposition, which seek to gain or exercise state power and justify their objectives in terms of nationalist doctrine", Billig (1995) introduces the concept of "banal nationalism", to argue that nationalism is an everyday construction, not necessarily limited to the dissenter, or those at the margin. Using the Western experience, he contends: "Banal nationalism is introduced to cover the ideological habits which enable the established nations of the West to be reproduced". Furthermore:

> These habits are not removed from everyday life, as some observers have supposed. Daily, the nation is indicated or flagged in the lives of its citizenry. Nationalism far from being an intermittent mood in established nations is an endemic condition (p. 6).

In established nations, Billig notes, national identity is unconsciously but routinely a priority in habits and ways that turn out to produce the nation. Barely noticeable, regular identification instruments like flags, anthems, language and currency (Grosby, 2005), which represents particular nations revive nationalism on an everyday basis.

In other notions, the question of commonality of culture, collective memory and pronouncement on equality are central in the determination of a nation (Hroch, 1996). Hroch (1996) stresses that nationalism is integral to social transformation through the growth of politics (Özkirimlii, 2000: 104-6). In continuing the argument that nationalism is a construction, Renan (1996) addresses the issue of principle through faithfulness and a common willingness of a people to invent a nation as grounds for its development. On the other hand, Brubaker (1996) would rather look at forms of nationalism arising from the nationalisation of "political space", as against previous ones that develop through the growth of political boundaries. Unlike Brubaker, Hechter (2000) discusses the subject using typologies. These are state-building nationalism, where a distant cultural group joins a particular territory; peripheral nationalism, where a distinct state resists merger; irredentist nationalism, where an integration attempt is made against a homogenous group; and unification nationalism, where the assimilation of homogenous group is consensual.

Attitude to territorialism and the understanding of this are crucial in the above analysis. Others say the way of appreciating the past and present are equally important. Smith (1991, 1994, 1995, 1999), for instance, argues that integration of the national past and the present need consideration in the understanding of nationalism. He adds that the "two-way relationship between ethnic past and nationalist present lies the secret of the nation's explosive energy and the awful power it exerts over it members" (1994:9). His integrated approach views the subject from the notion of the old and the new. Old in the sense of an appreciation of the *homeland*, (as a historic place), and agitations to protect the territory and valued centres, while it is new in the sense of concern for its evolving or shared culture, customs, traits, languages and thoughts. On the other hand, Smith (1991) writes that nationalism creates an "identity myth", from a multi-dimensional form, adding that it, amongst other things, carries political and social meanings. Greenfeld (1995) works on types and times. He argues that nationalism develops both individually and collectively to produce its three types including individualistic and civic nationalism; collectivistic and civic nationalism; and collectivistic and ethnic. The important ethnic question is present in Hastings' (1997) reply to Hobsbawn, wherein he distinguishes between ethnicity, nation, nation-state and nationalism. He writes:

An ethnicity is a group of people with a shared cultural identity and spoken language…a nation is far more self-conscious community than an ethnicity…a nation-state is a state which identifies itself in terms of one specific nation whose people are not seen simply as 'subjects' of the sovereign but as a horizontally bounded society to whom the state in a sense belongs…nationalism is strong only in particularistic terms, deriving from the belief that one's own ethnic or national tradition is especially valuable and needs to be defended at almost any cost through creation or extension of its own nation-state (p. 2-5).

Besides its temporal determination, Hall (1992) put more emphasis on the spatial element. He notes that nation and nationalism are not easy to construct because of their temporal and spatial processes. For Gilroy (1993, 2000), he argues that the appearances of nationalism are not necessarily pre-given. It is a result of mixing variables over time and space. Through difference, as well, Brass (1979) argues that nationalism is best from the viewpoint of ethnic and national identities' activities in the struggle for power, prestige and wealth.

Kedourie (1960) refers to the course of history and the expressions of nationalism within. He situates his analysis on the expressions of shared thinking amongst groups with similar language over time. The struggle for decolonisation amongst colonial and post-colonial Asian and African nation-states (Nairn, 1977; Nkrumah,1964; Wilmot,2006) are also important in the definition of the concept, as well as the several agitations in the Middle-East, and the distant imagination of the *homeland* amongst diasporas which, Anderson (1998) dupes "long distance nationalism". Fanon's (cited in Ashcroft, et al, 1995: 117) analysis, which has roots in anti-colonial agitations, however, fears that the "national bourgeoisie" could usurp state power for their own good after the agitations. Brennan and Bhabha (1995) also note that the importance of nationalism lies in the rise of the novel alongside it in Europe and in places where their influence spread (cited in Ashcroft, et al, 117).

Often conflicted with patriotism, ethnicity (Jaffrelot, 2003:3), tribalism, ethnocentrism, xenophobia, and sometimes racism, nationalism may imply a bit or all of these. It is still possible to express nationalism without any. Its conceptual diversity explains why a theory is inadequate for the concept (Calhoun, 1997:123), and because its "historical record is diverse, so too must our concepts" (Hall, 1999:1, cited in Jaffrelot, 2003:3). If this is taken as a license and I tow a trial and error path to view nationalism as partly a product of feelings, belonging, behaviour or attitude towards an entity that the individual relates with, (leading to ideas that emanate from social, political, or economic process), it would amount to viewing nationalism simply as a psychological construct (Deutsch, 1969:16; Anderson, 1983). Then if there is an overemphasis on the dimension of the state (Breuilly, 1985) in its understanding, it could again amount to reductionism in an affair that is a product of mixing social occurrences. Some of the occurrences are, for instance, ethnicity, which is central in the discussion of Daniele (2004). There is also modernisation, as Smith (2002) notes. Religious conviction that is obvious in the works of Smith (1998) is as well a part. Civil activity, which Brown (2000) reveals, additionally matters. It also includes free enterprise as Anderson (1983), Smith (1998), and Hecter (2000) theorise. Leadership manipulation, according to Billig (1995) and boundaries that Anthony Cohen (1985) explains, apart from civilisations, which is explicit in the theory of Huntington (1997), are significant aspects of the occurrences. These, therefore, justify the problematic nature of nationalism, as it tends to take a little, and sometimes, everything about most things, while defining the relationship between individuals, peoples and the state. The concern here, however, is about possible nationalism amongst diasporas and migrants. This "crystallise independently of the demand for self-determination (and) are not even territorialized" (Jaffrelot, 2003:7), but is useful enough to impact on institutions they relate with. In modern times, communication enhances these relationships. What does this mean regardless for nation and nationalism?

How do we identify the multi-stranded activities of the person in dislocation in relation to the nation? Nationalism can be defined through a migrants' state of attachment with a departed the *homeland* over time and space. And it is possible to evaluate this condition in relation to different aspects of life. The aspect of communication with a focus on the Internet is partly the pre-occupation of this work, not from a limited position like Bastian (2004) did on Nigerians, but from a critical assessment of the online actions of Nigerian migrants. Also related to the discussion is the question of identity, which I shall now examine.

IDENTITY: CONTESTED CONSTRUCTION, PROBLEMATIC DECONSTRUCTION

Identity is a concept that implies fluidity and change, sometimes used to address "everything and nothing" (Georgiou, 2006a:39). A contested concept, it has been addressed through theories on its meaning and construction (Hall, 1996; Bauman, 1996, 2004; Gilroy, 1993, 2000), rather than its shape (Woodward, ed, 2000; Hoffmann-Axhelm, 1992). The division is almost certainly weak, and overlapping. They even up to reveal the problem in conceptualising matters of belonging that identity partly represents. Hall locates identity from two sides (1996:2). The first involves "naturalism" through similarity of origin, ideology, or group. Raymond Williams also visualises naturalism in his reference to place, or rootedness as source of identification (cited in McRobbie, 2005: 43). The second, according to Hall, is through the "discursive approach", involving ongoing construction. The question of construction, instead of a fixed identity, currently has a dominant theoretical appeal (Ang, 2000:2). The predominance of arguments that identity is a construction and the critique to the essentialisation of identity relates to the complex human condition and position that results from class, ethnicity, gender, sexual orientation, location, age and place (Calhoun, 1994:3; Clifford, 2000:95).

The course of identity construction, Hall notes, cannot be essentialist, nor have roots in the past. It is simultaneously in the past and the future (Ang, 2000). Hall (1996) particularly remarks that its building process:

> Accepts that identities are never unified and in late modern times, increasingly fragmented and fractured; never singular but multiply constructed across different, often intersecting and antagonistic discourses, practices and positions (Hall, 1996).

This process, though through the point of view of "ethnic sameness and differentiation" is what Gilroy (1993: xi) calls the *"changing same"*. Acknowledging Leroi Jones as the initial user of the oxymoron (Gilroy, 2000: 29), the changes challenges absolutist ideas of identity, particularly through migrancy and diasporic experience. It locates the evolution of identity within the prevailing conditions of space and time, which are continuously in motion. This results in a newness that undermines the essence of a past. Gilroy sums it thus:

> This changing same is not some invariant essence that gets enclosed subsequently in a shape-shifting exterior with which it is casually associated. It is not the sign of an unbroken, integral inside protected by the camouflaged husk....The same is present, but how can we imagine it as something other than an essence generating the merely accidental? Iteration is the key to this process. The same is retained without needing to be reified. It is ceaselessly reprocessed. It is maintained and modified in what becomes a determinedly non-traditional tradition, for this is not tradition as closed or simple repetition (Gilroy, 2000:29).

The theme is also present in Bauman's (1996) metaphor of the pilgrim that is in motion, but who is enmeshed in uncertainties, in her/his routes. Through the desert path, the pilgrim constructs an identity-building place, but soon discovers that the desert lacks lasting structures. "The easier it is to emboss a footprint, the easier it is to efface it. A gust of wind will do. And deserts are windy places" (p. 23). To Robins and Aksoy "identity has functioned as an ordering device, but at the same time, and more importantly, we can see it historically as a device of cultural engineering: put simply, a person who becomes the bearer of an 'identity' becomes a particular kind of person" (2001:687). Implied here is that identity helps differentiations, and is a process of determining the ways of a people, groupings, or categorisations. It assists in the appreciation of varieties, through the labelling of differences.

Identity can, therefore, surface through a construction, destruction, shifty or alteration process. The processes can be gradual or immediate. It can come with ease or pain, slowly or quickly, individually or collectively. Individuals can also make identity (Marx, cited in Gilroy, 2000:127). Its definition may come internally or subjectively, implying how the self is seen, or from external conditioning through social definition of the person in interaction (Woodward, ed, 2000: 7). Identity helps in the definition of individual and society, partly through the questions of "Who am I? And where do I belong" (Gleason, 1995: 194). The conception of the self nevertheless goes through regular review via reflexivity (Giddens, 1991, 2000), and could conflict, or struggle with the social or external perception of the person (Woodward, ed, 2000: 7; Bauman, 2004: 16). The process is either rewarding or unrewarding, simply as there could be a balance, or a tilt on either side at intervals. It could also be at margins as is the case of migrants and diasporas (Bhabha, cited in McRobbie, 2005: 5). Emerging in the exchange is an infinite construction process, which Ang refers to as "incremental and dialogic" (2000:11). Extending Hall's seminal discourse on identity, Ang argues that its construction process come through the differences "between being and becoming". Importantly, "being is enhanced by becoming, and becoming is never possible without a solid grounding in being" (Ang, 2000:11). The discourse implies an understanding of one's past, the present, in relation to future projections, and probably the margins in between. Identity can emanate from many sides, and can help positioning. The positioning could be between the self and others, or the self within the context of time, or others against a collective, within time or space; or others against the self, in a spatial or temporal context, as well. In these circumstances, reflexivity enables the proper discerning of position.

As identity is common to matters relating to ethnicity, race, nationalism (Hall, 1995:435; Gilroy, 1993, 2000; Georgiou, 2006a) and other criss-crossing concepts, possessions like the passport (Woodward, ed, 2000; Hoffmann-Axhelm, 1992) can demonstrate identity in political and institutional terms. Politically, the passport may figuratively associate a person with a nation-state, simply as organisation or institutional identification could relate a person to the group. These further reveal that identity has multiple faces, because it can show in symbols, through documents inscribed via a brief textual narration of the self, or ascribed through an accident of birth. Identity can as well come via accomplishments. The passport document, for instance, represents simple features of an individual, like name, age, profession, and nationality, but also excludes other vital pointers of the self like ideology, feelings, or what Woodward (ed, 2000) describes as "how we occupy these positions or about what they mean to us" (p. 9). While the possession of the passport enables movements across places (Hoffmann-Axhelm, 1992), the participation of the state as the issuer in identity formation is evident. It adds to the understanding that the phases of identity construction are not only multiple, but goes across geographies and homogenous peoples (Hall, 1998, 1992). Other than that, it justifies the thinking that a person comprises of "multiple social identities" (Rojek, 2003: 180).

Nevertheless, the basis of defining identity is varied and conflicting (Woodward, 1997:1), which is why essentialising its meaning, is hugely unrealistic. While class, nationality, gender, ethnicity, and modern technologies of communication are some sources of its construction, it needs reflexivity (Giddens, 1991, 2000), and narrativisation to situate these variables. This is why Gilroy (1993; 2000) argues further that its shaping cannot be absolute. The shaping takes place in motions and movements and through reflexivity. In addition, the reflexivity is about a consciousness of "thoughts, feelings and bodily sensations" (Giddens, 2000:249), which needs protection in the contradictory age of globalisation (Ang, 2000).

Further to this, Castells (1997: 7) sees identities as "sources of meaning for the actors themselves and by themselves, constructed through a process of individuation", in an age of immense global changes. Three "forms and origins" of identity namely legitimatisation, resistance, and projecting are proposed by Castells (ibid., 8). In all, the role of the self and the society are part of its determination, through a conscious facilitation of reviews. More categorically, the reflexivity of identity, according to Giddens (1991), does not make it stationary or hereditary, but a product of an individual imaginative power. It emerges from a reflection on the dialectical interplay of the self and actors in interaction, in a continuous narrative. Close to this again is Gilroy's (1993; 1997) highlighting of the implication of space in the construction of identity, simply as he stresses its characteristics as a model for "understanding the interplay between our subjective experience of the world and the cultural and historical settings in which that fragile subjectivity is formed" (1997, 301). It, therefore, becomes relative or relational (Hall, 1989), as it is not a fixed phenomenon, but a progression arising from the "relationship of the other to oneself" (Hall, 1989). The dual logic of one and the other, illustrates identity as a contextual term, one that is dependent on judgements of parties in interaction.

Wendt (1994:395, cited in Fearon, 1999:4) extends this further by defining the contested word as a perception of the self through role expectations and shared societal understandings. It proceeds from a personal understanding of social role and the characterisation of it by society. Hogg and Abrams' (1988:2) approach is simpler. They note that identity is "people's concept of who they are, of what sort of people they are and how they relate to others". This may appear normative as it takes rationality for granted, but construction is also obvious. Race, religion, and language are in Deng's (1995:1, cited in Fearon, 1999:4) opinion, additional sources of identity construction. Jenkins (1996:4, cited in Fearon, 1999:4), refers to them as ways of differentiating "individuals and collectivities". Many of these underline its shifting, imprecise, and yet real nature. Though Gilroy's concept of the *"changing same"* implies these, through the main notion of construction, through reflexivity and narrativisation, and through being comparative or relational.

The absence of a common definition of identity does not change the reality that certain themes are common to it. These include its relevance in understanding what a person is, and is not, and how the person defines the situation either in agreement or in disagreement with others. It can, therefore, be complex, divergent, and a product of social and cultural processes, as it can be an individual or social construction, whether tangibly and intangibly. The concept is an individual, social and historical construct, which partly flows "from a tool kit of options made available by our culture and society" (Appiah, 2005). In relation to diasporas and migrants, identity becomes deeply intertwined to spatial, physical and symbolic mobility, arising from travelling and dwelling, and being insiders and outsiders in communities, localities and nation-states. It is not a thing "inevitably determined by place or nationality (or) for visualising a future where new bases for social solidarity are offered and joined, perhaps via the new technologies" (Gilroy, 1997: 304). The Internet as one new technology offers a unique platform for investigating identity amongst individuals, groups and peoples, because its dimensions are diverse and are increasing.

Notably, therefore, time, space and individual conditions are elements that could contribute to the construction of identity. The process might be subjective, through relating with fellow humans, or modern technologies, but possibilities of contestation shape these subjectivities, resulting in a shared social pattern. Amongst migrants, identity can be more ambiguous. This is because of dislocation that begins from source to destination and the associated challenges of self-representation in the progressions. New technologies offer fresh grounds for the reconceptualisation of identities (Gilroy, 1997). The Internet is principally dynamic in helping a redefinition of the self and groups via its confines (Turkle, 1995). How then does the technology affect Nigerian migrants' identities, or how do their activities affect the network? This is as well the concern of this work. The question of space and place of home and the *homeland* and the related idea of homelessness are central to the construction of identity in the light of the broader representation it offers. More specifically, its significance in the conceptualisation of the dynamism of migration is important. These are the reasons why I will now turn my attention to it.

HOME AND THE *HOMELAND*: A QUESTION OF IMAGINATION AND CONSTRUCTION

In line with its multi-levelled contexts, theories of home have come in different ways. Naficy (1999:6), for instance, sees it as a place that can be anywhere. It is not fixed. To this extent, "it is temporary and it is moveable; it can be built, rebuilt, and carried in memory and acts of imagination". As flexibility reigns in Naficy's argument, so are other elements like security evident in others. Brah describes home as a "mythic place of desire in the diasporic imagination", "a place of return", and "a lived experience of a locality" (Brah, 1996: 192). It all points at its contrasting make up and understandings amongst peoples, groups and individuals. These different appreciations also draw attention to its complex character, further leading to Tsagarousianou's (2004: 57) reference to it as a thing of subjective experience. In other terms, Rapport and Dawson, (1998: 6) describe it as a "physical centre of one's universe-a safe and still place to leave and return to, and a principal focus of one's concern and control". On the other hand, Hammer (2007), regards home as a "constructed institution" with which a relationship takes place. Also quoting Sagar (1997: 237), Hammer agues that home produces "bodies, borders, subjects, positions, discourses, and ideologies and mechanisms of surveillance". While the first definition talks about location, the second sees home as progressing from a complex motion. Obviously a value laden (Morley, 2002:16; Mallet, 2004: 84) concept, Bammer (Cited in Morley, ibid.) additionally perceives it as an "enacted space within which we try on rules and relationships or…belonging and foreignness". For Suasek, home is an analytical tool, suitable for gauging the processes of "territorialisation, deterritorialisation and reterritorialisation" (2002: 514). Therefore, home could be a place of habitation, or dwelling, or yet again, a town, or city, or place of birth. Mallet goes further to add that a home could be:

> The place where something is invented, founded or developed: the US is the home of baseball; a building or organisation set up to care for orphans, the aged etc **b**, an informal name for a mental home; **a home from home** a place other than one's own home where one can be at ease; (and) **at home in, on, or with** familiar or conversant with (Mallet, 2004: 3) (*Emphases in the original*).

Mallet's explanations stress its multiple applications. This is why it is a trans-disciplinary concept appearing in architecture, sociology, psychology, history, philosophy and geography. Conception of home may relate to family, when it is about an inhabited place in space; or a place and space for relaxation and retreat (Moore, 1984). Yet, it can be a space of belonging (Ahmed, 1999), where some space is controlled (Douglas, 1991: 289); or gendered, when it is about the traditional idea of the home as the preserve of the woman (Somerville, 1989), while the man plays the role of the breadwinner. It can also be that:

> The home is a major political background-for feminists, who see it in the crucible of gender domination; for liberals, who identify it with personal autonomy and a challenge to state power; for socialists, who approach it as a challenge to collective life and the ideal of a planned and egalitarian social order (Saunders and Williams, 1998:91).

Home is also, "the symbolic and real place that becomes a synonym to familiarity, intimacy, security and identity against the unknown, the distant and the large" (Georgiou, 2006a:85). Therefore, home is a place of rest, peace, winding up, association, leaving and returning. It is a place where the hope to return (Case, 1996; cited in Mallet, 2004: 77), and as Rapport and Dawson above attest to, remains. In the home, the wish to be in it, in the "new and disorienting global space" (Morley and Robbins, 1995: 87) could linger. In spatial or relational sense as in the foregoing, it becomes *homeland,* when land adds to it, which in itself assumes another round of abstraction.

The *Homeland* is again a constructed place in space, where a sense of identity comes. While "the concept of 'home' for many is mobile and nomadic, more synonymous with family than a particular place" (Pattie, 2001: 5), the *homeland* represents that physical or imagined place. It becomes a "cultural hearth" given the emotional attachment to it (Connor, 2001: 53). To Naficy (1999: 6) again, "*homeland* is absolute, abstract, mythical and fought for..." This is because of constant challenges to the places of the *homeland* leading to cases of homelessness. His understanding also implies that the *homeland* can be a variation, a relative phenomenon that depends on the choice of an individual.

The vision for the *homeland* may be blissful in the face of insecurity or persecution abroad. It could also be one of well wishes in the face of strong idealisation of return. Sometimes synonymous with fatherland, motherland, country of origin, land of my birth, mother country, the *homeland* is constructed through "memory and commemoration" (Appadurai, 1997: 189); historical association, or physical habitation. "Through the normalising processes of forgetting, assimilating and distancing" (Clifford, 1997: 255), the imagination of the *homeland* may witness a gradual reduction or erasure. Instead of any of these taking place, however, modern media like the Internet, camcorders, tape recorders, telephones, television "reduce distances and facilitate two-way traffic, legal and illegal, between the world's places" (Clifford, ibid.: 247), and in this circumstance, between the modern diasporic or migrant person and the *homeland*. It moreover creates a "temporal convergence", which discourages thoughts of return (Tsagarousianou, 2004: 57 & 62). The Internet has particularly become a virtual *homeland* (Stamatopoulous-Robbins, 2005) for many contemporary diasporas and migrants. Myths of the *homeland* silenced by distance and displacement find a space in the Internet, which is yet understudied. Overall, home and the *homeland* experience construction in relation to place and space, or in between. This is in a wider context of trans-border activities of parties. The activity arises in a complex transnational space, as I would now examine.

CONCEPTUALISING TRANSNATIONALISM

Analytical themes on transnationalism are diverse, interrelated and evolving. While the word is sometimes understood as a variant of the migrant whose activities bestrides borders (Glick Schiller, et al, 1992: 1; Kearney, 1999: 521; Portes, 1999: 464), it also represents the present-day interrelationship of people across nations where state interventions are unnecessarily absent (Albrow, 1998:2; Vertovec and Cohen, 1999: xx; Kearney, 1999: 521). Kearney emphasises the citizen perspective further: "Transnational calls attention to the cultural and political projects of nation-states, as they vie for hegemony in relations with other nation-states, with their citizens and 'aliens'" (1999:521). Glick Schiller, et al, (1992:1) add that modern migrants are developing new "social fields", which cut across different sectors including economic, social, political and cultural. The activities occur between the countries of residence and with origin. The process to the theorists is transnationalism, while those involved are not simply immigrants but "trans-migrants". These activities of people produce relationships across borders in manners that undermine territories (Kirshenblatt-Gimblett, 1994), subsequently resulting in multi-stranded interactions. The intensity of the interactions is, in addition, dense as a network across borders (Portes, 1997). Beyond the intensity, Portes (1999) offers a more lucid definition. He writes that transnationalism:

> May be conducted by relatively powerful actors, such as representatives of national governments and multi-national corporations, or may be initiated by more modest individuals, such as immigrants and their home countries' kin and relations. These activities are not limited to economic enterprises, but include political, cultural and religious initiatives as well (Portes, 1999:464).

Yet again, Kalra, et al's, (2005) definition is useful in the light of what transnationalism includes and excludes, and in how it avoids what a key concept like diaspora implies. The authors note that the concept:

> is able to describe wider sets of processes that cannot comfortably fit within the diaspora rubric. Thus, we talk of transnational corporations rather than diasporic corporations. The transnational also manages to avoid the group or human centred notions that diaspora evokes. The term allows a sidestepping of the usual pattern, when discussing diaspora, of having to evoke Jewish or Greek archetypes. At the same time transnational is more precise, if somewhat tame, description of the contemporary world of nations-state that might otherwise be called the World System, Imperialism, Empire or New World Order (Kalra, et al, 2005: 34)

Vertovec and Cohen (1999: xxii-xxv) discuss transnationalism under five categories. Though not essentially exhaustive, the categories are a fair representation. First, they argue that it is a reconstruction of "place or locality". This involves the exchange of understanding across nations. It undermines place and elevates space, through greater movement of peoples and through developments in technologies of communication. The second is the rising movement of capital, whether from "above" or "below". The former is in the activities of transnational corporations (TNCs), now exceeding 50,000 worldwide (Webster, 2002: 69), and the latter involves remittances by "transnationalists". Third is their description of it as being a form of cultural production. This means the widespread exposure of cultural particularities amongst peoples, through fashion and visual means. Transnational television networks facilitate the flows of these cultural particularities across national territories in manners unprecedented (Chalaby, 2003, 2005a, b). The fourth is the expression of transnationalism through politics. This implies political activities that transcend borders, although with roots within borders. The activities of international non-governmental organisations (INGOs), inter-governmental organisations (IGOs), Transnational Social Movement Organisations (TSMOs) and ethnic groups that act across borders are cases in point. The fifth and the last category is the understanding of the term through the views of sociologists and anthropologists as being a network of communities across borders. The works of Leslie Sklair (1998) on the growth of a transnational group of capitalists, politicians, bureaucrats, and Castells (1996) on the network society and a networking people, through increase in information exchange helped by developments in communication technologies, are important in Vertovec and Cohen's analysis.

In what emphasises the significance of communities in transnationalism, Portes (1997) examines the rise of these communities that are "neither here nor there". He arrives at three vital points that leads to their growth. I shall as well, reproduce these points, given its position as an important contribution to the debate:

1) That the emergence of transnational communities is tied to the logic of capitalism itself. They are brought into play by the interest and needs of investors and employers in the advanced countries. 2) That these communities represent a distinct phenomenon at variance with traditional patterns of immigrant adaptation. 3) That because the phenomenon is fuelled by the dynamics of globalisation itself, it has greater growth potential and offers a broader field for autonomous popular initiatives than alternative ways to deal with the depredations of world roaming capital (Portes, 1997:4).

Portes arguments seek to identify the causes of transnationalism. The expansion of capitalism is central to it, through his notion that the opening out of capitalism equals a consequent need for more labour and probably a cheap one. This labour force is equally eager because of an exposure to consumerists' traits in their borders, through probably the activities of TNCs. Therefore, the transnational movement of capital brings about the need for labour and market. It invariably affects the new or potential labour force, as the local market benefits. The new exposure to consumerism triggers a drive to the metropolis. They also still keep contact with origin within the wider process of globalisation. This reasoning features in Portes and Rumbaut's early work on the *Immigrant America* (1996), wherein they argue that migration to the West, the main direction of movement, is a product of an exposure "to life-styles and consumption patterns emanating from the advanced world" (p.12). Moreover, "seen from this perspective, contemporary immigration is a direct consequence of the dominant influence attained by the culture of the advanced West in every corner of the globe" (p.13).

"Movement is better described as continuous rather than completed" (Ley and kobayashi, 2004:1), in the period of transnationalism, therefore creating "confusion as to where exactly is home" (Ley and Kobayashi, ibid.: 21). These happen because the sense of place becomes fluid, linked, and in progress. Dislocations and relocations are endless, as actors move at will between nation states' borders. Places that are far apart turn out to be closer, or integrated through the simultaneous activities of actors in the places. "In this social field there is no finality to movement, but always the prospect of another 12 hour flight and another sojourn", Ley and Kobayashi (ibid.:18) said in a study of middle class returnees from Canada in Hong Kong, where "astronaut family" has also developed (Ong, 1999). In the case of the astronauts, family heads redefine the linearity of migration from simply moving from country of origin to destination, by regularly circulating between both places, while family is left behind, usually in destination. Like the Chinese businessperson, discussed by Ong (1999), they are "ungrounded" (Ong and Nonimi, eds, 1997), and "can live anywhere in the world, but it must be near an airport" (Ong, 1999: 135). Though the closeness to an airport is metaphorical, it highlights a readiness to move; the reduction of the limitation of borders; and even the ability of actors to act as if the borders are non-existent. In this understanding, travel plans are "continuous not finite" (Ley and Kobayashi, 2004:6).

A word "in the air" (Smith, et al, 1998: 3), transnationalism is taken as a buzzword that addresses a condition within globalisation, and also a specific word that describes cross, or trans-border activities of globalisation agencies and people. The many definitions of transnationalism also involve two forms of analyses. One is that transnationalism can be "from above" (Smith, et al, ibid., 3), through the activities of multilateral organisations and transnational oligopolies. The other is that it functions from below, at the informal segment, through global migration, diasporic movements, and a resulting mixing of cultures (Smith, et al, 1998: 3; Bhabha, 1990; Vertovec, 1999; Georgiou, 2006a).

More like a process, rather than an end in itself, the understanding of transnationalism can come through the hybridisation of cultures. This is because of the increase in migration and a possibly resulting change in identities (Appadurai, 1990; Bhabha, 1996; Clifford, 1997). The activities of some institutions can also help illustrate a process of transnationalism. The global network of the Catholic Church, as an instance, is an avenue for the understanding of transnationalism from the religious perspective. The activities of global bodies like the United Nations (UN), the European Union (EU), the African Union (AU), the World Bank, the International Monetary Fund (IMF), the Paris and London Clubs of Creditors, global non-governmental organisations represent the political and economic agents of transnationalism. Activities of transmigrants and diasporic communities (Karim, 1998) standing as "counter-narratives of the nation" (Bhabha, 1996:300), complement them at the micro-level. Though a tension exists between this formal sector of organised public and private institutions, and the informal sector of moving peoples and cultures, it is rarely unhelpful (Smith, et al, 1998: 5).

Noting themes through which scholars portray the concept, Vertovec (1999: 1) discusses it as representing "a social morphology; a type of consciousness; a mode of cultural production; an avenue of capital; a site of political engagement, and as a reconstruction of 'place' or locality." He subsequently defines it as a:

> Condition in which despite great distances and notwithstanding the presence of international borders (and all the laws, regulations and national narratives they represent), certain kinds of relationships have been globally intensified and now take place paradoxically in a planet spanning yet common-however virtual-arena of activity (p. 1-2).

These thematisations indicate some of the themes easily associated with the concept. A few of them are those of "weaker", but complementing players in a universal networking age. The definition of the term as a process is clear in viewpoints that the agencies of global bodies, transmigrants and diasporic communities are instances of transnationalism. Glick Schiller, et al, (1992:11), stress that transmigrants construct "fluid and multiple identities grounded both in their society of origin and in the host societies". It is within this framework that they negotiate citizenship though "self-making or being made" (Ong, 1999: 112), sometimes resulting in a hybrid or "new ethnicities" (Hall, 1991, cited in Vertovec and Cohen, 1999: xxiii).

Transnationalism is, therefore, about cross border movements and interrelationships of peoples, groups, communities and their cultures (Glick Schiller, et al, 1992; Vertovec and Cohen, 1999; Kalra, et al, 2005). It is also about the exchange and movement of capital (Sklair, 1998), and about interweaving cross border social and political relationships (Portes, 1997:199). In modern times, the media simplify transnationalism, because they function across geographical divides, in real time and in nearly no time. "New possibilities of being in two places at once" (Scannell, 1996: 91, cited in Tsagarousianou, 2004: 62) comes into focus. In doing this, transnationalism undergoes shades of reshaping, which open new avenues for scholarly investigations.

Robins and Aksoy (2003) depart from discourses of transnationalism situated from the viewpoint of imagined communities, or from culturalist diaspora perspectives. They argue that this models can be restrictive as they centre on issues around "community, identity and belonging" (ibid.: 90), originally derived from a national framework. The common, national perspective prevents the location of new meanings possible in the course of transnationalism. Individuals' power of imagination should be significant in itself, rather than concentrations on a collective imagination. Using their investigation of Turkish migrants as a reference, they argue that transnational television, for instance, brings everyday reality of the *homeland* life closer to the migrant. Then therefore, "the 'here and now' reality" of the *homeland*, disrupts the thoughts of the *homeland* as being "there and then". It thus works against notions of idealising the *homeland* and "the romance of diaspora-as-exile (making) transnational television…agents of cultural de-mythologisation" (Ibid.: 95). The model highlights the manner in which migrants' transnationalism becomes banal, and everyday. Recent rise in transnational media, particularly television in the case of the investigated Turkish migrants, facilitates this. The *everydayness* of cross-border mediation between hostland and the *homeland* expands the imagination, thereby upsetting the old believe in the idealisation of the *homeland*.

As with other migrants and diasporas, transnationalism for the Nigerian migrant is banal through regular engagements with people and places, especially on the Internet. It emerges via a routine exchange of e-mails with fellow migrants, with host community members and with some people in the *homeland*. The everyday desire to familiarise oneself with current affairs in origin, through surfing online editions of the *homeland* newspapers, or in the course of visiting news inclined websites of fellow migrants, and in an interest in cross border businesses online, reflect this. The process, as Robin and Aksoy (2003) argue, upsets the previous belief in migrants and diaspora idealisation of the *homeland*-an idealisation that was probably likely in the past because of greater difficulties in accessing transnational media. Consequently, like the Internet could facilitate seeming expression of nationalism, as earlier explained, it is also the case that transnational activities, amongst migrants can be facilitated online through cross border networking, information exchanges, and interactions in real time, across different nation-states. The online activities of Nigerian migrants as one of many transnational groups make a compelling case study. It represents a changing form of transnationalism, one that is highly mediated-especially via the Internet. The absence of literature on this subject matter is a gap, which this research plugs. In proceeding, I will now examine the social, economic and political situation of Nigeria in the African context, debates on the country's history, and its present condition.

CHAPTER TWO:

UNDERSTANDING THE AFRICAN DIASPORA: MIGRATION AMONGST NIGERIANS

This chapter attempts a critical analysis of some key issues about Africa and the specific case of migration amongst Nigerians. It proceeds from the position that the presence of Africans and Nigerians in the West historically originates from their slavery and slave trade experiences. The dispersal evolves into discussions on the African diaspora. Even then, scholars are still trying to find a common ground to describe it. Contending theories however agree on the usual dispersals from continental Africa as a reference point for conceptualising migration amongst them. The chapter begins by overviewing the dispersion of Africans through forced migration. It then examines how the experience and subsequent migration and resettlement occurrences progress into debates on African diaspora. It locates the Nigerian case as a specific picture of the changes. In considering the concept of the African diaspora, the section situates competing arguments on what it should mean, or how to define it. The essence is to establish the moving people within space and time, to situate their identities and communication agency, which is partly the object of this work.

THE BEGINNING OF THE DISPERSION OF AFRICANS

Africans experienced no fewer than 27,227 slave trading voyages during their dispersal to the "new world", between 1650 and 1867 (Shillington, 1989). A typical migration occurrence, it marked the beginning of black presence in the West (Dubois, 1970; Nwolise, 1992; Gilroy, 1993, 1997). Debate on it start date is nevertheless still inconclusive. While some scholars record 1532 as the time when the first set of Africans sold into slavery went across the Atlantic (Shillington, 1989:172), others note 1550 (Stalker, 2001). It is, however, safe to say that the Portuguese who made the first slave trading contact with Africans from the West Coast began exporting Africans from the early sixteenth century. There are academic disputes on the number of Africans affected. While some say it is 12 million in the three centuries of the slave trade (Shillington, 1989:172), others record 15 million (Stalker, 2001). Given the difficulty in specifying the exact figure of displaced Africans through slavery, partly because of sorry tales of deaths, due to disease and torture enroute destinations, arguing that it involved more than a dozen million Africans seems safest. Eventually, more than 40 million blacks, presently resident in the Caribbean and the Americas, are descendants of these slaves (Nwolise, 1992; Stalker, 2001).

They were "deposited Africans in the Caribbean, Mexico and Brazil-each case to work on tropical plantations" (Cohen, 1997: 34).

Some schools, however, argue that blacks foray into the West predated slavery, even though slavery heightened the process. Frank Tannenbaum and George Shepperson (cited in Wilson, 1997:1) note the 1440 presence of blacks in Northern Europe. Critical of the undermining of black movement in the pre-slavery era, Wilson himself adds that black appearances in "classical Greece and Rome or the early Muslim presence in Spain and Portugal" (1997:1), are worthy of note. Harris (1982, cited in Wilson, 1997: 119) was detailed on the pre-slavery movement that saw Africans in ancient Europe, Middle East and Asia. The moving people were then missionaries of different sects, and included soldiers and merchants. Importantly, pre-slave trade movement was largely voluntary as those of the contemporary world. However, movements in the slave trade period were not. There is an emphasis on the slavery period because of its mass effects, its dehumanising consequences, and because it began a chain of occurrences that still linger up to the modern world. Some of these are colonialism, post-colonialism, imperialism, and fascism (Shillington, 1989: 178). It includes the continuing accusation of socio-economic and political subordination of blacks (Fanon, 1967; Rodney, 1972; Shyllon, 1977; Wa Thiong'o, 1981).

Significantly, there have been different viewpoints on the dispersal of Africans. The slave trade period is nevertheless central to them. Scholars are either explaining African migration before then, during the period, or after its abolition. One is the pre-slavery period characterised with sparse, voluntary migration. The other is the slavery and slave trade period associated with massive involuntary migration. Third, is the post-slavery period. This is a little less massive, as it is a mixture of involuntary (caused by war, famine, disease) and voluntary (caused by economic, education and cultural) reasons. Shyllon (1977) argues, for instance, that the coming of blacks to Britain began from the "generally accepted date of their arrival in 1555". This was when:

> Five Africans were brought into Britain. Over the next century, more and more Africans were imported. By the middle of the 17th century, at least, a thriving black community had been established, and Britain had ceased to be a white-man's country (1997:3).

From that year, the experience of blacks in Britain began to assume different dimensions. Though they came as slaves, an initial covert activism in 1756 began a process of flight and resistance. Olaudah Equiano, Ottomah Cugoano, and Ignatius Sancho were amongst prominent activists. Slavery began declining in 1772, and with the 18th century rise of industrial capitalism, which the trade aided (Skinner, 1982:13), its economic importance reduced. The effective outlawing of slavery took place in 1807. From the beginning of the 20th century, therefore, black influence began to rise in Britain. Black population now comprises children of slaves and of black soldiers and seamen who settled in Britain after fighting in the Napoleonic wars. There were also Africans including students, business and sports people, apart from Caribbean professionals employed in sectors of the British economy. By the end of the Second World War for instance, 20,000 blacks in Britain were living in "dockside areas of London, Liverpool, and Cardiff" (accessed at www.chronocleworld.org on 06/03/2006). More migration of blacks to Britain took place from 1950 to 1960, from especially Jamaica. The 1962 Commonwealth Immigrants Act and other laws coming six years later in 1968, then 1971 and 1981 began restricting immigration of blacks to Britain. However, by 1991-1997 regardless, "Black Londoners numbered half a million people in the 1991 census, of which an increasing proportion were London or British born" (accessed at www.chronicle.org on 06/03/2006). Many settled in places where communal networking was probably easiest. According to Gates (2000), while some are London's Island immigrants:

> Trinidadians are in Ladbroke Grove; the Barbadians in Finsbury Park, Notting hill Gate and Shepherd's Bush; and the Jamaicans (who then made up-as they continue to do-more than two-thirds of the West Indian population), concentrated in Brixton (Gates, 2000:169).

Nigerians are in Brixton, Southwark, and Peckham like Jamaicans. While contacts through slavery and slave trade marked the major beginning of the scattering of Africans, it evolves over centuries into other forms of transnationalism. One of this is diaspora, which I will discuss below.

THE AFRICAN DIASPORA

Like the concept of diaspora, the meaning of African diaspora is still a subject of theoretical debate. Though some scholars maintain that the application of the word to African dispersal experience began from the 1950s (Edmund, et al, 1999:284), others argue that it began in the 1960's and specifically 1965. This was at the Tanzanian International Congress of African historians on "Africans abroad or the African diaspora" (Harris, 1993: 4). There are cases of opposition to the use of the word at all. This is because using the word diaspora to describe dispersing Africans means viewing them through the experiences of others-the Jewish particularly (Martin, 1993:441). Yet some feel it is accurate to the extent that it brings about senses of a common belonging (Shepperson, 1993, cited in Edmund, et al, 1999:284). Again, a number of writers note that the African diaspora is right as a phenotypical construction (Padmore, 1956; Dubois, 1973; Edmund, et al, 1999:285), because it denotes people of sub-Saharan African origin. Others see it as a cultural narrative as it relates to peoples of African ancestry (Mintz, et al, 1976; Herskovits, 1990; Thompson, 1983, cited in Edmund, 1999: 285). It adds into an expansion of the construction of the African diaspora concept through the commonality of skin colour. Furthermore, a few see it when employed to Africans as borrowed (Shepperson, 1993: 41). Shepperson (1993: 41) adds the scriptural dimension. He refers to Psalm 68:31, "Envoys will come out of Egypt; Ethiopia will quickly stretch out hands to God". He again notes Acts 8: 26-39, which refers to Ethiopian movement as predicting the African diaspora.

The idea that the word represents sub-Saharan African descents living outside the continent is meaningful. It refers to a people bounded by colour, as against geographical origin. Though changing (Akyeampong, 2000:183), the centrality of displacement, settlement, and possibly resettlement is, as well, a trait of the African migration experience. Harris (1993: 8-9, cited in Akyeampong, 2000: 187) captures the changes and stages thus:

> The primary stage is the original dispersion out of Africa (especially through the slave trade); the secondary stage occurs with migrations from the initial settlement abroad to a second area abroad; the tertiary stage is movement to a third area abroad; and the circulatory stage involves movements among the several areas abroad and may include Africa.

The stages are significant because they portray not only life in the diaspora, but also transnationalism. It is nonetheless too fluid to allow the location of their dimensions. Therefore, St. Clair Drake's in his Pan-African perspective argues that "Diaspora studies should include an analysis of the processes and implications involved in the mutual interpretation of the *homeland* culture and diaspora culture" (cited in Wilson, 1997: 120). Moreover, through the cultural perspective to the discussion of African diasporic experience, Leopold Sendar Senghor, Aime Cesaire, Jean Rabemanjara and Leon Domas, came in from the *negritude* standpoint. Negritude rejected the prevailing Western culture, with which migrants were interacting. While elevating the African belief system and history, the literary activism of Cheikh Anta Diop, Pathe Diagne and Alioune Diop (Asante, 2002: 112) supported negritude. Even as the cultural activists continued their campaigns, some other scholars sought an understanding of migration from the economic plights of Africans. Its roots are in history as the plundering impact of slavery on Africa testified (Rodney, 1972; Gunder Frank, 1971, 1975, 1978; Amin 2000, 2004, 2005). The contacts further eroded culture and self-believe (Fanon, 1967; Shyllon, 1977), which led to agitations for return. The Garvey's "back to Africa movement" and African-America's pan-africanist inclinations (Akyeampong, 2000: 185) are examples. These lines of thoughts are "absolutists" in the arguments of some theorists as the identities of the migrants have transformed overtime into new realities, possibly unrelated to any fixed idea (Gilroy, 1993). These differences broaden daily in the late modernity. Particularities within, including the Nigerian dimension, compete for analytical attention, which is why studying the Nigerian element represents an important input. In the meantime, I will now analyse Nigeria migrants.

THINKING THROUGH MIGRATION AMONGST NIGERIANS

Discussing African diasporic experience within the context of individual African countries is rather rare. The phrase "African diaspora" tends to become all embracing. It has been easily permissible because the dispersal of Africans during slavery and the subsequent push for return to the *homeland* after its abolition resembles the Jewish experience. The concept, as it relates to Africans, is therefore acceptable given their collective experience of "servitude, enforced exile, and a longing to return to the *homeland* that (they) shared with the Jews" (Shepperson, 1993: 46). This is despite arguments by some authors like Tony Martin (1993: 441) that the use of the word diaspora in describing the plights of Africans is wrong, as it means seeing the history of Africans in the light of other people's plights. "Let us use some other terminology. Let us speak of the African dispersion or uprooted Africa as somebody suggested or scattered Africa", he adds. The point nevertheless is there was an interference (Gilroy, 1993) that unsettled Africans for years. Those happenings involuntarily began in the pre-slavery period. It increased in the slavery period, while voluntary and involuntary migrations continue today. There are, all the same, more cases of involuntary migration than otherwise.

That aside, the dispersal experience of Africans from different continental African countries initially appear insignificant, because of the cover the African framework gives. It may no longer be the case, as the collective experience of slavery accounting for the greatest number of dispersion ended about two centuries ago. Colonialism, which succeeded the trade in slaves, began ending from the 1950's, up to the 1970's, leaving many African countries to be politically autonomous. Though the end of slave trade witnessed the physical return of some Africans to settlement countries like Liberia, Sierra Leone and many nations along the West coast of Africa, the fact of political divisions indicate a level of sovereignty. The succeeding colonial delineation and administration, as finalised at the 1884-5 Berlin partition of African Conference, further prepared the grounds for the political structuring of the continent. It then set the stage for the ultimate political re-grouping of the African people. The eventual end of colonialism, and the beginning of indigenous rule in many African countries, initiated new socio-economic and political experiences. Discussing the experiences still from the common African perspective hides the details in the life of individual countries. It also amounts to essentialising African countries into a homogenous whole.

Examining the Nigerian diaspora is significant in the light of important studies of the Indian diaspora, the Filipino diaspora, the Chinese diaspora, the Afghan diaspora, even if they can similarly be in the broader Asian diaspora. It is sensible to discuss the Nigerian diaspora because the Palestinian diaspora, the Iranian diaspora, and the Lebanese are, for instance, distinctively identifiable, instead of classifying them only as the Arab, or Middle-Eastern diaspora. The chart should place them independent of the African context, and away from being simply a part of the broader black diaspora, or migration studies. The focus is on the Nigerian case, even if through the realm of communication as a way of situating understanding through a particular case study. Notably, various scholars including George Shepperson (1958); St. Clair Drake (1978, 1990); Colin A. Palmer (1981); Joseph Harris, ed, (1993); and Folarin Shyllon (1974), have amongst others made references to the "Nigerian" born in the African, or Black diaspora. More meaning would emerge from the studies if a concentration had been on the Nigerian alone. The same meaning that an independent analysis of dislocations amongst Ugandans, Kenyans, or Ghanaians (Akyeampong, 2000), would produce. Furthermore, if the Cuban and the Mexican diaspora can be located in the US; the Magrebs are similarly examined in Germany (Safran, 1991; 83), while the Lebanese are discussed in their West African location (Cohen, 1997:98), analysing the presence of Nigerians in Britain seems proper. However, what is the state of the country's economy, and how do we understand it as it relates to migration?

NIGERIA: POLITICAL ECONOMY AND MIGRATION

Though the Nigerian topography is appropriate for agriculture, petroleum constitutes more than 90% of foreign exchange earnings (Castells, 2000: 101; CCDI, 2003: 3). Maier's (2000) description of the country is useful. He writes:

(Nigeria) is the biggest trading partner the United States has in Africa. It is the fifth largest supplier of oil to the US market, where its low-sulphur Bonny light crude is especially prized because it is easily refined into gasoline. As the worlds' tenth most populous country, Nigeria represents an inherently sizeable market that could provide trade opportunities for North American and European companies. It is a vast land, stretching from the dense mangrove swamps and tropical rain forests of the Atlantic coast to the spectacular rocky outcrops of the interior and the wide belt of Savannah that finally melts into the arid rim of the Sahara desert. Its 110 million people are an extraordinary human potpourri of some three hundred ethnic groups that represent one out of six Africans. It is the pivot point on which the continent turns (2000, xix-xx).

Nigeria became politically independent in 1960, after British colonial rule. The Immigration and Nationality Directorate (IND) country report on Nigeria says it is:

Heavily dependent on crude oil production, which now represents over 90% of her export revenue. All these have contributed to the lack of investment in Nigeria's physical and social infrastructure, which has resulted in a marked decline affecting fundamental sectors such as transport, health and education. Living standards for the mass of the Nigerian population have deteriorated markedly in the last 15 years. Nigeria's per capita income is about $280 at present, which is amongst the lowest in the world. **(Accessed at www.asylumlaw.org/docs/Nigeria on 11/04/2006).**

Disturbed by the increasing migration of Nigerians in the early 1980s', the military government of General Buhari campaigned against it. The government promoted "patriotism" and "nationalism" to discourage it. Mr Enebeli Elebuwa acted "Andrew", the passionate prospective migrant who soon changed his mind to stay back in a celebrated television advertisement against *checking out.* As Maier argues, Nigerians are in most countries of the world, with many in the US and in Europe. The continuing globalisation contributes to the push and pull. The new gains in international communications and the systematic increase in international finance capital are also encouragements (Nworah, accessed at www.nigeriansinamerica.com on 22/10/2006).

The depressing economic state generates frustrated migrants who end up taking risks attached to migration, in their effort to find better living conditions. Some use "the 60 mile (96-kilometre) crossing to Lanzorote or Fuerteventura, the Canary Islands nearest to North Africa-a 20 hour trip by rowing boat" (Stalker, 2001:56), to get to Europe via North Africa. Authorities caught about 400 Africans trying to reach the Canaries in April 2006. The figure when compared with the 4,757 in 2005 (accessed at www.csmonitor.com/2006 on 11/04/2006), is alarming. Wilmot (2006: 2) puts it rather simply: "Africans die crossing the Sahara Desert to reach the so-called promised land of Europe". Others forge identities, while some travel as visitors, but would never return. They manipulate host country's immigration rules over years, to regularise their stay (Portes, et al, 1996). The long period this may take is unimportant, because the initial reason(s) for migration is strong enough to sustain the desire to live a better live abroad. Though drawing a class line is inappropriate, many in this group are largely desperate illiterate or semi-literate. They have lost hope in the Nigerian system and now believe solution is abroad. The educated elite are a little more organised. Some of them migrate as visitors that may never return (Stalker, 2001), while some cash in on migration schemes of destinations. Many of the skilled migrants often lose their careers back in Nigeria. They rationalise the troubles of possibly re-starting a career in hostland by dwelling on the difficult circumstances that regularly prompt departures from Nigeria. Host authorities may sometimes apprehend and deport illegal migrants. Many, including especially the regular migrants stay in foreign lands, for years, partly enabling the thinking on the gradual evolution of a Nigerian diaspora (Maier, 2001: xxiii). Their length of stay and the emergence of generations of the scattering people further justify this notion. This is however still open to debates because of the increasing criticism of the use of the word diaspora to qualify dispersing people (Tsagarousianou, 2004; Robins and Aksoy, 2005).

Economic reasons constantly determine migration amongst Nigerians, whether in a military or civil government. However, political repression remains a one-off reason that forced many to migrate. The repressive military regimes of Generals Mohammadu Buhari (1983-85), Ibrahim Babangida (1985-93), and Sani Abacha (1993-98), led to the flight of many Nigerians (Adebanwi, 2001). Whereas Babangida's harsh economic policies impoverished millions, (including the middle class), the Abacha regime was highly intolerant of virtually every critic. Search for asylum by many critics, political and human rights activists in many Western nations was common (Ajibewa and Akinrinade, 2003). Indeed, the activists regrouped abroad, raising international awareness to what was a problem of origin. The resettling people became a "Nigerian in diaspora". The Nigerian press also found this a suitable name to call the re-settling Nigerians. However, what kind of diaspora is this? It may appear that exile has been mistaken for diaspora (Naficy, 1999), just as travel, or even tourism (Braziel and Mannur, eds, 1993). While exile is more of an individual experience, diaspora is collective, but again often runs into a danger of overgeneralisation. Yet again, tourism tows the adventure, or pleasure line, but diaspora is more of a sober, trying experience (Gilroy, 1997). In some of these cases, as well, time has not passed (Safran, 1997) to fit them into the term in its critical sense. The word nevertheless suits their understanding in as much as it describes those who live, or are finding a home outside Nigeria.

Many migrants in these circumstances deliberately move for economic or educational reasons. The economic migrants may include those searching for advantage or those seeking to invest their resources in safer environment (Brah, 1996:178). The educational migrants could be those who travel for further education, complete their course and are reluctant to return because of the difficulties of life in Nigeria. A few stay behind after the initial push of military high-handedness. These people dwell for years and are gradually developing, or have developed into a generation. Some could be idealising returning home even though it is hardly ever feasible. Return therefore becomes "ambivalent, eschatological or utopian" (Shuval, 2000:2). Others think of an origin; an ancestral home that would be a better place to return. Yet several may have independently migrated, while others are offspring of migrated Nigerians. They collectively form the new Nigerian diaspora.

What however is the basis for the thinking that survival lies abroad? I shall discuss this next.

THE CULTURE OF MIGRATION AMONGST NIGERIANS

Nigerians tend to be keen to migrate. It is always the next ambition of one living with a disappointment, or the adventurous citizen (Nworah, accessed at www.nigeriaworld.com on 24/03/2005). To them, all forms of movements, temporary or permanent are "travels". This is not necessarily in the common sense of movements, but an expression that describes positive dislocation (Momodu, accessed at www.thisdayonline.com on 28/12/2007). The migrant seeks to move probably to begin a new economic life elsewhere, preferably at any of the Western countries. The prevalent migration interest is almost certainly a result of years of frustration, or years of non-achievement. It is not always a result of individual incapacity, or lack of requisite qualification, but because of years of successive leadership failure. Migration here, Castles and Miller wrote, "is often a way to escape crushing poverty, or even death due to malnourishment" (1993: 139). Many also see migration as an immediate response to a pain, or a momentary disappointment. Instances of this are victims of robberies, rape, road accidents, bewitchments, and house demolitions (Ajibewa and Akinrinade, 2003). Frustrations in the work place, in marriages, over childlessness, or unemployment also lead to migration. This is because of an assumption that a new environment could be soothing. The overarching economic reason subsumes these factors.

The migrants may as well be professionals or non-professionals. The first comprise medical doctors, nurses, lawyers, lecturers, pharmacists, and engineers. They include workers who migrate for a better economic life, for better job experience, or for improved security (Parnwell, 1993; Maier, 2000). Because of their social status, and a likely concern for their reputation, migration amongst this group is usually legal. They are the regular set of migrants. Their determination to emigrate also leads many to accept lower status job in the first instance on arrival in host society. In some cases, a planned temporary job may become permanent. Some initially gain a work permit or a leave to remain through which they may become citizens. A few may well turn out to be people who move in and out of Nigeria.

The non-professionals who could as well be university graduates have different skills. Migration amongst them is a cherished desire (Smith, 2006). Amongst this category are those who overstay their visa requirements. It is amongst them that those with forged passports and identities (Stalker, 2001) can emerge. They are sometimes, however, able to remain, first living as illegal/irregular migrants, then eventually legalising their stay through a number of processes. Some of these processes are the application for asylum, bogus marriages (accessed at www.bbc.com/Africa on 04/12/06), or patiently working through a complex statutory requirements.

Generally, these migrants face diverse challenges. Apart from allegations of discrimination in the host country, the more entrenched native black population may as well be prejudiced (Christian, ed, 2002). Their accents become an issue, adding communication problems to their trials. Loneliness takes it toll, following the immediate loss of communal attachment that was available in the more traditional African society. In most cases, the migrant do most things her/himself, given the absence of a likely usual family, paid, unpaid, or underpaid assistance. While these changes are continuing and sapping, friends and families at home may now be restless, should the desired economic advantage that could lead to remittances be late in coming (Adeniyi, 2006). The migrant who is to meet their needs, becomes a disappointment! Meanwhile, the migrant qualification from origin could have become irrelevant. Concern is no longer with career or job satisfaction, but with "survival". Perhaps desperate, as is possible, they therefore make do with what Stalker (2001) called "dirty, difficult and dangerous" jobs.

In moving, they settle in different countries of the world with the Western industrial societies predominating amongst destinations as a "natural" endpoint (Braziel and Mannur, eds, 2003: 285). These popular destinations include the US, with preferences for cities like New York, Washington, Atlanta, Chicago, Dallas, and Florida; the United Kingdom (UK), with a high preference for London, Manchester, Birmingham and Leeds; and Canada, with Ontario and Toronto as major receivers of the migrants. Then France is one more hostland with Paris as a point of attraction. Berlin, Frankfurt, and Verda Bremen in Germany are also receivers of the migrants (Castles and Miller, 1993; Stalker, 2001). They as well go to other Western countries like Sweden, Norway, Greece, Spain, Italy, Turkey, Austria, Switzerland, amongst others. Non-Western societies like China, Singapore, South Korea, are alternatively attractive to them. Then countries that Akyeampong (2000:1) calls "non-traditional points of migration", including Australia, New Zealand, Israel, Taiwan, and Japan as well fascinate them. A few of them who cannot reach Europe divert to other African countries with better economy, or with greater stability of politics, like South Africa and some North African Countries like Egypt, Libya, Algeria and Morocco. United Arab Emirate (UAE) is another prominent option because of its growing financial prowess.

Interestingly, Nigerians are sometimes going to destinations in accordance with ethnic preference (Odi, 1999; Zachary, 2005). For instance, while the Igbos which is a major ethnic group in the country of over 250 million ethnic groups are fond of the US with Huston, Dallas in Texas as a major point of settlement, the Yorubas, another major ethnic group prefer London, England. With commerce in their minds, the Igbos easily associate with notable trading countries like the UAE, and the rising industrial societies of Asia and the Pacific Rim including Japan, Singapore, South Korea and China (Odi, 1999:2; Zachary, 2005:1). As previously noted, the Igbos are known to moving because of 1967-70 succession war, as it pitched them against other major Nigeria ethnic groups. It has ever since created "re-assimilation" problems of a sort, notwithstanding the "no victor, no vanquish" declaration of the then opposition, following their loss of the war (Odi, 1999:2; Zachary, 2005:1). As an instance of a vibrant diasporic presence, the Igbos in America have an annual celebration day, the *"Igbo day"*, where they gather to celebrate their culture, with the participation of prominent natives from Nigeria, following invitations.

The Yorubas travel mainly in pursuit of educational accomplishments, while the third major group, the Hausas, travel to further business interests. They (the Hausas) also travel for religious and cultural reasons, especially as it relates to the Islamic faith. This they share with oil rich Saudi Arabia and the stable monarchies of North Africa (accessed at www.nigeriamasterweb.com on 22/08/2006). Educational attainments of the migrants sometimes define destinations. While the well educated tagged "highly skilled", by some Western countries, prefer the developed West, the less educated are indiscriminate about destination. This is all to say that there remains a high level of flexibility on migration trends. While abroad, their activities eventually turn into a network, as I will now examine.

NETWORKS OF NIGERIAN MIGRANTS

The migrants, like many others, function within networks. The networks thrive around the cultural, the social, the economic, the religious, and the political. Though the boundaries around these are probably weak, they are cultural when hometowns or home villages within the larger state context come together like the London based *Odoziobodo* club of *Ugwashi-Uku*. They aim to foster the shared beliefs of their people, besides working for the progress of the hometown (Van Hear, et al, 2004: 10). Aims could be social as the US Igbo Association that regularly organise an annual Igbo Day, while ensuring the presence of prominent Igbo citizens in, and outside Nigeria. Group aims could be political when the National Democratic Coalition (NADECO) was for instance formed abroad to fight former dictator, Gen. Sani Abacha (Adebanwi, 2001). It could be religious when the groups cluster in churches to fulfil spiritual needs like the estimated 15,000 worshippers in the 50 different assemblies of the Christ Apostolic Church in London (Ajibewa and Akinrinade, 2003:6). There are foreign branches of many churches with headquarters in Lagos. Some of these are Mountain of Fire and Miracles Church (MFM), the Redeemed Christian Church of God (RCCG), and the Deeper Life Bible Church (DLBC). They command thousands of Nigerian migrants' followerships across Europe and North America. The aims and functions of these networks may be applicable to some, or all of the groups above, it is necessary to note that migrants form clusters for various reasons. They range from assisting prospective migrants to improving the lots of irregular/undocumented or regular/documented migrants, and for the development of country of origin (Ajibewa and Akinrinade, 2003:6). These groups importantly represent themselves online through websites, newsgroups, *blogs*, listservs, and usenets. Besides a representation, some of the groups are online solely for virtual interactions. Beyond this, many sites, news groups, listservs, and usenets with Nigerian interest multiply to embrace these "minor" groups. They combine to constitute what are becoming Nigeria migrants online, which represents a variation of diaspora network.

Some professional elites find themselves clustering in groups and associations like the Nigeria IT professionals in America (http://www.nitpri.org/index.html); Association of Nigeria Physicians abroad (http://www.anpa.org/); Nigerian lawyers Association (http://www.nigerianlawyers.org/ index.asp); and the American Association of Nigerian Pharmacists (http://www.aanpweb.org/); amongst others. The professionals, in most cases, form the core of the "influential" migrants as the less skilled easily ease out of international migration process (Parnwell, 1993: 50).

With some of the migrants changing status to permanent, naturalised settlers in a process of mixing cultural structure (Gilroy, 1987:161), some integrate into loose communities (Cohen, 1997: 180) in the bid to associate with fellow migrants. This unsteady character of migrants and migration results in different shapes of Nigerian migrants. For instance, a 1980 and 1990 official US government figures says one third of black immigrants to the US are Nigerians; while Georgiou (2000) notes that they represent a good chunk of labour migrants in Greece from 1985 to date. A 1991 US census estimate also says that 21,000 Nigerian physicians are in the US. British Home Office Statistics show that higher number of Nigerians sought asylum between 1994 and 1990, period of military dictatorship, while it went down between 1999 and 2002, a period of democratic reign. Becoming "migrants and vagrants" (Adebanwi, 2001: 49), many often feel a sense of dejection, while returning may not be a solution (Olaniyan, 2003: 1).

Besides this, the people are sometimes constituted into groups and associations like the Nigeria Community Leeds (NCL), Association of Nigerians Abroad (ANA) and the transcontinental Nigeria Diaspora Organisation (NIDO). It is significant to note that an advertisement of the existence of these bodies take place online. The NIDO, for instance, has a detailed site, where Nigerian migrants desiring information can choose from a drop-down menu on their country of location. Country-specific information, which may be in demand, is accessible. Apart from dispersion onto various countries, before reconstitution into associations and professional bodies, the web has become a space where the people cluster in different sites depending on interests for networking. Researching the limitless extent of the Internet will however be overwhelming, if not impossible. While I shall record their online interactions across territories, I have chosen the UK as a case for the investigation of their activities, and particularly, for understanding their online and offline communication practices in migration.

MAPPING NIGERIAN MIGRANTS IN THE UK AS AN INSTANCE

The UK census figures of 1971 say 27,000 Nigerians are in England and Wales (accessed at http://www.ukcensusonline.com on 02/06/2006). Hardly was there a significant increase in the number until the early 1980s when Nigeria's oil economy began to decline. From the figures, 30,045 were in the country in 1981. It moved to 46,231 in 1991 (Van Hear, et al, 1998:10). From the 2001 estimate, 88,105 Nigerian born were living in Britain. From the BBC records, it means, "0.15% of Britain's population was born in Nigeria by 2001". The figure indicates that Nigerian born UK residents are the largest set of Africans after South Africa and Kenya. (South Africa posts 140,201 and Kenya 129,356) (Accessed at www.bbcnews/uk/bornabroad/nigeria. on 11/04/06).[13] The figures above may have largely excluded the growing number of undocumented migrants who perhaps avoid counting for fear of arrest. The point is that a significant number of Nigerian migrants are in the UK. In addition, as a world economic power, it remains an attractive destination for troubled Nigerians, given its soothing promise. A focus on it could therefore represent the experience of Nigerian migrants elsewhere, perhaps in the Americas, in Asia, the Middle East, or to some degree, other African countries.

According to the World Fact Book (accessed at https:// www.cia.gov/cia/ publications/factbook/geos/uk.html on 07/12/ 2006), Britain is the fourth largest economy in the world. Its GDP estimate was $1.664 trillion, going by a 2003 figure. The Office for National Statistics (ONS) recorded a 3.1 percent growth rate in 2004. Generally, the economy has witnessed a steady growth from 1992. The country has such resources as natural gas, silica, oil, gypsum, lead, tin, coal, Iron ore, limestone, salt, clay and chalk. Its over 60 million population is the third largest in the EU. It is also the 21st largest population in the world. Its capital, London, is the largest city in Europe, registering over 7 million residents. Employment level is high at above 74.6

---

[13] The population is between UK areas including East Midlands; East of England; London; North East; North West; Scotland; South East; South West; Wales; West Midlands; and York and Humber. Thirty six million, fifty-three thousand of the population are however in London and they are between Peckham, Southwark N, Hackney S, Camberwell Green, Deptford N, Vauxhall N, Shoreditch, Vauxhall S, Bermondsey and Canning Town.

percent, just as literacy rate is at over 90 percent. Communication networks are wide ranging, and are still growing. A 2001/02 assessment says 65 percent of households have mobile phones, representing an increase from the 1996/97 figure of 17 percent. Forty percent of household have Internet access. The same figure is nearly the case with satellite, digital or cable receiver (accessed at www.statistics.gov.uk/ on 05/08/2006). Credit facilities are available in different forms from many financial institutions. Comfort, convenience, or ease of life is likely, depending on the status and preference of a prospective beneficiary. Against this trend is the tendency to abuse the process by sections of Nigerians, and other immigrants. Citizens may as well be culprits sometimes. A Chatham House 2006 report notes that:

> Nigerians arriving in Britain suddenly have access to benefits not available at home. Even though British governments have been putting in place tougher conditions for paying housing and unemployment benefits, there are still plenty of opportunities for defrauding the system. For some people used to receiving abuse rather than benefits from the authorities in their own country, the opportunity is too good to miss. 'They are not used to being treated decently,' says one banker, 'You now have people who have found an open system and exploit it'. **(Accessed at www.chathamhouse.org Page 23, on 11/12/2006).**

The story is often not about abusing an advantage. For many, it is in relation to rewarding investment. Lots of them seek productive employment, while they reinvest credits in Nigeria with a determination to repay. Importantly, the UK is a habitual destination. A concentration on it, with London and Leeds as sample areas is not only reasonable, but also helpful when cost and convenience are in consideration.

Some individuals with historical connections with Nigeria, who have made marks in Britain, are again an evidence of a significant relationship between Britain and Nigeria. The eighteenth century feats of Olaudah Equiano-a Nigerian slave migrant whose anti-slavery campaign reached across the Atlantic, is a case. Richard Akinwande Savage also made his mark at Edinburgh University between 1897 and 1905, where he was a student leader, and assistant editor of *The Students* and co-editor of the *Edinburgh University Handbook* (Shyllon, 1993: 235). Bandele Omoniyi, another Nigerian student at Edinburgh contributed to African consciousness through his piece, *'Defence of Ethiopian Movement'* (Shyllon, 1993) in 1908. In recent times, Britons of Nigerian descent have made marks in the UK in different fields. Some of these are Ben Okri whose novel, 'The Famished Road', won the Booker Prize in 1991. There is Shade Adu, the musician, and John Fashanu, the former football star, amongst many others. Of course, several quiet achievers exist in different niche businesses. The list further supports my argument that Nigerian migrants' activities in the

UK can be a representation.

Again, the migrants form a notable number of the British 2.2 million foreign populations, which is 3.8% (Stalker, 2001:16) of the country's total population. Besides, colonial affiliation lingers since the British departed Nigerian shores in 1960. Other pull factors are the English Language (British native language), which is Nigeria's official language. Nigerian people's exposures to the British educational system and to some extent, its way of life, as learnt from the period of their rule, are also encouraging. The two countries' membership of the Commonwealth (the association of Britain and her former colonies), supports these arguments. London being only six hours away from most Nigerian cities is another reason. The short distance, relative to the distant Americas and some recent economic powers of South-East Asia, could mean cheaper fares.

In 2007 a book "Nationality: Wog, The Hounding of David Oluwale", was published in Britain. It details the story of a Nigeria immigrant murdered in cold blood by security agents in Leeds in 1969. The writer, Kester Aspden, discusses the problematic issues of racism and particularly Britain's true readiness for multiculturalism. Aspen reconstructs an incident, which occurred nearly thirty-nine years ago, as another reminder of the centrality of the Nigerian migrants to issues of travelling, accommodation of foreigners in Britain, in the past, the present, and in determining its future. The realm of communication that my own work represents finds an importance in its new modern day significance, as an inquiry into a multi-sided relationships, and in this case migrants' mediation of distance, the mitigation of longing and the negotiation of belonging.

CHAPTER THREE:

METHODOLOGY

The work examines the Nigerian diaspora members' chances of using the Internet to communicate with their country of origin. The research seeks to know whether the Internet is useful for communication, for sourcing information, or whether it has a more complex role for communication. How different is it from previous media, like the radio, television and the press? Besides, the research investigates whether the Internet activity has implications in the experience of transnationalism. This experience could arise because migrants and diasporas are transnational communities. And the present age of globalisation features cross border activities of moving groups and communities. Do the migrants and their communication practices contribute to our understanding of transnationalism? Besides, are migrants' engagements with the Internet useful for insights into nationalism? If the answer is in affirmative, how is it so? And if not, why? Then, does the Internet contribute to the shaping and reshaping of migrants' identities, in a world where technologies of communication have become an important means for its possible construction and re-construction?

These key points may not be fully exhausted in this study and analysis, but they are investigated in a detailed and multi-methodical process. Because issues being studied are multi-stranded, the research was multi-positional, long term, employing various methods. My empirical study took place both online and offline. Participant observation was primarily online, while interviews and survey were the adopted offline methods. I did part of the research online as it was necessary to examine participants' activities on the Internet. It was offline because the migrants exist in the real world, and are possibly using the Internet to be informed, and to relate with real life issues and concerns. As such, qualitative and quantitative methods were used in both spaces. While qualitative method allowed the understanding of relationships, thoughts and dispositions (Grix, 2001; Silverman, 2005; Goldbart, 2005:16), quantitative methods permitted standardisation, the formation of categories, and the figurative expression of results (Frankfort-Nachmias, et al, 1996; Blaxter, et al, 1996; Berger, 2000; Fowler, 2002). Mixing qualitative and quantitative research advanced the technique of triangulation. It ensued that the methods were mutually supportive and enhancing enough to minimise margin of errors (Blaxter, et al, 1996; Grix, 2001:83). In triangulating, therefore, interviews, and participant observation, which are variants of qualitative research, were used. Survey, a quantitative method, was also used. Though some techniques were simultaneously applied online and offline, others were exclusive to one space. For instance, while participant observation was both online and offline, survey was offline. Notably, investigating online connections, disconnections, and possible meanings requires a high degree of diligence. And the status of the web as a domain of different structures with several social, economic, cultural and political elements (Schneider, et al, 2005:157) further encouraged different investigative approach.

Importantly, this study was ambitious in its aims as it explored the complex issues of identity and belonging in a multi-spatial context. The use of various methods helped the maximisation of resources and access so that the study records the depth and width of diasporic experience and the condition of diasporic connections on the Internet. Additionally, as diaspora and migration have been studied from different disciplinary positions and with the use of various methods, the design reflects this experience and tries to learn from previously conducted projects in various disciplines. I will now proceed to discuss the methods used, why and how they were adopted, as well as their limitations.

QUALITATIVE RESEARCH

INTERVIEWS: INQUIRING THROUGH DIALOGUES, CONSULTATIONS, DISCUSSIONS AND INTERROGATIONS

A major research technique, interviews are a way of collecting opinions (Barbour, et al, 2005:41) on issues relevant to a research hypothesis (Frankfurt-Nachmias, et al, 1996:232). Many professionals use it, for instance the police when interrogating suspects; the journalist when engaging a source; and the medical doctor when consulting a patient, amongst others (Keats, 2000; Berger, 2000:111; Barbour, et al, 2005). It is different from ordinary conversation because of the existence of controls in the gathering of information (Keats, 2000:1). Through it, a questioner (the interviewer) seeks to obtain information from a respondent (interviewee), who is knowledgeable in the area. The interviewee may know enough in some circumstances to volunteer information on an issue. An exchange between the interviewer and the interviewee, the process often offers an investigation more information than observation would do (Berger, 2000:111). While the present, actions, contexts and what is happening characterises observations, interviews are about past and present, attitudes, motivations, hearings and probing (Berger, ibid.:113). A researcher may consider interviews in the case of limited empirical data or the need for detailed assemblage of information. It is usually based on expectations that a prospective source is familiar with a subject, or the need to dig deep because of the views and opinions of interviewees, so data can be fresh, raw, and insightful (Creswell, 1997; Denzin, et al, 1998; Guion, 2007).

There are different types of research interviews. Most notably, they are structured, where the researcher consistently follows a set of questions. They are semi-structured, where questions are a guide but conversations sometimes go off the plan, and are unstructured, when the investigator exercises little control on the process, following the outlining of questions. A fourth, informal interview, as Berger (2000:111-2) notes, is one where controls are absent and "they just take place; are not organised; or focussed; and are generally used to introduce researchers to those being studied" (p.111-2). Interviews seek to find meanings, motifs and themes through a guided conversation with the subject. Probing of an interviewee takes place for clues, leads, facts and data about a subject matter. They are a means of digging deep into subjects' worldview in a discursive circumstance (Barbour, et al, 2005:43).

There are various procedures for the usually dynamic course of interviewing (Keats, 2000:21). Notable is the face-to-face, where a direct engagement with the subject takes place; or the administration of questions through means in a non face-to-face contact. The distribution can be through the post, through telephone, or through e-mail. It can also be through other delivery methods like hand-to-hand. The researcher's goals of credibility, validity and convenience are often a reason in choice of interview techniques. Clarifications, interpretations, recordings, thematisations, designing, transcribing and analyses essentially symbolise the processes (Creswell, 1997; Keats, 2000; Guion, 2007). Much as interviewing can be rewarding, questions can be on its overall relevance. For instance, appropriating single or few meanings to a complex process of interaction can be a problem, as it could be reductionist. In addition, subjects' statements are likely to vary between what the interviewer hears and what the true picture is (Gubrium, 1997, cited in Silverman, 2005: 45). Silverman (ibid.: 45) also refers to Holstein and Gubrium (1995), on the question of whether respondents are natural with responses or simply volunteering "constructed narratives". Data from interviews are likely helpful, but it consequently raises questions on information from the "real self" or the "constructed self", the "natural" from the "artificial" and/or the "stage-managed self" and the "unmanaged self".

"CONTROLLED" DIALOGUES

In this study, the interview technique was a means of getting close to the migrants. It gave a first-hand view of the sampled people's lives, from a close range. It would have made little or no meaning investigating a people without talking to a sample. By meeting and questioning them, it was possible to hear them and get their impression of the Internet; Nigeria; and to identify and collect information about their cultural and communication practices. Interviews revealed intervening or moderating variables unseen in other methods like survey and observations (Blaxter, et al, 1996), such as peoples concerns, fears, and emotional dilemmas. Supple and possibly result yielding, it was however costly and time consuming (Keats, 2000). In this case, I shuttled between London and Leeds about half a dozen times and spent periods in London, which is not my base, and had to incur an anticipated extra-cost of living temporarily away from my residence.

My interviews were semi-structured. They combined standardised questions with in-depth discussions (Burns, 2000:423; Berger, 2000: 112). Because of many evolving leads that needed follow-ups, several easily resembled unstructured interviews. Some sessions moved from semi-structured to unstructured interviews, even though many participants actually preferred the semi-structured format, probably in a bid to be guided. The chosen semi-structuring was good for the larger sample. It enabled a better control of the process, apart from ensuring uniformity. With a notebook, a mini-recorder and the outlining of my questions on paper, I had no difficulty managing different interviews' sessions. Apart from containing drafts of the questions, the notebook was mainly useful for noting of facial demeanour, body languages and other forms of non-verbal communication. I had to be careful to ensure the notebook did not distract interviewees by periodic engagements with it. Interviews and note taking were rewarding in many instances, as facts recorded complemented my observations.

Those interviewed lived either in London or in Leeds. Cost and convenience influenced location of the study. Participants were chosen through a purposive nonprobability sampling. (See footnote on Page 17). They were to have spent a minimum of five years abroad, to give room for a relatively good level of migrancy experience. The five-year minimum period of residency was also to ensure that a temporary resident or visitor was not taken for the unintended long term migrant. While this judgement might raise questions, every interview session began with a question on number of years abroad. The sampling was to include all classes of workers including skilled and unskilled, educated and uneducated, middle class and working class. Across these samples were medical doctors, pharmacists, lawyers, lecturers, political and union leaders, sales assistants, security personnel and local Nigerian shop owners. The sample also included the young, middle aged and senior citizens. *Snowballing* (Georgiou, 2002), however, took place in cases where some classes were missing, like it was when I needed to talk to a union leader, and had to seek help from a trader. Forty-six interviews were conducted. This number included ten under 30's; fourteen between ages 30 and 40; seventeen between ages 40 and 50; and five persons were above age 50. Different numbers of people were interviewed in each of the above age group, because of access, rather than by design. Those between the age groups of 30 to 40, and 40 to 50, which posted fourteen and seventeen interviewees were more readily available than those under age 30 and those above 50, which recorded ten and five people. Some satisfaction however came from having more people between the age groups of 30 to 40 and 40 to 50 because they are relatively of the active age, and therefore likely very familiar with issues under investigation. The 46 interviews included 23 men and 23 women, further divided between London and Leeds. A first set of 40 interviews took place between February and June 2006. I conducted six more interviews between February and March 2008. The additional six interviews focussed on issues around use of alternative media, other than the Internet. These media include television/cinema, radio and press. Issues around nationalism were also further discussed (see appendix 1). These themes featured in the first instance, but it required further investigations in order to position the Internet in the context of media culture and consumption. Roughly put, each Interview session lasted a minimum of 40 minutes and a maximum of one hour.

Venues were different. Some interview sessions were conducted in pubs. Many of them were initiated at meetings and later conducted in residences, offices, pubs, and in cars. Some of these meetings included a christening ceremony in Holborn Terrace, Leeds; a Nigerian group meeting at Memorial Drive, Meanwood, Leeds; a birthday gathering at Alwoodley in Leeds; a religious event at Central library in Leeds and another birthday celebration in Kirkstall, Leeds. They were also conducted in areas like Kirkstall, Morley and Chapeltown. In London, they were mainly initiated or conducted in restaurants, pubs, parks, hotels and in residences. Many of these were in public places like Brixton, Liverpool Street, Peckham, Leytonstone, Pimlico, Canary Wharf, Notting Hill, Thamesmead, Hampstead, and Vauxhall[14]. Venues mainly depended on the preferences of the interviewees. It was only in London that two interviewees opted to meet me in my accommodation. Different locations could be a pointer to the diverse state of migrants' places of residence. The locations also gave room for situating them in multiple geographical contexts. The ability to adapt or not in those circumstances can become evident, and could be beneficial to analyses and discussions. Different venues may prevent predictability, but can complicate geographical categorisations. To provide for relative evenness, not more than three were done in a particular place. On interview points in geographical areas, I preferred to have them done where the interviewees wanted rather than losing the chance because of disagreements

---

[14] The interviews in Holborn Terrace, Leeds took place 18/05/2006, while the Nigerian group meeting at Memorial drive, Leeds' interviews were done on 15/04/2006. Other interview dates are as follows: Alwoodley, Leeds, 18/02/2006; Church Function, Leeds, 19/02/2006; another birthday in Kirkstall, Leeds, 28/04/2006. Many interviews in London tool place on 22/02/2006; 23/02/2006; 10/06/2006; 17/06/2006; 23/06/2006 and 31/03/2008. Dates of interviews useful for analyses appear beneath excerpts.

on specific location.

It was difficult to make a distinction between the legal and the illegal migrants. While it is easier with the former, because of some level of confidence, it was hard to ascertain the latter even in cases of indicative hints. Differentiating them may not however matter much in answering the research question, given the likely similarity in the experiences of those who travel and dwell as one of travails (Portes, et al, 1996:156). As expected, some respondents were enthusiastic, while a few were not. Many wanted extra reassurance that the aim of the interview was academic. I gave a further guarantee on the importance of their anticipated statements. Apart from formal interviews, there were information from casual conversations and discussions. Though informal, they were useful sources of data that enriched analyses because the atmospheres were usually less controlled (Lipson and Meleis, 1989:106, cited in Braakman, 2005:41).

On some occasions, however, I contacted interviewees again on issues they raised, for further clarifications on themes under investigation. The repeat sessions were always agonising, sometimes implying extra-cost, but always very useful. In doing the interviews, I used a mini-recorder for reasons of accuracy and credibility. This was however with permissions of the participants. I transcribed interviews as I went along, where doable. In some cases, it was after a couple of interview sessions. Thematisations began after the entire transcription. In doing this, I outlined themes on key grounds. Themes were on the subject matter of online connection, disconnection, expression or sense of nationalism and leads on identity construction and experiences of transnationalism. With many transcribed materials on hand, notes, impressions, and recorded observations from the interview, the sieving and refinement process was characteristically messy, maddening and sometimes overlapping. To deal with this therefore, I used the Constant Comparative Method (Maykut, 1994; Hewitt-Taylor, 2001). This means the inductive identification of categories and units of meanings; separating the categories or meanings with a code or label; and re-reading of the transcriptions again to check if there are valuable themes missed, while initially identifying and separating the categories and meanings. If this emerges, new categories were created or the freshly identified meanings were integrated into those previously sorted. A fine-tuning of the processes followed these. Then the examination of relationships amongst the categories was done and lastly the integration and analyses of data. The key meanings identified from the transcriptions were as they relate to the communication ability of the Internet, or lack of it; nationalism evidence or its absence; indications of transnationalism; and identity construction and reconstruction. I added return as a theme during a review of the categories, because of its relative importance and its usually controversial state. The issues may not be exhaustive, but they were central in the general confessions of participants and are core enough to the exploration of the relationship between theory as discussed in Chapter one and the activities of participants. The entire exercise required further sifting many times over for reasons of credibility.

PARTICIPANT OBSERVATION: A WITNESS TO MIGRANTS' ONLINE AND OFFLINE AGENCY

Participant observation seems an improvement when compared with simple observation. Instead of simply observing, the researcher is involved in the investigated activity. Earlier associated with anthropology and now with different forms of ethnography (Silverman, 2005:379), it involves the application of the sensory organs, to wit: the eyes, the ears, the nose, the mouth and the hands for the discerning of meanings (Jones, et al, 2005:138). Significant as a method, sieving and evaluation of the data progress as "the researcher understands 'being in the world (ontology) and the nature of knowledge (epistemology)" (Jones, ibid.: 141). Observations come through details like the researcher's worldview, preferences, biases, background and identities. Also regarded as a unique form of observation (Jorgensen, 1989:7), it could imply a deep integration with the group being studied or some defined membership status (Frankfort-Nachmias, et al, 1996: 282). Success in it is dependent on the skills, flair and friendliness of the researcher (Jorgensen, 1989:8; Berger, 2000:167). It may as well require the learning of the "language, habits, work patterns, leisure activities, and other aspects of (subject's) daily lives" (Frankfort-Nachmias, et al, 1996: 282). It enables the researcher to see the world of the subject, not from a distance like mere observation, but probably like the subjects see it, through a first hand experience. Helpful to interpretative studies, the method gives further room for the analysis of both verbal and non-verbal communication (Gunter, 2000:5). Participant observation requires a simultaneous or close process of joining, integration, monitoring, watching and note taking (Jorgensen, 1989; Frankfort-Nachmias, et al, 1996; Gunter, 2000). Though note-taking time often depends on the researcher's judgement, it should not be too far from the time of activity to avoid forgetting (Gunter, 2000). It should also not be often enough to constitute distraction to subjects.

A form of qualitative research, participant observation requires the establishment of understanding with subjects (Hammersley, et al, 1983). Though the atmosphere may become less controlled upon involvement, the responsibility is on the researcher "to balance two roles: that of being participant and that of being observer" (Berger, 2000:161). There is a need to avoid "going native" (Berger, ibid.), meaning "becoming so identified with this group that they lose their objectivity" (p.161). Objectivity, credibility and reliability require the researcher to be reflexive,[15] and to be

---

[15] I shall discuss reflexivity at a latter part of this chapter.

reviewing of her/his role in relation to the study. A concern for this could help to minimise its drawback, which is to a degree, the difficulty in determining the complexity of human action (Jones, et al, 2005:138). Berger (2000: 166-7) also raises several problems. These are the possibility of losing focus and the problem of "reactivity". There is the issue of whether or not subjects are behaving in a certain way because of the researcher's presence. Problems arising from errors in what to note and not to note also matter. Then temptation of mind reading, implying an assumption of what the subject of study means through actions and inactions is also noteworthy. Other than this is the ethical question of identity disclosure: should subjects be aware of researchers' motive or not? However, it makes sense to say that participant observation allows for a more integrated scrutiny of groups, in their natural setting, even while the result is dependent on the researcher's worldview.

PARTICIPANT OBSERVATION IN USE

My approach in applying participant observation to this research was multileveled. One of its elements was the gathering of facts from chanced insights into the manners of the Nigerian diaspora members. These insights occurred in interactions with them at meetings, in shops, restaurants, and through participating in Nigerian religious activities. It also took place through casual listening to stories, reports and experiences of Nigerians abroad. The insights were at formal and informal forums, with friends, family members, colleagues and acquaintances and host society members. Significant data was collected in this way. Some of this includes gripping stories of some migrants' experiences: how they began, how they have settled or failed to settle; deportations; work experiences; educational and health services' experiences and such others. Complementing techniques reinforced or reduced some of these facts to nothing. Again, I also occasionally took part in newsgroups' discussions, chats, and e-mail exchanges. I sometimes started lines of debates on areas where I wanted specific insights, for instance (on one occasion) their thoughts on changing accents in post-migration. Interpretations of Facebook, *Bebo, Orkut,* and Myspace discussions were a part of the research. Other than this, cross and multiple postings of information revealed data that gave clues and directions for analyses.

More specifically, I observed a newsgroup, naija-politics@ yahoogroups.com, during three periods over 2006. This stretched through the first weeks of March, April and May of that year. Choosing the periods and the newsgroup was for purposive nonprobability reasons. Averages of ten contributions, -long, short or medium-come to the list every hour. I observed them for three hours on each of the working weekdays as defined above. With the ten postings per hour contribution, it meant I examined an estimated thirty articles on each day. By the end of the third week, I had observed roughly 450 contributions. This is apart from other chat rooms of observed websites (Details in typology on pages 87-88). This process was productive because it was inexpensive, and was useful for learning about migrants' interests in discussions. It was sometimes tiring as it involved prolonged surfing. Excitement came at intervals through jokes and thrilling contributions of some participants. The overall objective of examining a people in an online setting was motivating. Its representative capacity may raise questions, but mixing techniques balanced each method's limitations.

As an ethnographic method, participant observation is helpful in the generation of meanings, not necessarily in the quantitative, positivistic dimension but through a complex interplay of actions, and in the interpretation of the actions (Hammersley, et al, 1983: 1; Goldbart, et al, 2005:18). In the precise case of the Internet, which Tapper (2001:15) calls "internetnography", it involves integration, or immersion with the group studied. A simultaneous writing about groups was a key characteristic (Fetterman, 1998:1; Denzin, 1998; Silverman, 2005:49; Goldbart, et al, 2005: 18). What is written is not necessarily selective but largely inclusive to depict the routine lives of the people, in the bid to examine their behaviour and thoughts (Fetterman, 1998:1), as expressed online.

Moreover, for a broader ethnographic context, participant observation becomes important for the study of the Internet. Now an important location for the modern ethnographer (Fetterman, ibid.), the Internet has become a huge resource base for the ethnographer's search for meanings, embedded in the cluster of human offline activity. The density of online activity can as well represent the practice. While the former is natural and traditional, the latter is technological, implying mediation through technology, as against the physical, face-to-face character of offline field (Hine, 2005:1; Beaulieu, 2005). The possibility of a technological based "field" of the Internet is however still an issue in ethnographic methodological debate (Hine, 2005:1; Beaulieu, 2005:183). The closeness of life online to life offline means there is an alternative to life offline. This encourages the thinking on the possibility of virtual ethnography, which Tapper (2001: 15) describes.

A typology of the more than seventy websites studied can be found below. This may however not be perfect, but it is simply "to provide the framework for interpretation" (Hiller and Franz, 2004:737), and to make a sense (Chalaby, 2005c: 155) of the wide range of online interests. While the typologies may overlap with one another, they are based on prevailing concerns. The search for meanings as they relate to key theoretical themes like possibilities of communicating, transnationalism, nationalism, and identity shaping and reshaping led to the study of the sampled sites. The attention paid to every site could not be equal, as some were obviously more informative than others were[16]. The supposedly less popular sites were also studied when necessary. A number of issues led to the sampling of some websites. These were confirmation from websites that pose to keep record of traffics like www.alexa.com[17]. Then volume of online and offline references to these sites were considered. The references came in offline interactions and more in online spaces like Nigerian related homepages, newsgroups, chatrooms and usenets. Many respondents to the survey questions also refer to these websites as their favourites. The interview sessions revealed as much. Sites easily trust up in these circumstance are the www.nigerianworld.com, www.nigeriamasterweb.com and www.nigeriannews.com, amongst many others. There were chance encounters of few others. The controversial ones were easier to identify, particularly through the propaganda concerns they cause Nigerian governments and elites. The worries were through their daring, unconventional, non-equivocal, but sometimes flawed reportage of exclusive stories, which web editions of Nigerian newspapers would ordinarily not report. The criticisms most times serve as leads or online sources for other news agencies, and even local newspapers. Offline and other online references to them by migrants' were always common. Examples of these are www.saharareporters.com, www.elendureports.com and www.pointblanknews.com. Apart from these, I coincidentally came across some other sites through a regular use of the Internet, and a usual use of search engines, like Google, Yahoo, Hotmail, and Alta Vista. Rather than being inadequate, it was quite a constant challenge to reduce, via sorting the "relevant" from the "irrelevant". In working through the data, there is however the element of human errors through missing out valuable items or by way of leaving out potentially useful themes or sub-themes. The outlining of key issues offered a sense of direction. Besides, the harmonising effect of triangulation is valuable enough to take analyses closer to the general picture. Though the interests of sampled websites are sometimes vague, I have grouped them on the strength of themes that regularly prevail.

---

[16] An example of an informative one is www.nigeriaworld.com. An instance of a less informative, but useful one is www.pointblanknews.com.

[17] Alexa.com is a "web information company", which specialises in traffic ranking of websites, under different categories like language, country, and influence, amongst others.

Figure 1: A Typology of Observed Websites

TYPE OF WEBSITE	DESCRIPTION	EXAMPLES
Type A: News and current affairs' websites	These are migrants' websites. The interests are diverse, and they focus on different Nigerian, and other related issues. The issues could be political, economic, social, professional or family. They operate like the traditional mainstream media, particularly the press, with sections and sub-sections on different sectors.	• www.nigeriamasterweb.com • www.nigeriaworld.com • www.nanka.com • www.saharareports.com • www.elendureports.com • www.pointblanknews.com • www.naijapages.com • www.nigeriaweb.com • www.dawodu.com • www.odili.net • www.nigeriawatchnews.com • www.naijamailnews.com • www.thetimesofnigeria.com • www.nairaland.com • www.worldskipnews.com • www.amebonews.com • www.wazobia.com • www.netnigerianews.com • www.nigerianation.com • www.nigeriainfornet.com
Type B: Specialised websites	These concentrate on a limited aspect of life. They promote particular ideas like fashion, ideologies, profession, gender matters, religion, and sports to serve specified interests.	• www.winnerscanaanland.org • www.mfm.com • www.rccg.com • www.ana.com • www.chitafrik.com • www.nigeriawomen.com • www.nigeria-arts.net • www.nitpri.org • www.anpa.org • www.nigerialawyers.org • www.aanpweb.org
Type C: Ethnic sites	This, as the name implies, includes pages of migrants' groups interested in continuing with their Nigerian ethnic cleavages.	• www.edonation.com • www.arewaonline.com • www.asaba.com • www.zumunta.com • www.yorubahomepage.com • www.oduduwa.com • www.Igbo-net.com • www.biafraland.com • www.arochukwu.com • www.egbeIsokanyoruba.com • www.warri.com • www.uromicommunity-ny.com • www.rivnet.com • www.amanaonline.com • www.irinnews.com
Type D: Blogs and individual websites	In this category are *bloggers*, and individuals devoted to propagating an idea, or an interest. They are also of occasional pages	• www.nigeriamuse.com • www.uchenworah.com • www.nigerianthoughts.com • wwww.naija-politics.com.

	of those who set up sites for an event and then fail to continue with it.	
Type E: Organisations/corporate bodies' websites	These are of groups and migrant associations, concerned about Nigerian migrants in general, despite ethnic group or creed. In this group are also corporate bodies' sites.	• www.nigerialeeds.com • www.nido-nl.org • www.nidoeurope.com • www.yahoo.com • www.google.com • www.msn.com
Type F: Official websites	Official sites include government sites like the Nigerian governments', alongside other foreign missions.	• www.nigeriahighcommission uk.com
Type G: Other websites	Here I include sites not necessarily Nigerian related but have sections or resources on Nigerians and perhaps on the migrants.	• www.cnn.com • www.bbc.com • www.allafrica.com
Type H: Nigerian websites	In this classification are online versions of Nigeria based media. They help to understand how migrants relate with Nigeria, or how the site owners may perceive the absent people, and for any other themes that may relate with the research.	• ngrguardiannews.com • thisdayonline.com • www.punchng.com • sunnewsonline.com

While the first six categories above are either constructed, or administered from outside Nigeria, the last comprise of those administered from Nigeria. Some from the Nigerian sites, like www.worldmissionagency.org, has migrants as its targets. Other than these specific cases, there were other "floating" but relevant materials. They are not necessarily in websites, but came up in search engines. Many times, the intention may be to while away time on the Internet. The act of idling away may lead to valuable discoveries that became helpful to understanding key issues under investigation. It is also noteworthy that many of these websites share addresses between and within themselves. With one site having links to other useful sites, a surfer is often tempted to move between them, such that surfing one site could translate into surfing many others at every other time.

Observation was used as this study worked through the massive space of Nigerian migrants' online life. It was through participation, via the examination of virtual materials in bits and pieces and as best possible. Observation was also through understanding and interpretation of the materials not as a distant observer, but as a submerged investigator interested in key details of a people's online activities. These were all towards the discovery of key meanings, in an evolving Internet culture. Again, I took notes as the observations of the resources went on. Images and figures useful for illustrations were also considered. Subsequently, the meanings from there were indexed around communication with Nigeria, or lack of it; manifestation of transnationalism; expression of nationalism; and indications on identity. *Return* question also counted as a sub-theme. These were compared with similar exercises that followed the transcribed interviews, for purposes of establishing relationships, or lack of it. It explains why discussions and analyses will feature a simultaneous mix of relevant quotations from face-to-face interviews, quotes, statements, figures and images from websites, listservs, newsgroups, chat rooms, e-mail lists and news pages. Apart from this, the third method adopted, which is survey, (I will explain this shortly) is often times part of the analytical process. It is a way of figuratively illustrating ideas. The illustrations come before or after narratives, where they could further support arguments. These are especially common where materials from interviews and observations were inappropriate. Other than this, qualitative methodology complemented the quantitative in a triangulated process of balancing. Nevertheless, quantitative method was limited to survey, which amongst other things, helped in the formation of categories; in achieving a fair geographical representation of the migrants and in the specific mapping of their activities. I will therefore now discuss this and then follow it with how the exercise went.

QUANTITATIVE RESEARCH

SURVEY: PARTICIPATION THROUGH A RESPONSE TO SET QUESTIONS

Survey research usually seeks to produce numerical statistics about a sample proportion of a population. This is always through questions that would later be analysed (Fowler, 2002:1-2). The sample frame is to represent that population (Hutton, 1990:8, cited in Blaxter, et al, 1996:77), from where meanings come through a well thought out process. The aim is to understand identified differences amongst respondents. It brings forth results that could represent the larger sample (Blaxter, et al, ibid.: 79). While the questions should avoid prejudice, Berger (2000:188) notes two types namely descriptive and analytic. The first seeks information on "age, gender, marital status, occupation, race or ethnicity, income and religion and to relate this information to opinions, beliefs, values, and behaviours", the second is concerned about "why people behave the way they do". The importance of the first type is the formation of categories and identifying differences between groups in a sample. It gives an inner picture of those studied and offers an opportunity for a comparative analysis of data, mostly in the figurative sense. This form of survey is more popular than the analytical variant, usually needed for the development of hypotheses, testing it and the investigation of casual relationships between variables (Berger, 2000:189-9). Survey techniques can be through interviews or the administration of questionnaires. The interview can also be face-to-face, or on telephone. Distribution of questionnaires can be in various ways including the post, e-mail or physical, which is hand-to-hand (Berger, 2000; Frankfort-Nachmias, et al, 1996). The choice of a technique is dependent on the skill, experience and perception of the researcher. The core goals of reliability should however be an important consideration, to ensure the validity and the usefulness of data (Gunter, 2000:23).

Importantly, survey is good for structuring and standardising. Survey also helps the consideration of bits and pieces of differences amongst groups. Understanding possible relationship to each other can come from there. A limitation of the survey is often in the certainty that data is more in figures and diagrams. The exclusion of inner details may emerge (Blaxter, et al, 1996:79). These details come in the nuances embedded in people's conducts, but easily lost in figurative expressions. Other more expressive research methods mainly of the qualitative variety challenge the attempt of survey analysis to reduce the complexities of human behaviour to numbers. Survey process could be costly, time consuming and could yield poor response rate (Frankfort-Nachmias, et al, 1996). The survey in this project is descriptive as it complements the qualitative techniques, through the formation of typologies, the identification of migrants' particularities, and in the making of meanings out of their complexities-a basic character in human interaction.

THE SURVEYING PROCESS

Thinking of questions to ask respondents began nearly the same time as the research programme. A higher momentum came from around December 2005. The questions were finally ready in early February 2006. There were thirty-five questions in all (See Appendix 3). Piloting took place between early February, and early March 2006. This was in Leeds, with seven people. Their responses were quite helpful. For instance, one or two respondents called my attention to the possible future difficulty in analysing a section, where intensity of cases was to emerge through numbers (one, two, three or four). However, analyses would still have been possible, but making responses straightforward was an improvement. I agreed with the suggestions, did some modification and then went fully back to the field. Prepared with 250 questionnaires, distribution began in Leeds and then London. Each questionnaire was with a self-addressed envelope, with my university address. This was preferred to the home address, to give a sense of educational purpose to the respondents, even if the home address may do no less.

Distribution of questionnaire was done through a purposive nonprobability sampling. In Leeds, I began distributing the questionnaires at meetings, to members of the Nigerian local community; at religious gatherings and at colleges and university campuses, to selected Nigerian students. Volunteers came from those who promised to give friends and family members not necessarily known to me. The promises were either seldom fulfilled, or perhaps those contacted failed to respond. My direct intervention always encouraged replies. *Snowballing* took place in many ways. It was one questionnaire per respondent (Bradley, 1999: 1). In London, the distributions were at meetings, and at Nigerian and African restaurants. It was also at religious gatherings and to friends, and colleagues. Interestingly, on an occasion in an African restaurant, some non-Nigerians including a Cameroonian and a Ghanaian heard about my task and sought participation. "We are all Africans, our problems and experiences are the same", one of them said as he sipped his drink. It took a polite rejection statement to discourage his jocular persistence. The brief incident was nevertheless a reminder of the need to be careful with the origin of respective respondents. The investigation, on this occasion, was about Nigerian migrants and I had to avoid distractions.

I distributed a hundred questionnaires in Leeds and London. Fifty were reserved for chanced encounters. Twenty-one questionnaires of the 250 produced were reserved. And like a forewarning I received from a leader of the Nigerian Community Leeds (NCL), Mr Kayode Alabi, through whom I snowballed, " responses may be very, very poor", it was indeed so. The distributions were between March and June, a period of four months. Again, the processes took me back and forth London and Leeds. By the middle of April 2006, just about 79 questionnaires had come back to me. I keyed the responses into the SPSS file I had opened for analyses as they came. "Data keying delays are eliminated" (Watt, 2005:1) through this systematic, one-after-the-other approach. Alongside the 21 leftover questionnaires in file, I rolled out a hundred more. Again, 50 were distributed in London and Leeds through the same method, including sampling and snowballing at the migrants' gatherings. This time, it was with a heightened aggression, perseverance, and pressure for those still with the questionnaires to respond. I also sent some through the post to sourced addresses. In ones, twos, threes, fours and fives, they started trickling in. By the end of June 2006, I recorded 73 more responses, making the total to be 152. Two responses could not however be used. This was because, while one was strangely and surprisingly vulgar, the other commented outside the tick boxes, making it impossible to recognise preferences. I eventually worked with 150 responses. In the process, I was again conscious of the need to reach all groups: men/women; old/young; rich/poor; skilled/unskilled; and the employed/unemployed. The determination of these, particularly age, nature of work and whether employed or not was through simple inquiry from the respondents, or as shown in the relevant sections on the questionnaire. The efforts made are in the analyses of differences. I applied the same method of initially asking prospective respondents, to the determination of duration of residency, which should be long enough to reveal migration traits. The labours are hopefully productive, as will be shown in the findings.

Importantly, the sampling procedure was of the nonprobability type. It was so because respondents were indiscriminately chosen from across the two, out of the many migrants' bases, due to cost and convenience. The respondents were also from groups, associations or communities in the cities. Through careful judgement, I ensured a fair representation of all migrant groups, classes, and identities, as already explained in the sections above. The survey expectedly helped the research process chiefly in the area of mapping, or situating participants in terms of their categories, class and attitudinal characteristics. Survey helped on how these differences relate to variables in the analyses of key themes. London and Leeds is perhaps a small case for a globally dispersed people, but their dispositions therein are typical of migration experiences in many ways.

TRIANGULATED TECHNIQUE AS A BASIS FOR TRIANGULATED ANALYSES

Significantly, the Internet presents a diverse and interweaving analytical theme that often makes the selection of method for its study difficult (Guimaraes Jr, 2005:141; Schneider, et al, 2005: 157). Sometimes, the diversity makes it difficult for its content "to be classified according to a handful of categories" (Chalaby, 2000:24). A combination of methods for investigating matters related to it has therefore become attractive. Mixing methods can be useful as it sieves personal prejudices possibly inherent in a method (Denzin, cited in Franfort-Nachmias, et al, 1996:206). Triangulation represents an important strategy for maximising the use of various methods. Also regarded as convergent methodology or multitrait (Campbell and Fiske, 1959, cited in Jick, 1979:1), it defines the complementary nature of qualitative and quantitative research. Rather than being contending methods, it establishes a compromise between the two broad research types (Jick, ibid.: 1). The idea of triangulation is derived from surveying, through the practice of finding a spot from different reference points (Smith, 1975:273, cited in Jick, 1979:1; Blaikie, 2000: 263-70, cited in Grix, 2001:84). Social researchers use it to achieve validity, accuracy, reliability, and credibility. It can be "between (or across) methods", and "within methods" (Denzin, 1998: 301-2, cited in Jick, 1979:1). The first refers to the application of distinct methods, while the second is about using different techniques within a given method. Jick (1979:2) sums its relevance thus: "'Within method', triangulation essentially involves cross-checking for internal consistency or reliability, while 'between methods', triangulation tests the degree of external validity". Triangulation eventually enables comparisons and the objectification of findings. It allows greater confidence in results, given the chance to compare and contrast outcomes of used techniques.

Nevertheless, triangulation could as well be delicate and confusing if a research question is unclear. Because a "whole picture" anticipated through triangulation may be illusory, as according to Silverman, (2005: 122) it can "speedily lead to scrappy research based on under-analysed data and an imprecise or theoretically indigestible research problem". For triangulation to achieve its aim, therefore, research questions need to be clear and conceptual. For this work, triangulating lingers between qualitative and quantitative research. It involves interviews, semi-structured survey questions and participant observation. Included in participant observation are direct observation and participation. In this work, and as seen in the foregoing, triangulation has been useful for comparisons, for testing the validity of meanings through comparisons with results from other techniques. In another sense, triangulating led to triangulated analyses, as examinations of findings was not from the result of one method, but also from the viewpoints of others. It led to comparing and contrasting, mutual enhancement of techniques, and sometimes the elimination of facts in cases where other methods point to the contrary. Figure 2 illustrates how the methods converge and interrelate. It gives a picture of how the approaches differ, but are dependent and balancing. It also points to fact that the understanding of methods is different, but analyses and discussions of research can be more credible when techniques come together.

Figure 2: Relationship between the Adopted Methods

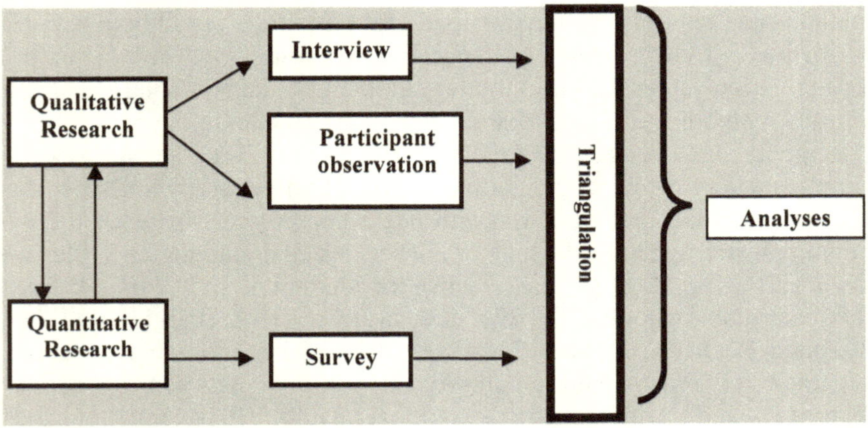

MATTERS OF ETHICS IN ONLINE RESEARCH

Though the investigation was not completely done online, it is important to remark on the basic rules expected in an online research. Lankshear, et al, (2005:327) quoted Sharf's (1999:254) suggestion that online researchers should:

> (i) introduce themselves clearly to online groups or individuals who are the intended focus of study with respect to their identities, roles and purposes; (ii) make concerted efforts to contact directly and obtain consent from individuals who have posted messages they want to use as data; and (iii) seek ways to maintain an openness to feedback from the e-mail participants who are being studied.

This comment is made because of debates on appropriate method for online research. The comments explain an approach to online research, which this study partly sets out to do. Much as the recommended processes were in consideration in some cases, a wholesale adoption of the procedure could take a time without end, given the many participants. The suggestion is again mostly useful for a research that is wholly online, not one that adds offline data. I can also argue that the Internet is a public space and contributions should be public materials that can be a subject of miscellaneous uses (Dochartaigh, 2002; Hewson, et al, 2003; www.aoir.org, accessed 20/05/2007). Materials not meant for public consumption can be restricted through security controls like encryptions, passwords, and registrations. Such would necessitate permissions and applications for entries. This is if at all, materials in those domains are useful for analyses. Though registrations for participation took place in a few cases, a majority did not require it. All materials were freely accessed in the open "field" of the Internet.

Nevertheless and because of a concern over Denzin's, et al, (1998: xiii) position that: "subjects now challenge how they have been written about (Lee & Ackerman, 1994:343) (and that) the writer can no longer presume to be able to present an objective, noncontested account of the other's experiences", care manifests in the representation of participants. I attribute quotations to people's first names, not to their full identities. It was not possible to conceal names only where materials are practically verifiable, in online archives, or through downloads and in few official or government sites. Some contributors use only pseudonyms or no name at all, which further helps the process of confidentiality. Associating, or crediting them becomes therefore difficult, adding to the general concerns around identity problems online.

Tapper (2001:15) notably dwells on this question of identity in online research. He argues that anonymity is not necessarily a problem, as participants are still humans discussing concerns. Therefore, identity problems online may not affect the credibility of a research. This is true to some extent, but could again be up for disputes because of possibilities that pets, particularly a dog may as well receive trainings to surf (Bonchek, 1997: 9). Bonchek (ibid.: 9) quotes P. Steiner in *The New Yorker* as stressing, "On the internet, nobody knows you are a dog". This could imply many other things apart from complicating identity. The quote may mean that a user is acting like the animal, or behaving in an unexpected way. It may also be a metaphor to describe the different characteristics of users. The quote can as well lead one to think of the possibility of a dog using the Internet, if not already being done.

Again, a multiplied false identity that Tapper talks about, offers fewer chances for diversity, representations and originality. A contributor who comes up with different identity may become repetitive, boring and may lack further creativity. Monopolistic thoughts would then give a picture of a dominant thinking, which could be misleading, apart from being an unfair imposition. The advantage of a multiplied contribution could however be in the provision of quantity, if it matters to an analyst. Core to the arguments is that there is a crisis of identity on the internet. These however invite the researcher to be cautious with online data. Efforts were also directed at keeping the researcher's distance. Interest is therefore limited to analyses, deductions, as against undue judgements. Any such indications are certainly unintended.

REFLEXIVITY

Reflexivity invites us to develop an interrogation that considers our position and biases in a research process. It nudges the researcher's courage through revealing personal circumstances that may affect objectivity. "A process of critical self reflection" (Schwandt, 1997), it partly answers the question: what is my place in the endeavour? (Ibid.: 1997). An evidence of a "researcher's deep learning and unlearning" (Kleinsasser, 2000:2), reflexivity challenges a researcher's claim to neutrality. This challenge is not adverse to objectivity, but highlights its limits. Reflexivity allows a constant consideration of the self in the research, and an admission of limitations in relation to the study. An honest approach to this increases credibility (Gillespie, 1995; Schwandt, 1997; Yanow, 2006), because feigning a natural objectivity in social research raises suspicion. However, admitting biases and preferences is an acknowledgement of human frailty, which may not be absent in a research project, just as it does not strip the research of its value. It rather gives the reader space for reflection (Yanow, 2006).

Finlay (2003) argues that reflexivity is different from reflection, because it is "more immediate, continuing, dynamic and (a) subjective self-awareness" (p. 108), while reflection is more detached and deferrable (ibid.:

108). Reflexivity should take place at the same time as the research work for reliability purposes. The researcher needs to define her/his role in a subjective way in the interest of a better understanding of claims (Hammersley and Atkinson, cited in Georgiou, 2001: 85). The process has to go simultaneously with the investigation, not afterwards. Learning comes from maintaining this balance (which is the goal of the research), and unlearning (Kleinsasser, 2000:2), representing the impossibilities in the process. Most times "discussed in relation to a researcher's empirical work" (Brown, 2006: 2), reflexivity invites an acknowledgement of distance from the subject of investigation. In this circumstance, the scholar should be reflective, and should explain how the likely assumptions that influenced the study arose (Ruud, 1998 cited in Stige, 2002:3).

With reflexivity, the reader, following a perception of the researcher's epistemological background, better understands meanings. Though limitations may feature in reflexivity course, it may not affect the scholar's analytical ability (Georgiou, 2001: 83). It shows that findings are a construction, which went through several defining processes, between the research and subject, and within the researcher as an individual. Reflexivity implies that the scholar is mindful (Gillespie, 1995: 67) in investigating subjects to whom one is familiar. This posture could help to avoid some pitfalls in interviews, or ethnographic data collection like "reactivity", and "going native". I shall now discuss reflexivity as associated with this research.

FORWARD AND BACKWARD THOUGHTS ON POSITION

Previously a journalist, academic research was a relatively new terrain. Some of the participants who therefore knew me, or have read my reports in Nigeria, regard me simply as a journalist. An acknowledgement as an academic researcher was new. In approaching them, it was possible that a memory of journalistic interview lingered. For me too, warding off the feeling that this interview was no longer to beat a short deadline, dateline, and to get a by-line as journalistic interviews were, was challenging. While it was possible to embellish, and strive to keep the interviewee as a regular source, the style and purpose of this interview was different. My skills as a journalist may have helped in terms of approach, persistence in the face of an evasive response, or a disinterest to participate, the present need to be more formal and less flowery in the use of materials were moderating. The journalism zeal to be the first with the story, also sustained the research process, as the migrants are yet to be a subject of intense academic research, as this. The outcome is new, in a way that makes the researcher a pioneer, or being the first to unearth a phenomenon in the mould of a well-driven investigative journalist. My mindset hovered between a past and present role, but found a balance in the differences in objectives.

Positioning featured also in my objective in the UK. Here I am as a Nigerian migrant like those under investigations. Though mission is different, circumstances sometimes cross paths. While the people under investigation are mainly economic migrants, my mission is for further education. I use the Internet as they do. Therefore, I experience aspects of its mediation possibilities as well. Again, I remember Nigeria like the typical economic migrant. Perhaps, the idea of return is common for me, as well as for some of them, because of statutory limitations on residency. Also, I am officially still on study leave. Like the typical migrant however, thoughts of return as I adapt more to life in the UK, becomes more frightening as time passes. It is therefore possible to sometimes put oneself in the position of participants. This situation enables the practical appreciation of migrants' experiences, particularly in relation to thoughts on return, and race relations. The positioning may occasionally blur the difference between researcher and subject, even while tasking the scholars' sense of objectivity. The solution during these processes was the development of a more critical disposition.

Negotiating the research course through my ethnic identity was of concern as well. Nigeria is a country of over 250 ethnic groups, and a 36 state federation. There are three major groups in this multi-ethnic state, which are Yoruba, Igbo and Hausa. Tension always exists in their effort to co-exist. Sometimes, this trait features abroad. I am of the Yoruba group, but a minority one. This ethnic group reputedly prefers the UK as destination during migration. They are also more cosmopolitan, because of an early exposure to Western education through colonisation. Chances were therefore that they would be easier to approach, not only because of my name that suggests a Yoruba affiliation, but also because of their relative higher educational standards, and an attendant disposition to be more receptive to an academic endeavour like this. I made a conscious effort to reduce my *yorubaness*, and to try to get the perspectives of migrant groups from other ethnic groups. This experience was similar both offline, and online. It was however easier to sample other groups online than it was offline. The Internet was an important balancing space to counterbalance my offline subjective limitations.

Another sensitive issue was that of gender balance. Many interviews with female participants were in the company of others. They were mainly with their spouses, partners, boyfriends, or children. The presence of others in the course of some of the interviews might have influenced comments, or led to some self-censoring. Talking to a male interviewer may in addition add some other biases, which interaction with an "Other" could bring about. Thoughts on these possibilities continued, as it was when on two occasions I considered the level of rationality of two men interviewed while drinking alcohol. The men had insisted at different times in London that they would only meet me at their relaxation points, which were restaurants. In such circumstances, I needed to make sure I knew which thoughts were rational and which were not. Overall, I tried to engage with the situations I encountered with critical consciousness, in the determination to be as close as possible to the truth.

CHAPTER FOUR:

THE NIGERIAN DIASPORA MEDIASCAPES: INTERNET USE AND THE COMPLEMENTARY ROLES OF OTHER MEDIA

> It is important to acknowledge that not all migrants use the Internet and, even when they do so, not all migrants use the Internet in the same way or at all phases of the migrant cycle. However, the purpose and experience of online usage characteristically changes with each phase and it is our **(my)** goal to sketch the functions, roles and abilities of the Internet particularly to support the migrant experience **(Hiller and Franz, 2004: 737).** *(Emphasis mine)*

This chapter discusses online connections amongst the Nigerian diaspora by examining their activities in cyberspace and the mediation possible on this domain. The section examines the Internet as a medium, routinely used by many people, aside from analysing non-use, or sparse use observed in some cases. The relationship between the Internet and other media like telephone, television, radio and the press are explained. The examination is done despite the focus on the Internet's position in the mediation of participants' relationships amongst themselves, with Nigeria and with the hostland. There is an analysis of variations in use across class, age, and gender, as the main divides. Analyses in this section are partly based on all the typologies of websites except Types F and H (See pages 87-88). The analyses also come through interviews and survey.

PATTERNS OF ONLINE MEDIATION OF DISTANCE

SUSTAINING CONTACT WITH FELLOW MIGRANTS THROUGH BASIC INTERNET FUNCTIONS LIKE E-MAIL, CHATTING, BLOGGING AND NEWSGROUP INTERACTIONS

This section examines the basic use of the Internet by participants and explains the role of the network in helping the migrants relate with each other. The explanations take place from the study of the migrants' activities, through the performance of simple Internet functions like e-mail exchanges, chatting, blogging, discussions in newsgroups, engagements with the social networks, posting to e-mail lists and frequent visits to familiar websites. Abati, writing for *The Guardian* (of Nigeria) [www.ngrguardiannews.com], for instance, notes this as he highlights the multiple role of the Internet and the increasing participation of the Nigerian diaspora in online activities:

More persons are spending more time daily on the World Wide Web, which they now rely on for a broad range of activities including conversation, romance, therapy and education. The number of Nigerians, especially in diaspora, who falls into this category, continues to increase, the same with internet sites on Nigerian affairs, with the most active and the most interactive being in my estimation, the Nigeria Village Square. **Abati, accessed at <u>www.nigeriavillagesquare.com</u> on 13/04/2008**

Another participant, Coker joins Abati in emphasising this point. She describes in general terms the activities of the Nigerian diaspora on the Internet, ending her comments with a criticism:

Nigerians abroad are everywhere on the Internet. They have many websites, where they write articles on Nigeria. These sites are crowded, with topics and subtopics. Some are very interactive. The Internet keeps them busy and might help them cope with exclusion. However, my grouse with them is that they are too presumptuous and impatient. **Coker, accessed at <u>www.ngrguardiannews.com</u> on 29/06/2008**

The exclusion that Coker refers to reminds us of the main status of the migrants. They are blacks from a major African country. In terms of colour, they share this status with many Black-Caribbean, and other black migrant groups. As a result, the Nigerian diaspora members belong to the non-White ethnic minorities in Britain. Some other groups in this classification include people of Asian origin, like Bangladeshis, Pakistanis and Indians. The Nigerian diaspora also belong to the larger African diaspora, whose ancestors were enslaved. Britain, the present host of the migrants, is also Nigeria's former colonial master. The exclusion question in Coker's comments may have been because of the issues above. As minorities, a number of disadvantages like stereotyped representation in the mainstream media, and an inability to get suitable jobs may result (Heath, et al, 1999). The Internet, according to the above statement, becomes a space of connection, given the chances of being disconnected in hostland.

Other than this, observations reveal that resort to virtual exchanges indicates the discovery of a system that can again bring them together despite dislocation. The country of origin is a possible place to remember, while the Internet presents an opportunity for this remembrance. The physical setting of the *homeland* may be far off. Return may also be a myth[18]. Establishing contacts with the *homeland* probably becomes a

---

[18] Though some literature still regards return as a myth, it is, nevertheless, a contested subject in other works. This is because viewing it as a myth implies impossibility. However, some authors refer to actual returns. As this happens infrequently, regarding it as a myth amounts to generalising. (See for instance Braakman, 2005). Other writers also allude to the alleviation of the myth as *homeland* and hostland are experiencing

problem given mobility and disparity. The supplementary effect of virtual connection via e-mails, newsgroups' discussions, SMS messages, and participation in other forms of online interaction sustains the myth and imagination of the *homeland* (Georgiou, 2006a: 40). The exchanges also keep memories and commemoration (Fisher, 1986; Boyarin, 1994; Ben Amos & Weisberg, 1999, cited in Georgiou, ibid.) of the distant origin, amongst the diaspora members alive.

In connecting migrants, the Internet replaces the interactive spaces of the *homeland*. These interactive spaces could include the media space, and the physical spaces of interaction like town, city and hotel halls; conference venues; open fields; abandoned parks; party venues; *Bukas*[19]; shops; and community centres. For the migrants, the Internet space is a substitution for the possible regular verbal articulation of issues about Nigeria known by past experience of the country. Christy (Female, age unknown, Leeds: Interview date: 19/04/06), brings out this point:

> I cannot determine the time my friends come online, but I buzz friends I happen to meet while there. A lady I met at the airport in Abuja, who was heading for Canada, while I was on my way to London, met me online the other day and we compared notes on chances of marrying abroad, as against going back to marry in the unpredictable Nigerian social climate

E-mail exchanges, newsgroups' activities and presences in websites, amongst migrants are soothing solutions to loneliness, longings and a likely crisis of belonging in the hostland. As e-mail connection initiates meetings, or serves as a medium for exchanging information about meetings, it illustrates a need for migrants' linkages. Being e-mail correspondents or agents in network activities, participants feel a sense of presence despite physical absence. A presence in these contexts eases the probable complexities often associated with dislocation. They construct relevance in virtuality through participation in a space, suitable for dialogues. Production of ideas go on while exchanging e-mails, surfing websites and in chatting with fellow migrants in interactive online spaces. A sense of importance may mix with existence in the diaspora, where integration is probably still a subject of negotiation. While this may mitigate nostalgia, remembrance also occurs, and it can create amusement rather than despair. Online connection between migrants, therefore, amounts to a virtual replacement of traditional media and other physical spaces of interaction in origin. The traditional media includes conventional forms of communication namely, word of mouth, the postal services, newspapers, radio and television at origin.

---

integration through new gains in some technologies of communication, like television and the Internet (Robins and Aksoy, 2003, 2005; Tsagarousianou, 2004).

[19] *Buka* means restaurant in Nigeria.

As is seen in the testimonies below, the Internet is a place of assembly. E-mail exchanges, sharing of photographs, domination of news/discussion groups, mailing lists, and usenets are common practices. Also frequent are social networking activities in locations such as Facebook, Myspace, *Orkut*, *Bebo* and in E-journals. The exchanges are amongst members in different migrant locations. It could also be within a particular location, or both. Participation in discussions and the management of websites is wide ranging. They arise from the Americas, European countries, rising economies of South East Asia, and some African countries particularly South Africa. Virtual interactions amongst the migrants initiate the sharing of a collective memory of Nigeria, as the many to many communication qualities of the Internet guarantees. Sometimes, they agree on topical issues about Nigeria. Other times, they disagree but in most cases, the debates are inconclusive. Importantly, the chance to engage in dialogue and communication exists. The sample quotations below from the point of view of scholars clarify this position. The masthead immediately beneath is an online Journal on African migration, where Nigerian migrant academics play key roles.

ISSN #1540-7497

ìrìnkèrindò: a journal of african migration

Figure 3: Masthead of an African Scholars' Online Journal

The journal says of itself:

> *Ìrìnkèrindò:* a Journal of African Migration will make online research material on African immigration and migration available. It will facilitate connections between the users of the technology and research scholars, analysts and writers in the area of African immigration and migration that enable them to debate, dialogue, present the results of their research for immigrants and migrants, a record of their life experiences. The use of online technology will enable the ease of communication across vast geographical expanses. It also facilitates linkages between scholars and professionals and institutions or individuals that need their expertise. **Accessed at http://www.africamigration.com/ on 17/01/2007**

Ìrìnkèrindò is a Yoruba word meaning wanderings. In Yoruba mythology, it is etymologically associated with adventures to strange or lonely places. Such places could be a forest, or a foreign land. The naming of the journal after the African word connects with the scholars' stated bid to discuss "African immigration and migration". It also relates to their bid to "debate, dialogue, (and) present the results of their research for immigrants and migrants, a record of their life experiences". Many US based scholars like for instance Mojubaolu Okome and Julius Ihonvbere[20] have written several times on the problem of Africa, partly based on their experiences abroad. Okome writes in one instance that:

> The unequal access to information that the technology divides causes is a typical example of the antinomies of globalisation. Tragically, many African countries are still on the negative side of the information divide. There are not enough computers, telecommunication links, and definitely, there is not enough money to purchase new, and sometimes, even old technologies. It is unbelievably difficult to engage in instant communication when one is dealing with power failures, (and) unreliable Internet service providers. **Okome, Female, online, 21/12/2006**

Okome paints a problematic picture of connection in Nigeria. The description is one of the dearths of infrastructure, which is central to connections, and which is more readily available in the hostland. She laments the poor state of the infrastructure by listing many obstacles to the development of Internet communication. Though US based, the problem hardly affects her. It becomes therefore more convenient for her to interact with peers in diaspora than with those in Nigeria, because of the connection problems of those in origin. Another scholar, Adebayo, (Male, age unknown. Interviewed in London, 27/06/2008) says the existence of online journals "expands the chances of publishing research works particularly for those who may be finding it difficult to break into themes of mainstream journals". The scholars' use of the Internet for the projection of African migration experiences is one instance of an increasing improvement in learning patterns. Participation in this regard identifies them as active agents in an age of growing and complex connections. The scholars can individually or collectively identify the relevance of this participation. However, the fact of being enthusiastic users, invites thoughts on the existence of a multi-centred network. As well as the scholars' example above, the statement below explains the sustenance of contacts with fellow migrants:

> The Internet to me is another home. When I do not have anything to do, I do it on the Internet. In addition, when I should be doing things that are more "serious", the sight of the Internet distracts me. I surf and surf until I become tired. I am usually everywhere on the Internet, connecting with friends in the US, UK and everywhere. I also go to fashion sites, personality sites, government sites, etc. The technology electrifies me. **Angela, Female, 39, London. Interview date: 16/02/2006**

---

[20] Ihonvbere later relocated to Nigeria to work with the country's federal government.

The importance of the network to the above participant is, from her statement, multi-layered. First, it is an alternative home, with her description of it as "another home". Second, it is a solution to idleness, because it offers her an opportunity to be active. Third, the Internet is a nuisance that prevents serious work given the manner in which the network distracts her. Fourth, it helps maintain multiple connections, as she can be "everywhere" through its space. Fifth, the participant finds an emotional attachment to it, as it "electrifies" her. The dominant theme of connection and an assurance that the network offers that service is noticeable.

The next participant also gives insights into how networking relates to sustaining contacts with family members and the discussion of intimate matters. Online interactions with acquaintances show that the Internet is relevant to personal and impersonal uses amongst migrants. Its unreserved space points to a possibility of a multi-purpose application depending on the interest of the user:

> My parents are not in Nigeria. My father is in America, while my mother is in London. I communicate with them as often as I can. I talk to them on the telephone. Sometimes, I use the text messaging system. When I want to talk to my father on something extensive, I send e-mails, especially when I want to brief him on marriage plans. Moreover, he replies in same way. **Bola, Male, 24, Leeds. Interview date: 21/03/2006.**

The speaker below also refers to the network as a way of interacting with friends, and fellow migrants. The sharing of ideas extends the boundaries of relationships beyond what it is with intellectual colleagues, like networking amongst scholars above. Alaba testifies:

> I have connection at home, so I network with friends and family members around the world. I also network with members of the Nigeria Community in this city; we share ideas on outings, and we share postings on issues. **Alaba, Female, 53, Leeds. Interview date: 12/04/2006.**

Networking and the sustenance of contacts online is not necessarily for its own sake. Many think of it as a way of building contacts with fellow migrants, and as a stepping-stone to easing life when they merge interests with the individuals with whom they establish relationships. Observations reveal that these interests have to do with being relevant to Nigerian issues and the quest to attain success in hostland. Easier access to the network upon relocation is an encouragement, according to Jide below. The telephone may sometimes be a little more expensive, and hence his preference for the Internet for connections, and even research:

For me, access is free as I use the university facility, so it makes the Internet use cheaper than telephoning, which entails buying of card. However, it can be more convenient. My e-mail box attracts me, when I want to see messages from sites I subscribe to, either for my research, or for my personal knowledge. I hardly watch television, apart from when I go to watch football matches in Pubs and in people's homes. **Jide, Male, 29, Leeds. Interview date: 01/04/2006.**

A few times as well, people agree to meet through appointments made online. The meetings lead to the establishment of physical contacts for the purpose of continuing discussions that begin on the Internet. This is mostly the case when the parties live in the same town or country. The parties may not have known each other before. Sometimes, they were acquaintances. In cases where meetings are new, the Internet takes credit for being the stimulator of such interactions. A participant additionally notes its relevance in initiating physical contacts across multinational spaces. He says:

I arrived in the UK about four months ago from the United States, where I had gone for a post-doctoral programme. The chap who accommodated us for a few days before my family and I found our feet was contacted online. You can imagine the wonder that the technology is. **Ahmed, Male, 38, Leeds. Interview date: 14/05/2006.**

Ahmed reveals that he links up with the prospective assistant through his e-mail address on his webpage. "I told him to educate me about life in the city and he was kind," he stresses, adding, "His Nigerian name was the initial attraction to him". The expansion of social relationships though the Internet is an evidence of the networks' ability to advance sociability. The possibility of advancing sociability is not entirely dependent on it, as the process is complemented by face-to-face relations or other mediated connections. The message below sent to migrants is an instance of how e-mail helps networking, or how it leads to social gatherings:

Hi Fellow Nigerians, very warm greetings in this period of winter. Find below useful information from the newly elected NC (Nigeria Community) Leeds, UK, members. There are also updates and plans for activities in the near future. Please do not hesitate to make your positive contributions as we always welcome good ideas. Many thanks for your support.
Femi Philips, Sec. Gen. NC UK.

An attached message posted 17/12/2006 includes programmes for a party for Nigerian students. It also includes notices for a New Year Party, for meetings and for new members to register. Information for meetings is given online most times. There are notifications leading to gatherings on key Nigeria anniversary or commemoration dates. It could be political like the October 1st anniversary of independence, or the May 29th democracy day ceremonies; or religious like Christmas, New Year or *Sallah*. When they gather for political events, observations show that tales of regret on the unpredictable and turbulent politics of the source country are always expressed. The prevalence of corruption and the siphoning away of funds to the hostland they dwell are factual or incorrect issues for discussion. Importantly, the conversations demonstrate dissatisfaction with the state of origin. When the events are religious, fond memories about its celebration while in Nigeria prevails. Fundamental is that the gatherings are initiated in cyberspace, while the subsequent expression of feelings are products of the efficacy of online networking.

The conventional media take the lead in Nigeria for networking, for information dissemination and in the performance of simple communicative functions. Cost considerations, time differences and amount of information sent may hardly be in calculation in terms of news dissemination when in Nigeria. In migration, economic considerations come to the fore. Because most diaspora members are economic migrants, prudence guides their expenses. Many migrants do not use scarce resources for costly telephones in interacting with each other across migrant locations that are far apart. This is also because of a concern for the time when a call is right or wrong. The unease is even more relevant in the case of some very distant migrant locations like the US. In the US, a prospective caller may be unsure of a reasonable time to call, as California and New York, are for instance, in different time zones. The Internet network is more convenient concerning cost and time, to reach each other at a personal or group level. In their distant locations, therefore, the migrants find themselves via computers, which reduce the sense of absence. Apart from sustaining contacts, information sourcing also emerges in their pattern of online mediation of distance as will be discussed below.

4.2.2: Connecting For Information: A Dependence on Cyberspace for Updates on Nigeria

Other than networking with each other as above, participants also get on the computer to learn about Nigerian events. Connection here happens in different ways. It can be through visits to the websites of local Nigerian newspapers, or through exchange of e-mails, e-mail attachments and photographs with family members and some friends back in Nigeria. It can also be through news/discussion groups' activities with the *homeland* parties, or through chatting with folks in Nigeria in their favourite chatrooms. In engaging with the system at this level, they are not only seeking to improve their knowledge of Nigeria, but also to be active in debates on Nigerian affairs. The process eventually contributes to the evolution of their impression of the place. This varies over time, but is more likely to progress from familiarity to forgetting. The individual process is dependent on the interest and disposition of the migrant. The preferences also relate to class, gender, cause of dispersal and overall objectives.

Nigerian newspaper sites are amongst the most popular sites usually visited. One of this is, according to observations, *The Guardian* (of Nigeria) [www.ngrguardiannews.com]. This is a newspaper with elitist tendencies. Founded in 1983, the paper is a clone of *The Guardian* of UK. It appeals to the elites, who respect its editorials. Migrant elites prefer the site in order to get the truest, non-sensational picture of events in Nigeria. *ThisDay* [www.thisdayonline.com] is another widely read newspaper, which is slightly more colourful than *The Guardian* (of Nigeria). It enjoys the confidence of sources in high places, translating into faster reportage of breaking news. In addition to this, it has regular exclusive insights into events. A talented journalist, Mr Nduka Obaigbena, publishes *Thisday*. Its edge in political and economic stories is always appealing to migrants. *The Sun* [www.sunnewsonline.com] is a different newspaper, which attempts to be a copy of the UK tabloid paper, *The Sun*. It has been largely successful within this context because of the professional experiences of its founders, Mike Awoyinfa and Dimgba Igwe, in this journalism genre. Its tabloid form and expertise in reporting the "man and woman on the street", which many other newspapers look away from, endears it to migrant readers. *Business Today* [www.businessdayonline.com] is a newspaper with a business orientation, as the name implies. Migrants with interests in the analysis of economics of origin prefer this site.

The location of *Daily Trust* [www.dailytrust.com] is in the Nigerian capital, Abuja. Its publishers are journalists from the Northern part of Nigeria. They report stories mainly from their region. Www.gamji.com, and *New Nigeria* [www.newnigeria.com], also have roots in Northern Nigeria, in spite of their diverse interest in news reporting. Similarly, *Irinnews* [www.irinnews.org] has roots in the culture of South-West Nigeria. *Vanguard* Newspapers [www.vanguardngr.com], and *The Punch* [www.punchng.com], are other national newspapers of repute, with interest in competing with papers like *The Guardian* (of Nigeria) and *Thisday*. www.naijanet.com and www.nigeriamasterweb.com are migrants' sites of substantial influence. Www.nigeriagovernmentnews.com and www.ebeano.com are government-managed websites. Visitors seeking official information, amongst other things, could use them. Many of these sites concentrate on news. They daily upload events from Nigeria, in a way that updates readers in a detailed fashion. Some interviewees' go further to validate this diaspora versus origin linkage:

The internet's role is for accessing information about home, not necessarily communicating with people directly, but getting information, through newspapers, news bits and those things. **Dupe, Male, 43, London. Interview date: 02/06/2006.**

I keep in touch with my country in many ways. I use the Internet to particularly get in touch with friends. That is mostly with friends who have access to the Internet. Sometimes, I am able to discover this when they e-mail me. **Emeka, Male, 46, London. Interview date: 02/06/2006.**

I am regularly online with relations and my fiancé who is happy to join me here any moment from now. We chat online, and he sends online cards as well. **Esther, Female, 42, London. Interview date: 22/02/2006.**

I often use the Internet. I use it to read newspapers, and to send e-mails to friends in Nigeria. **Jide, Male, 29, Leeds. Interview date: 01/04/2006.**

The statements above are a few examples of respondents who confirm using the Internet for sourcing information on events and current affairs in Nigeria. The computer terminal becomes a space for diasporic connection with home through the exploration of various information sites. The act of doing this momentarily transfers, even psychologically, the participant to the place of Nigeria. The act is capable of lessening nostalgia, as it diminishes the sense of absence from the distant origin. Imagining Nigeria through knowledge of its affairs can intensify a sense of connection across a virtual space. The social position of migrants in the hostland often defines the uses and meanings of Internet connection. The way the migrant fits in with colleagues abroad and other communities in the hostland and their experience of integration or exclusion[21] are important. By extension, an interest in connecting for information about Nigeria is dependent on shifting variables. Crucial is that the course of updating oneself about Nigerian affairs can become a routine for many, and an then turn into a solution to loneliness in the diaspora.

Figure 4 below provides additional evidence of the efficiency of the Internet in informing the migrants about Nigeria. Seventy percent of respondents say the network is highly effective in doing so. Those who say it is moderately effective are 21.8%, while only 0.7% says it is ineffective. Since those who say the network is highly effective are a greater number, it indicates that the Internet is a medium, with little territorial limitation, just as it has the capacity to inform, and educate across diverse spaces. Time and

---

[21] As blacks, they belong to the category of the others. Their colour also makes them easily differentiated from the natives, and other coloured people from, for instance, Asia. They are therefore confronted with a challenge of integration, which some slightly overcome through the claiming of citizenship. The multicultural posturing of hostland government is sometimes comforting for many of them, but absolute integration continuously remains a difficult task.

cost constraints become relatively less important, therefore highlighting the network as a medium unhindered by circulation or the problem of bandwidth, which occasionally troubles some mainstream media, and more likely those of Nigeria, as a developing country. Reading, uploading and downloading of information is not exactly dependent on deadlines, but on the choice of the user. For participants, probably threatened by exclusion in hostland, observations reveal that some sense of inclusion surface when informed about the *homeland*, as the network confers emotional relationship, participation and/or involvement, despite the 3100 miles (4988 Kilometres) distance between Nigeria and Britain (Accessed at http://www.mapcrow.info/ on 30/07/2008).

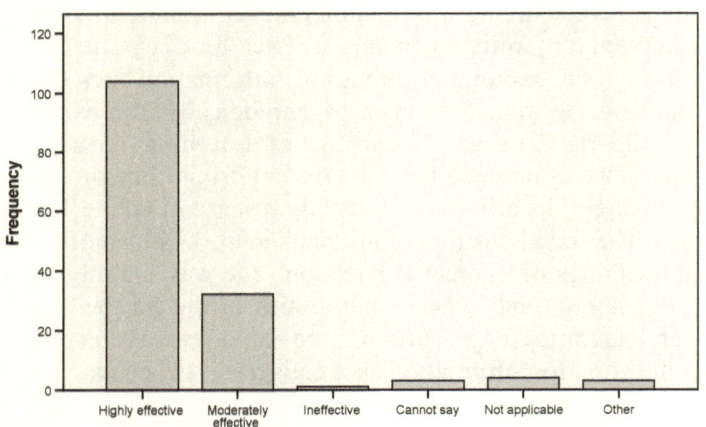

Figure 4: How the Internet Helps In Updating Participants about events in Nigeria

CONNECTING WITH HOSTLAND THROUGH THE WORLD WIDE WEB

As Marthoz (1999:73) argues, "The internet…enables individuals and groups hitherto marginalized to become involved", apart from finding the network as a means to enter "the world stage, of presenting their situations in their own words, of expressing their claims independently of governments and the channels laid down by the large media groups". Connection therefore takes place with the hostland, and it takes place in many shapes and forms. Through the Internet, visibility in a global network is taken for granted. Because the network is global, users have a limitless potential for exposure. The Nigerian diaspora members' activities as webmasters, bloggers, lists' owners, and as participants in web pages that relate to Nigeria increase their chances of being found out via search engines. A Google search of the key words "Nigerian diaspora website" on the 18/12/2006 brought up 1,300,000 links. When this was repeated on 30/07/2008 to see how it has recently performed, it produced 1,400,000, showing an increase of 100, indicating potentials for further increase. Opportunities to know them in unimaginable places through the screen symbolises a worldwide coverage. The chances of being visible are significant as it can be timeless. The visibility is for every user, regardless of location, or level of political and economic influence. It exposes migrants to distant peoples and places. This enhances some users' knowledge of the Nigerian diaspora. They are then therefore no longer simply in connection with fellow migrants, or peers in Nigeria, but with other interested parties in a global virtual community. This new experience marks a departure from older and more traditional forms of communication. Examples of these were the post, telegram, telephone, television and radio. In previous times, participants lived a more private life. They were likely to witness correct or incorrect representations in the mainstream global media. With the democratic, non-linear, and non-hierarchical credentials of the Internet as advantages, the migrants represent themselves in any manner they choose. Connection with the world is facilitated by, and only limited to the imagination and creativity of the migrants.

This site which promotes itself as being the "mother of all sites", adds that it is the "ABC of Nigeria…everything *Naija*" and works to make "Nigeria an ABC issue in cyberspace". Administered by Charles Okereke from the UK, it has various sections including directories on every Nigerian sector. The detailed website represents the migrants' way of making themselves available to web users investigating Nigeria. Its masthead usually appears thus:

Figure 5: Masthead of Notable News' Site

It is important to note that non-Nigerians wishing to reach the Nigerian diaspora members sometimes do this through some sites, like the one above. It can also be through newsgroups, which signifies availability in the open global Internet space. This testimony is revealing:

Embassies have had reasons to post messages on www.nigeriaworld.com in their bid to reach Nigerians, while the newsgroup naija-politics@ yahoogroups.com, have been used for announcements. **Accessed at http://nigeriaworld.com/articles/2005/Sep/041.html on 12/02/2006**

Interactions with people in hostland is central, despite the two other connections they experience, which are connection with fellow migrants and with Nigeria. The need to be in connection with the hostland is partly a bid to continue the process of negotiating integration. It may also be to seek an alternative to the difficulties attached to offline integration. The situation reflects the challenges of interacting with a new culture. Seeking integration involves an engagement with different social facets, like the health and educational sectors. The process could be online and offline. The online variant nevertheless allows for greater freedom. This is because "otherness" is more hidden on screen, which eliminates the downside of physical interaction. Notably, moods, mien, group, class, or age may influence physical interaction. These are less visible, or even become invisible online. Via the exchange of mails, with some people in the hostland, and in hitting hostland's related websites, migrants experience a temporary sense of freedom. A feeling of integration could come through a likely translation of the online sense of freedom to life offline.

The three patterns of connections above are not intended to generalise on Internet uses and functions. It may not also be comprehensive but simply to represent categories of online connection. Within the groupings are divides and limitations, which indicate differences in use. An understanding of the differences can come through some variables. These include occupation, class, age, duration in migration, frequency of use, degree of interest, and cause of migration. In turning to these differences, the analysis of the survey findings shall be useful.

DIFFERENCES IN THE USE OF THE INTERNET

Cross-tabulations reveal the details of participants' engagement with the Internet, in terms of differences in conditions that determine the tendency to use the medium. It also includes the degree of intensity. The question, "How effective is the Internet in informing you about Nigeria" is common as an independent variable in seven cases. The cases are illustrated with graphs. It is to see how the different dependent variables measure in terms of engagement with the independent variable. The example variable (question) does not undermine other dimensions of use. This can involve, for example, simple correspondence with people in and outside Nigeria, and use for research. It may also involve entertainment, and connecting with the world in general. Figure 6, for example, shows the relationship between the year of migration from Nigeria and the level of interest in the possibility of using the Internet to know about Nigeria. As seen therein, 61% of respondents who left the country in the period of economic depression/successive military regimes say the Internet is highly effective in helping them know about Nigeria. A little less than that notes that, it is moderately effective. However, 19% of respondents confirm this. Those born abroad are next in line, with 17% of them confirming the usefulness of the technology in relating with home.

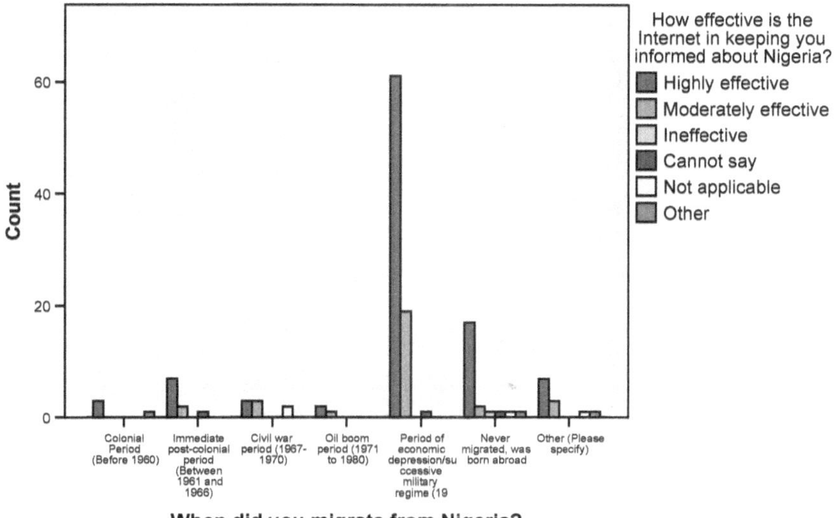

Figure 6: Relationship between Period of Migration and Internet Use

Figure 7 explains the relationship between the reason for migration and the chosen operational variable, which is the efficiency of the Internet in helping migrants know about events in Nigeria. Those who left for further education purposes mostly regard the medium as being highly effective. Forty percent answers in the affirmative. Those who left for a better economic life follow with 35%. Other causes of migration, which could include adventure account for 12%. Then those who escaped military repression follow with 9%. The highest, which was 40%, reflects level of literacy necessary to use the technology. Each of the dependent variable beneath also considers how respondents feel about the efficiency of the network. In general, the first two options, which are whether the technology is highly effective, or moderately so, occupy the high level of response.

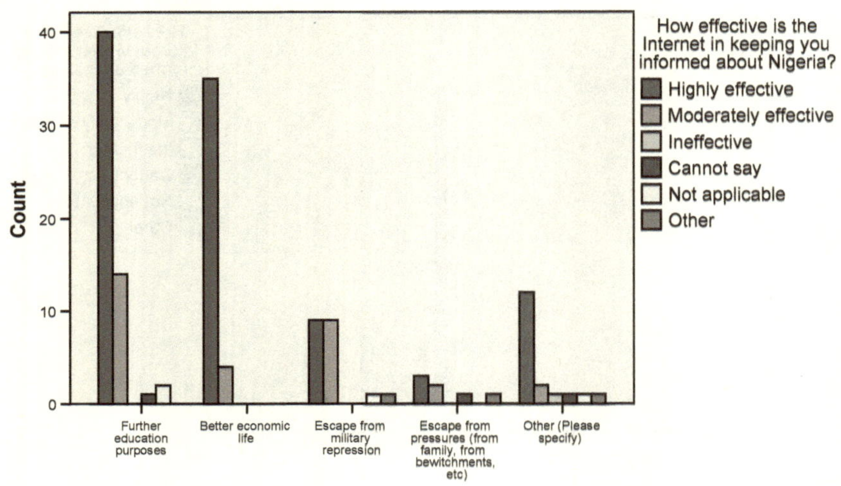

Figure 7: Relationship between Reason for Migration and Internet Use

Accessibility and computer literacy partly determine Internet use. The ability to read, at least, is a necessary condition for its use. An additional ability to write makes engagement with the technology easier. The chances of appreciating its functions increase with good literacy. It will be more possible with a mastery of the English Language-the most used language on the Internet. Local languages may feature in interpersonal communication, via e-mail, for fun, or creativity, but a mastery of the English language enhances a greater sharing of online information. The educated elites, mostly taught in English, are therefore in a better position to interact with the technology. The average education condition gives a sense of moderation concerning decision making abroad. The moderation means an "Inbetweeness" for a people coming from an origin with high illiteracy level. It then leads to an increased interaction with a medium that is still elitist to many in Nigeria. The educated migrants, therefore, delightfully associate with it as a demonstration of their enlightenment. Or, it may be reflecting Internet use as one that requires literacy. It shows in figure 8 why most migrant professionals[22] consider the technology highly effective in helping them to connect with Nigeria. Connection here may include

---

[22] The professionals include medical doctors, pharmacists, engineers, solicitors, lecturers and related jobs.

sourcing information about the country, personal communication, or group networking, and researching. Logging on frequency could be higher amongst this group because of a likely economic advantage, given their class. Because they are elites, sociability, or an intention to participate in Internet use is likely to be high. The Internet, therefore, becomes a place for its demonstration.

Thirty percent of professionals attest to this high efficiency, while the percentage decreases as the variable moves down to the less elitist professions.[23] Fewer professionals as seen from the correlations in the graph reply that it is moderately effective, while a negligible fraction notes that it is ineffective. The unemployed also relate less with the technology in terms of seeking information about Nigeria. One of many reasons that could be responsible for this includes pre-occupation with job hunting. The condition of unemployment may lead to a relative lack of interest for an imagined place. The extent of interest goes up amongst the self-employed to 9%. It also increases to 18% again, amongst those in school, and then to 33% amongst the unskilled/menial workers. It is 31% amongst clerks, secretaries and those who do jobs that relate to administration.

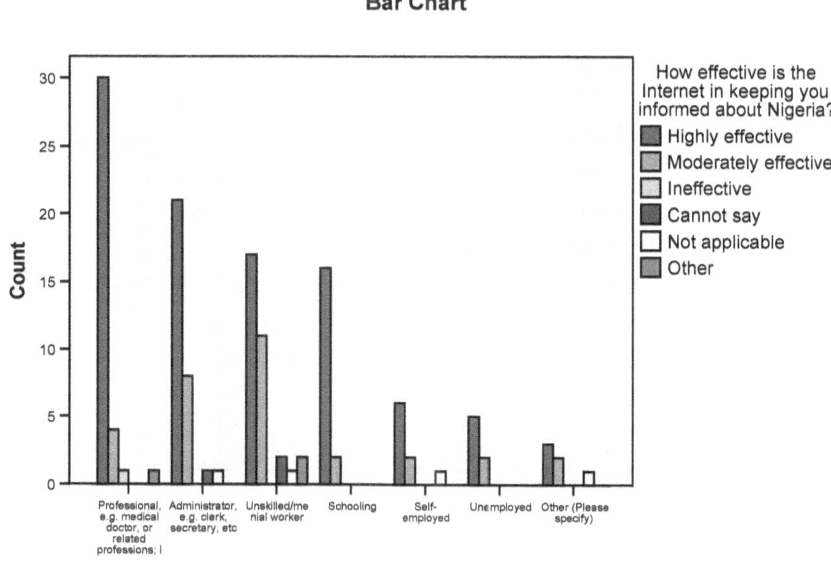

Figure 8: Relationship between Occupation in the UK and Interest in Using the Internet

---

[23] The less elitist professions are for the purpose of this analysis clerks, office secretaries, unskilled/menial workers, amongst others.

Figure 9 is another example of differences using "possible interest to know about Nigeria", as an independent variable. The dependent variable here is residency status, which is crucial to migrants. Other matters in migration like the level of relationship with origin, and the likely idealisation of return are dependent on it. Determining these may also be a conscious or unconscious process. While the extent of remembering is unpredictable and immeasurable, it makes sense to see if there are relationships between length of stay in the hostland, and the need to keep links with Nigeria. From the result, those who have UK citizenship consider the Internet highly effective in updating them about Nigeria. Those whose status is of indefinite stay deem it far less so. Migrants on work permit are greater than people in the indefinite stay category. Individuals on student visa follow those with citizenship status in terms of value of the technology. Asylum seekers and others have the same rating. In that order, therefore, citizens record 37%; indefinite stay, 14%; work permit, 18%; student visa, 23%; asylum seekers, 4% and others, 4%. The categories further vary in terms of how they appreciate the technology in other ways. These are for instance whether it is moderately effective or ineffective. There are categories such as cannot say, not applicable, and others. The figures in these groups are however insignificant in terms of determining their interest, or lack of interest.

Bar Chart

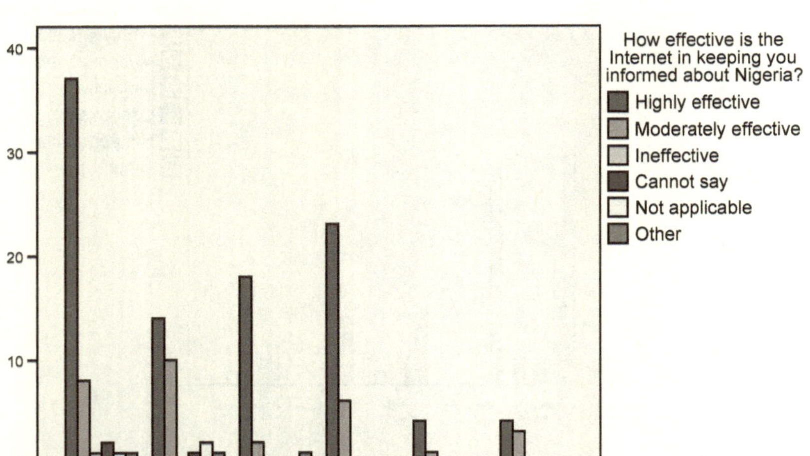

Figure 9: Relationship between Residency Status and Internet Use

Figure 10 examines the frequency of visits to Nigeria amongst participants in relation to the possibility of an interest in knowing about events therein. Again, visits to origin are dependent on a number of factors. Some of these are interest; affordability; family; adventure; health grounds; the mitigation of longing; and possible break from the trials of integration. There are also reasons like possible interest in revealing new experience of international travel to peers in Nigeria. There could in addition be other foreseeable and unforeseeable circumstances. These may involve death of close relatives, and sudden invitations to events. The scope of the establishment of physical contact sometimes determines levels of awareness with Nigerian matters. With the rise in media technologies, physical presence may not, nonetheless, count. It is however again dependent on other variables relating to different participants and groups. Important in the argument, nevertheless, is the probable significance of physical contact in the determination of online connections with Nigeria.

The majority of respondents rarely visit Nigeria. Thirty seven percent consider the Internet highly effective in updating them about Nigeria. The reasons for this may actually be numerous. The likelihood is that having settled in the hostland, the need or desire for physical visits might have reduced, or has become non-existent over time. This may lead to a regular desire to know, about events in Nigeria. Knowing about Nigeria could as well be to ease longing; register distant belonging; or to sustain memories of it. Persons who visit every two to five years make up 25%; annual visitors, 143%; six monthly visitors, 7%; and migrants who do not visit, rank similar with those in the category of the others, with 9%. The reduction in the percentage between every two to five yearly visits and six monthly is probably because an alternative mode of sourcing information exists. One of these is through the relative frequency of the establishment of physical contact during visits to origin. In these periods, the migrants may refresh and become aware of developments. Some of the new information may or may not be available online. Afterall, not everything can be online. The indication that those who do not visit at all, but regard Nigeria as their original home post 9% (which is 2% more than six monthly visitors), signifies the possible fading of memories of Nigeria. Yet again, the percentage decreases, for other response alternatives like whether or not the Internet is moderately effective, ineffective, cannot say and not applicable, between the "frequencies of visit" dependent variable.

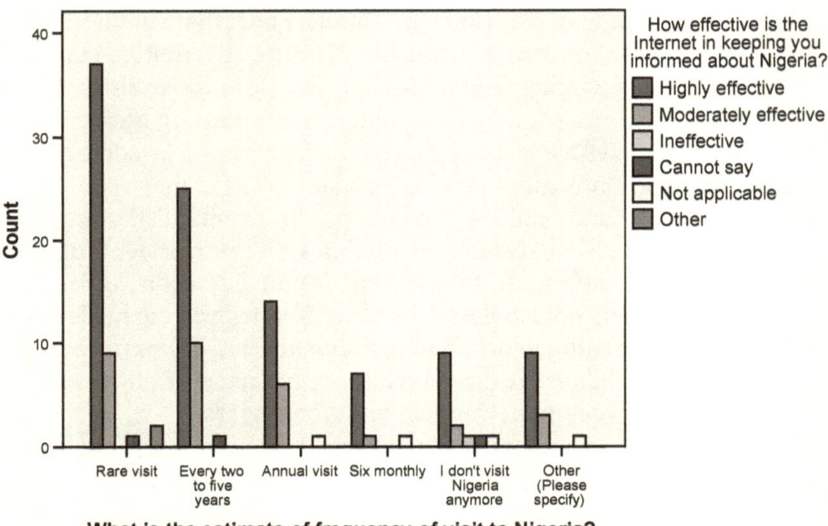

Figure 10: Relationship between Frequency of Visit to Nigeria and Interest in Using the Internet

Return largely remains difficult, if not impossible. It is often desired but unrealistic. However, it takes place in some cases, which is why ignoring it, is perhaps wrong. Like Nwaochei (2007:1), and other participants note, migrants consider retuning to Nigeria. Sometimes, it is mainly for the sake of some traditional belief. Related to this is the need to avoid the Western care home in old age. Preference is for the traditional care of the old in Nigeria, where there are extensive family and community support. Again, the cultural belief in the dignity of home burial is paramount in their considerations. Even then, hardly does this influence many. They are not able to actualise it, despite a desire for it. Sustenance of the return myth nevertheless continues until the feared old age, when the will to actualise it weakens, or becomes worn out. How, therefore, does the idealisation of return affect the remembrance of home through the Internet?

The data below shows the response options, which are seven and the measure of respondents in terms of how effective the network is. In addition, in terms of those in the "Highly effective" category, those who are undecided over return are more with 34%. Their ambivalent state might have been suitable for thoughts of Nigeria, which continues online. Persons who plan to return on retirement are 28%; in old age 16%; individuals not likely to return 13%, and migrants who have made up their minds not to return are 10%. Others are 3%. Importantly, all the response options find the Internet useful for connecting with Nigeria. This is possibly because of a continuing spatial or temporal desire to remember Nigeria. They either see it as highly or moderately useful in helping them know about Nigeria, as shown in the graph.

Bar Chart

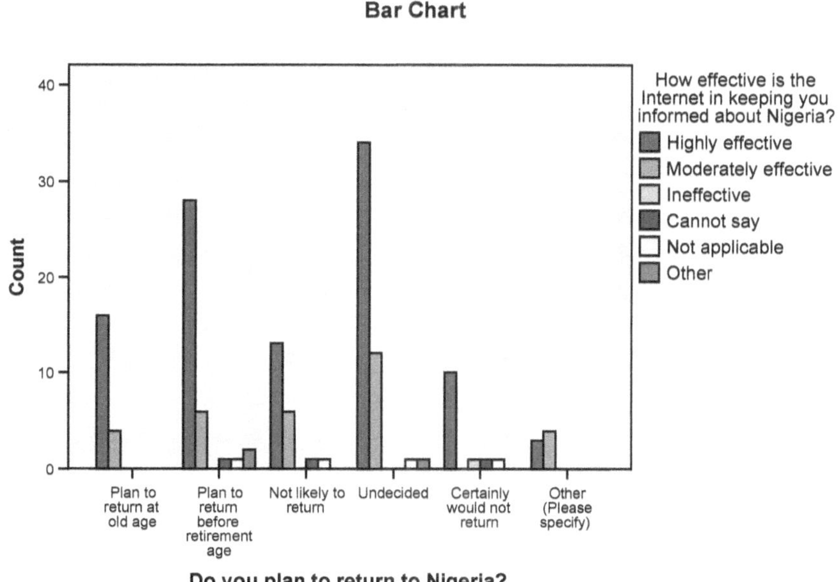

Figure 11: Relationship between plan to return to Nigeria and Internet Use

Similarly, participant engagement with the technology cuts across ages, as seen in figure 12. The illustration shows that more respondents across the age groups find it highly effective or moderately useful in knowing about Nigeria. It is important to say that the relation between age and Internet use is flexible. Using the technology across different age groups really depends on interests. Though reason for using it is common to all age groups, purpose of use is not. It goes through alterations with advancement in age. Younger people or teenagers may find it more useful for entertainment, but senior people are perhaps doing other things. Other spatial and temporal reasons like location, period and objective of use may vary across the ages, and as the user matures over the years. While the Internet possibly does not amuse the senior respondents (who are above 70), the middle-aged, might not be too detached from it, when they have reached their 70s. The younger respondents may witness a change in interest, as they grow older. The condition usually shifts, but in this circumstance, it is important to examine the correlation between the age of participants and level of appreciating the network in terms of connection with Nigeria. Consequently, those aged between 30 and 39 are greater users. This could be because the age group is

103

young and may be more enthusiastic. Due to foreseeing a brighter and better future, and because information is reasonably an important criteria to ensuring it, the Internet becomes a helpful medium.

Bar Chart

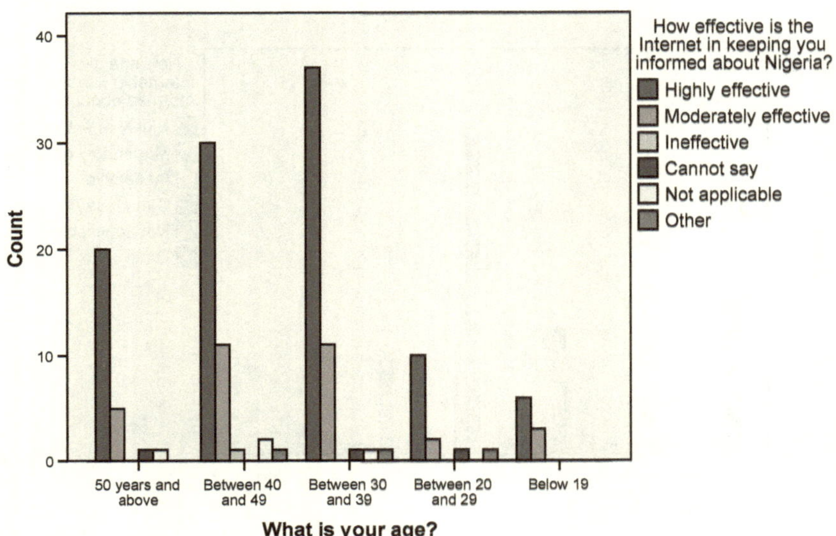

Figure 12: Relationship between Age of Participants and Internet Use

There are also gender disparities, even if they are not huge. From the survey, a nearly equal number of men and women say they use the Internet to know about Nigeria. While 17% of female respondents say it is highly effective in doing so, 14% of their male migrant counterparts give the same response. The results are also nearly equal in the category of those who say it is moderately effective. It is noteworthy here that the number of female respondents is a little larger in the survey, as against the trend of usage that runs through this research. While this is, according to this survey, statistically possible, it may mean that the female respondents include migrants who use the technology by proxy-through a dependence on their spouses, friends, or partners for sourcing information on Nigeria. This comes after the original user has done her/his work online. It may mean that there are less male respondents than female. However, it is realistic to argue that the use of the technology amongst migrants is not affected by gender.

These differences are by no means definite. I am aware of the different issues that could influence use of the Internet amongst participants, like availability of time or lack of it, and the ability to afford the cost of sitting by a computer terminal, whether in the café, or at home, despite its low cost. Use may also depend on whether the migrant is interested in being updated about Nigeria or not. The point, therefore, is that engagement with the Internet depends on so many variables. The examples above simply show the way uses relate to year of migration from Nigeria; reason for migration; occupation in hostland; status in hostland; estimate of frequency of visit to Nigeria; return plans, or lack of them; and age.

OPTIONS TO ONLINE CONNECTION

THE EDGE OF THE TELEPHONE

The combination of ease, accessibility, and cost are essential when personal connection between Nigeria and the host country is in focus. Emeka and Esther below note that the Internet is not a convenient medium to relate with their parents in Nigeria. Absence of enabling infrastructures for Internet use, illiteracy and age are some reasons they mentioned. Akinmade also hints at this, particularly as Internet does not guarantee intimacy. This makes the Internet what I have called a *detached* medium. The detachment occurs when participants have to go at length to gather information online after telephone conversations. It may be when sending or receiving further information through e-mail, instead of a long and rather costly telephone conversation. Then it may occur when the migrant desires to take time out to visit the café, or go through the process of connecting at home, or through concentrating on using it on her/his mobile phone.

The regular/routine roles of preceding media like the telephone are possible online, through sending and receiving e-mails; e-mail attachments; chats and Voice over Internet Protocol (VoIP), but the regular need to get detailed information is obvious from the viewpoint of participants, like Dupe, 43 (See page 110). This detailed information is not easily accessible on the phone. They are of the type from parties in Nigerian, who have impersonal relationships with migrants. Others probably simultaneously seek the information, instead of the one-on-one track of the telephone. The information is usually loaded online by website owners who desire to reach many, other than participants.

I cannot say that many Nigerians back home, (use the Internet) especially those I could have used it with. The economic differences between the UK where I live and Nigeria matters a lot… Of course, I cannot talk to my mother on the Internet. **Emeka, Male, 46, London. Interview date: 02/06/2006.**

Though we are connected to AOL broadband, we seldom use e-mail for reaching home. We may use it to reach friends and families in places where we go for holiday, maybe to send photographs, share ideas and forwarded messages, but not really to discuss matters that are more intimate. **Akinmade, Male, 48, London. Interview date: 02/06/2006**

I am regularly online with relations and my fiancé who is happy to be able to join me here any moment from now. We chat online, through the text and telephone, while he sends cards to me online as well. For my old parents back in the village, I ring them occasionally. Of course, they are not computer literate, and I cannot expect them to start learning computing at their ages. Therefore, it is convenient for me to talk to them on the telephone. **Esther, Female, 44, London. Interview date: 23/02/2006.**

This *detached* medium sends and receives further texts and figures. It has ample information from a variety of sources and users, and migrants use it as time permits. It is yet to be a highly routine/regular medium when everyday mediation with origin comes to play, as participants above argue. Its newness and the limitations created by the digital divides, despite its fast developing pace, is responsible for its present detachment. The Internet yet has a bias for economic development, class and is still elitist. Its pace and cheapness is mainly valid in the area of information sourcing, as against regular or routine communication. Higher literacy and degree of economic growth will eventually determine its everydayness. For now, the telephone seems to be the habitual media for relating with Nigeria, on a much more regular basis.

Importantly, most respondents testify to preferring telephone to reaching loved ones. This is either on a daily basis or once every two to three days, or weekly. Greater convenience and accessibility are some of the advantages of the medium over the Internet. As in previous points, the convergent character of the Internet includes the telephone, with facilities like Skype, SIP, IAX, and H.323, as Voice over Internet Protocols (VoIP). Though available, these newer devices remain relatively more sophisticated for use than the mobile phone or landline. These subsequently give an accessibility advantage on the non-Internet based phones. The minimum variant of the phone that can be in their possession at any time is the mobile. Sheriff, (34, Leeds. Interview date: 28/03/2008) notes this:

The mobile phone was the first thing I bought when I arrived the UK in 1999. At that time, the GSM was not yet in Nigeria. Therefore, it was thrilling to have it in the UK at low cost. Those concerned about my well-being, particularly my Dad, easily reached me. I was not computer literate then, so I was not attracted to the Internet. With the mobile, prospective employers reached me, and I called them too. That was how I got my first job. It was later that I began using the Internet and now, I am an addict.

International calling cards make long distance phone calls much more affordable. Landlines are also available, while the cards reduce the cost. The mobile phone is always with the owner, while the landline is readily available at home, or on the streets. However, the Internet terminal may not be readily available in comparative terms. It is always *detached*. It may indeed be possible to send and receive e-mails on the mobile, but it requires more time and concentration than simply dialling. Will it therefore be suitable at the time of need? It again brings up the convenience and accessibility component, which many participants easily associate more with the telephone, as Jide, 29 says (See page 107).

Observations and interviews like Sheriff's statement above show that the mobile phone is a priceless medium for many migrants. Access is not a serious issue in the determination of use. In Nigeria as well, it is very popular with the introduction of the Global System of Mobile telecommunication (GSM) in 2001. Contacts on the network from both ends are easier in most places and at most times. The likely illiterate village dwellers that Emeka and Esther talk about above, who are not able to interact with the computer, can engage with the phones. In addition, literacy hardly counts hear, simply as the ability to read or write in English language-the main Internet language. Migrants may use native languages in telephone conversations. The urban non-elite who is yet to embrace the Internet, and who is yet to have an e-mail account, can also hear or speak English. And just in case s/he cannot hear or speak, an interpreter can be engaged. These processes are less burdensome than reaching a computer terminal, which is dependent on an erratic power supply; an unaffordable computer system; a costly server; expensive or poorly managed cafés; and very slow and possibly outdated computer system. Okome earlier mentioned some of these. (See page 105). These show why the telephone is the most useful, non-*detached* medium in relating with Nigeria, as in the figure below, where many respondents regard the telephone as the most important when communicating with the *homeland*.

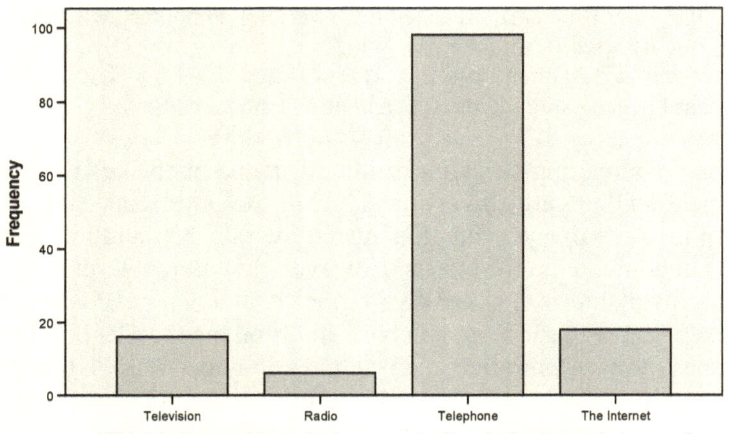

Figure 13: Most Important Medium In Terms Of (Possible) Every Day Communication with Nigeria

The statement of a participant below is also indicative. The prevalent use of the telephone when contacting people in Nigeria is emphasised. It is a reminder that the Internet is not the only effective medium. The voice advantage of the telephone, as against e-mails, is probably an additional encouragement, as it stimulates recollection of the likely familiar voice of the distant receiver. Perhaps, emotions are roused through it, just as it may minimise longing.

We are regularly in touch with home, through telephone calls, using international call cards or discounted numbers. The telephone work well in this (talking to people in migration source) regard. **Akinmade, Male, 48, London. Interview date: 02/06/2006.**

The statement that follows values the Internet but gives credit to the telephone for being another speedy medium. Immediacy features with the phone as it can be more flexible, as against the Internet, which requires a connected computer, a more suitable environment, and a lot more concentration. Even if the Internet can be mobile, it is not as much as the mobile phone. The reason being the less portability of relevant appliances and access problems in Nigeria, which is relatively not the case in the hostland:

Though, the Internet is fast, telephone is faster. You only have to click some buttons and you are through, but with e-mail, you have to sit by the computer, type in and send. You know what I mean. Telephone conversations can be on the go, but e-mail is a bit cumbersome. **Jide, Male, 29, Leeds. Interview date: 01/04/2006.**

The next participants' contribution is identical to the two above in terms of the primacy of the phone, but departs from them with the element of keeping record. While the written word of the Internet can most times be stored and retrieved, (informal) telephone conversations are often not on record. Even so, the relative speed in the dissemination of voiced information is vital in his consideration, which influences his preference for the phone:

I keep in touch with home mainly through the telephone. Sometimes, I write. I write because people sometimes like to keep records. So I send post cards and such other things. I use the Internet also. I send e-mails to some of my friends. However, for my parents and uncles, who are not educated, I communicate with them through the telephone. The telephone is more important to me because it is faster, and it conveys messages as quickly as possible. **Mohammed, Male, 27, Leeds. Interview date: 14/05/2006.**

The next participant finds a balance between the two media, but gives an edge to the phone given the access and educational disadvantages of Nigeria-conditions that could guarantee widespread use:

It is not everybody that you communicate with through the Internet, because of the educational level of our people. At least with my wife and with some of my friends, I do. With people in the village or may be in my local government where there is GSM, you have to use telephone. If we have Internet facility in my village, it will be cheaper and faster; you can write whatever you want to write and you do not have to pay as much as you pay when using the telephone, or the phone card. I have to use the telephone now, because there is no Internet connection where my parents are. **Magaji, Male, 36, Leeds. Interview date: 14/05/2006.**

On frequency, the majority of the respondents say they use the telephone at least once a week to call Nigeria, which further shows a high engagement with the medium. A little less use it every two to three days, and a fewer number than the second group use it on a daily basis, as seen in the table below. The table shows the frequency of telephone use to connecting with Nigeria. The question asks, Do you telephone Nigeria (on), a (a) daily basis (b) every two to three days (c) every week (d) every month (e) less often (f) not at all (and) (g) others (please specify). The responses show that those who do so at least once a week are the majority with 34.7 %, and then followed by two to three day contact basis with 25.3%, and on a daily basis

12.7 %. The remaining options are, altogether, less than 18%.

		Frequency	Percent	Valid Percent	Cumulative Percent	
Valid	Daily basis?	19	12.7	14.1	14.1
	Every two to three days?	38	25.3	28.1	42.2
	Every week?	52	34.7	38.5	80.7
	Every month?	3	2.0	2.2	83.0
	Less often?	13	8.7	9.6	92.6
	Not at all?	6	4.0	4.4	97.0
	Other (Please specify)	4	2.7	3.0	100.0
	Total	135	90.0	100.0	
Missing	System	15	10.0		
Total		150	100.0		

Figure 14: Frequency of Telephone Use in Relating With Nigeria

There is the probability of limiting conversation time on telephone due to cost considerations. It often makes participants to go the distance to complement its regular use with the Internet. Mobile phone Internet users or owners of wireless enabled laptop computers, among the participants could be relatively non-*detached*. However, because Internet use on the mobile needs attention, just as a position of settlement is required to use the laptop, adds to the fact of detachment. It is not the case with the telephone, which is always available to them for a flexible and faster use.

While the Internet is able to update the migrants about details of occurrences in Nigeria, the telephone plays the routine, regular and personal communication roles. This takes place through, for instance, saying a quick "hello…" to a loved one in Nigeria, with the additional advantage of voice communication in consideration, as observations confirm. The convenience, for participants, of getting everyday routine information about someone's well-being; whether or not remitted funds have been received, or a new need for it; marriage or divorce plans; children's well being; return plans, or its absence; job situations and conditions; and other general talk on the telephone is unmistakable. And this is not Internet based telephone or the Voice over Internet Protocol (VoIP), but mainly on the mobile or landline, with one of the many international call cards in hand. However, when the matter is about details on the politics of origin, migrants turn to the websites of Nigerian newspapers and magazines or the many developing news-inclined portals. The websites also help in providing information about the state of the economy; about the security situation; about celebrities and their world; and about the many evolving new rich, and the declining rich. Other than the telephone, television also matter in the migrants bid to mediate distance. I shall turn to this next.

AUDIO-VISUAL IMPACT OF TELEVISION

The roles of television and cinema in the expansion of migrants' imagination are important. This is because Nigeria Television programmes emotionally close the distance between origin and present locations, when it produces images, as participants say. The images may not simply remind the migrant viewer of the departed ways of life, but updates them about new trends. They (the images) prompt recollections, enliven remembrances, just as they elicit memories. When it becomes a regular act, the *homeland* ceases to be in the distant. Many networks have lately become available for the consumption of interested the Nigerian diaspora members. References to these networks in online spaces of interaction and revelations in returned questionnaires reveal the significance of such TV stations. The websites of the networks lay claim to making the migrants a target. These sites are alternative access points for the migrant consumers, as opposed to viewing them from the screens of "real" TV sets. Among these TV stations are Bright Entertainment Network (BEN Television); African Independent Television (AIT); Nigeria Television Authority (NTA); Kingsway International Christian Centre Television (KICC Television) and Channel 331 on Sky, which is devoted to the production of *Nollywood*[24] films. I shall now discuss these sampled networks as a means of understanding the mediation effect of the television on the migrant audience.

A Nigerian migrant Alistair Soyode established the most popular television stations amongst the migrants in the UK, BEN TV in 2002. Its target audience are black people. These groups, according to BEN TV, hardly receive reports in the mainstream media of the hostland. In their plans, BEN TV was an outlet of expression for this minority. Though the slant is frequently commercial, the originators are championing the cause of giving voice to an assumed voiceless. This voice, though significant, is different from the Internet voice. While one person, a few people, or a group, may establish the TV voice, the Internet voice can be more flexible. Even so, the advantage of satellite broadcasting to migrant communities is not lost in the process of globalisation. The owners note further that they are out to help the process of self-empowerment and self-actualisation. They promise to help migrant viewers realise their objectives in the hostland through the airing of appropriate stories, and through information exchange (Accessed at www.bentelevision.com on 15/03/2008). Its programmes centre on news, evangelism, and the production of music, videos, sports, personality interviews, and interactive sessions. One of its programmes, *"In*

---

[24] *Nollywood* denotes the Nigerian film industry.

Diaspora", appears 8.00pm every Tuesday. As named, it aims to reflect the absent status of its targeted consumers. As observed on the 19th and 21st of February and on the 4th and 11th of March, 2008, the subject of discussion by its anchor, Jide Iyaniwura, relates to migration, resettlement and host people's perception of the migrants. The degree to which the migrants can modify, challenge or change this perception was of interest to viewers who phoned to contribute. *"In Diaspora"* projects the mood of phone-in participants in the hostland on a chosen topic. Invited guests in the studio review issues from a probably more informed perspective. The station specifically describes itself as the:

> 24-hour black-oriented television service in United Kingdom, (BEN Television is) bridging and filling the gap created by mainstream broadcasters. The television introduces new cultured, black oriented programmes to European taste with good family ethos. Ben television is a Black oriented, urban, diverse and cosmopolitan family channel, established to provide a wholesome mix of entertaining programmes suitable for family viewing. It also includes a range of cultured programming to empower, transforms and challenge the conventional perception of Africa and Africans. **Accessed at http://www.bentelevision.com/2007/home/introduction.php on 11/02/2008.**

The channel's interests in airing programmes that are "black oriented", but tailored to "European taste" suggests that a new element in transnational communication is coming because the programmes are no longer going to be entirely African; neither are they going to be reproducing white, liberal Eurocentrism. They are black oriented television series suitable to the European environment, and acceptable to its migrant audience. Through a consumption of BEN TV programmes, therefore, the migrant may acquire a new worldview; one that is not entirely African. Robins and Aksoy (2005:14), call this experience "transnational disposition", as their study of Turkish migrants in the UK revealed. It may as well be a disposition as it relates to Nigerian migrants, but the process rather turns them into consumers of a modified culture. The culture undergoes modification, as it is new, in between, and sometimes shifting between cultural locations and ideological points of reference. The channel's claim to be airing programmes that could "empower, transform and challenge the conventional perception of African and Africans" is also important. While this is possible through educating viewers, it may be limited by the stations' capacities and to their viewers' expectations. This is so because not all migrants subscribe to Sky, even if the channel is a "free to air", meant for "blacks in Diaspora" (accessed at http://www.bentelevision.com/2007/home/introduction.php on 17/03/2008). Again, they are unlikely to compete with the developed networks of leading mainstream media, where misrepresentations allegedly take place. This argument does not however erase the significance of such a project that offers alternative representations of Africans and black people, compared to the mainstream media.

The Nigeria Television Authority (NTA) like most transnational television stations had until recently been concerned only with audiences within the country's national territory. The station yielded in late 2006 to the pull of changes in global satellite broadcasting, by reaching out to foreign audiences, most probably Nigerians in the diaspora. It is available online via AFRICAST (Accessed at www.africast.tv on 16/03/2008), and through BEN TV at 8.00 p.m. (This however varies in accordance with time changes between the two countries). MHZ Networks provide it in the US. Importantly, the programmes they show are the popular "Network News", which is a comprehensive daily report of key events in Nigeria. However, stories are official and have a government leaning. Through updating migrants about origin, a periodic connection with Nigeria manifests. Physical presence is likely taking place in the hostland, but thoughts of country of origin goes on through the hour that the broadcast lasts, or through the time that the viewer engages with the screen. "Transcultural dispositions" (Robins and Aksoy, 2005:14), may result when the act becomes routine. Because of the mindset that develops via the everyday practice of consuming NTA productions, other kinds "of mental and imaginative spaces", could evolve eventually helping to form a "capacity to function and think across cultural domains" (Robins and Aksoy, ibid.: 15). A US viewer, Dr Femi Ajayi comments on the NTA transnational production as follows:

> I am welcoming the NTA to Atlanta, Georgia. Thanks to NTA international for bringing this live broadcast to the corridors of CNN, telling Nigeria story as it has never been told before. Something good is coming from Africa. Here is NTA international, the first and the largest television station in Africa, broadcasting LIVE to the world, from Atlanta. What other stories do we have to write about Nigeria, more than this live broadcast on the Economic opportunities in Nigeria that have not being told by any other before? **Ajayi, accessed at http://nigeriaworld.com/columnist/ajayi/081407.html on 17/03/2008.**

The excerpt above is celebratory. It is a reminder of the core philosophy behind the creation of minority media, which is to challenge exclusion. In this specific case, the writer envisages a direct challenge to CNN, as the reference to the "corridors of CNN" implies. However, can this challenge be effective? The question arises because the capital outlay of NTA transnational network is no match to that of the transnational worth of the US based CNN. From the mindset of the writer, it does not have to be. Satisfaction comes from the ability of the network to tell "The Nigeria story as it has never being told before". They could possibly have been half-truths, negative or incomplete. The new voice from Nigeria sounds like a long muted one. The release of the voice is therefore a welcome to freedom in the distance, one that is particularly educative on the available opportunities in origin, if return ever takes place. In an opinion article in Nigeria's *The Guardian,* Owogbemi Modupe writes:

> If one of the motive of the NTA is to be responsive to negative Western reports through a basic rendition of news, then success would hardly be registered. The projection of Nigeria's heritage, in ways that are germane to explaining the dynamics of the period seem more sensible. The Brazilian example is a witness. **Modupe, accessed at <u>www.ngrguardiannews.com</u> on 30/11/2006.**

His argument was that rather than being defensive about so-called negative reports, the network could concentrate on positive things that may be attractive to the mainstream international media. Viewers note TV *Globo,* for instance, for its efforts in projecting the Brazilian culture to migrant Brazilians, and other countries within the range of its signal. *Aljazeera* (Arabic and English) is not essentially defensive in its reflection of Islamic civilisation, which the Western media allegedly misunderstands. Both TV *Globo* and *Aljazeera* (Arabic and English) have turned out to be important transnational television stations from the "south". They are epitomes of contra-flows (Thussu, 2007), while *Aljazeera* (English) has grown to become one of the "big three" (Chalaby, 2007). The other two are CNN and the BBC. Does the NTA reveal any sign of being a consequential challenge after nearly two years of transnational broadcasting? The question may not be fair, given the crisis of development the owner nation-state still faces. Nevertheless, the ambitious posturing could lead to the query after this period of transnational activity. As its programmes and workforce are still largely Nigerian, its limitations are therefore apparent. It is nevertheless a significant medium of information for the Nigerian diaspora in the light of its ability to offer a larger space for connection.

African Independent Television (AIT) is a private initiative led by a Nigerian, Dr Raymond Dokpesi, to compete with the state owned NTA. Watched through Globe Cast World TV in the US and Canada, and through BEN TV in the UK (accessed at <u>www.aitv.com</u> on 17/03/2008), its reputation for offering unofficial perspectives to news and current affairs is evident. It also broadcasts *Nollywood* products to viewers, just as it airs interactive sessions, through its popular early morning show, *"Kakaki"*. Though quality of production is suspect, it offers alternatives for migrant consumers.

Kingsway International Christian Centre (KICC) Television performs a similar role. Led by the Nigerian born Pastor Mathew Ashimolowo, the twenty-four hour television station, viewed through Sky Channel 774, specialises in the broadcasting of Church programmes, church conference proceedings and messages to viewers, such as women, businesspersons, youths, couples and singles. Apart from the lead pastor, the wife, Yemisi, is also a regular on screen. So are some preachers from America, Nigeria and elsewhere. Other than reaching those who do not attend their church services in London, and who may be living in a different place, the channel claims to be determined to "make champions", and to make people "the best". The programmes on air are similar to those on church television broadcasts in Nigeria. Classy aesthetics, an upbeat ambition, and an obvious panache symbolise the programmes. Other than the style of the church head, his Western exposure spanning over two decades may have contributed. To some viewers, the achievement of the church is a pride of blacks, and more particularly Nigerian migrants. To others, Pentecostal priests are businesspersons, who soon after establishing their churches become rich. The statements below represent these strands of thoughts:

> Pastor Ashimolowo is particularly blessed. He has brought a revival to many lost souls. The KICC station is a constant attraction to me. I like to hear the word. It is what I need to grow in the lord. The pastor and the wife know the word. I have been blessed many times, particularly at nights after work.
> **Lovett, Female, 33, Leeds. Interview date: 13/03/2008**
> I like to listen to Nigerian news sometimes. However, I have to be concerned about when I switch to these Nigerian TV stations, so as not to be bombarded with the theatrics of the many modern day preachers always on there. They are obviously always preaching to the wrong people. I do not need to hear them to get what I want in this country-all I need is to work for pounds, not to listen to somebody asking for ten percent of my earnings!
> **Demilade, Male, 39, London. Interview date: 31/03/2008**

To Lovett, the channel is appropriate for her spiritual needs. She feels a need to achieve a spiritual maturity and finds the station helpful. Many of these religious programmes are present in Nigeria. The reality is different in the hostland, as they are arguably less overtly religious. KICC TV therefore fills a spiritual void in migration. The overall impact of this is perhaps ambiguous, because belief systems are personal, but associating with the messages of the broadcasters makes her feel a sense of ontological security. Imagining co-viewers could also formulate a sense of belonging. Demilade however feels different. His mission in the hostland is economic. "I came here with a work permit, not a church permit", he boldly adds. He would therefore avoid distractions that could lead to a reduction of his resources on the grounds of satisfying a vague spiritual need. As it is, the migrants' perceptions of the religious channels are different. Nevertheless, the significance of the channel in contributing to migrants' paths to spiritual uplifts is clear.

Equally important is the representation of Nigerian images and cultures to migrants through *Nollywood* movies. Rated by *Time* Magazine as third in the world, after Hollywood and Bollywood[25], and "being worth over 22 billion dollars", (Accessed at www.naijarules.com on 23/03/08), the movies' impact on migrants' perceptions is considerable. Video cassettes, Audiotapes, VCD's, CD's and DVD's are sold in local Nigerian food shops. They are available for rent in these outlets, for a fee or are free in some circumstances. Viewing them may take place on different websites, again for a fee or for free, especially during a specified period of promotion. SKY Channel 331 now exclusively shows *Nollywood* films. The promoters are accessible at www.nollywoodmovies.tv., for subscription details. They began in January 2008. A subscription of £5.99 applies. The charges effectively started 29/02/2008 after a two-month free trial period. Plots are often around love, riches, witchcraft, politics, religion and cultural practices (Azeez, 2008). Production quality may still be relatively substandard, but they appeal to migrants for many reasons. The participant below sums it up:

> I watch *Nollywood* films when I am less busy. Particularly during Bank Holidays, if I am not doing overtime. I like to hear them because actors speak like me. Their pronunciations are clearer to me than Western films. Neither do I have to bother about reading English interpretations, if they were for instance, Indian. I also do laugh at some of the ways of our rich men as portrayed in the films. Though the storylines are most times predictable, I appreciate them for reminding me of home. **Maja, Male, 43, London. Interview date: 31/03/2008.**

The statement is revealing in two ways. First, it shows how familiarity and association with actors gives viewers a sense of comfort. Second, is the issue of accent when he says, "actors speaking like me". Connection with Nigeria takes place not only in the plot but also in the speeches of actors. This indicates an ability to relate better with them in communication terms than with Western actors. Watching the movies may therefore be less strenuous to his ears than non-Nigerian films. In the case of "other" films, he probably has to listen more attentively; watch the speakers' lips; or even rewind to keep proper track of the story line. There is therefore evidence of relief in his engagement with the movies. In addition, this relief heightens when he laughs. The amusement at the ways of the Nigerian rich in the film is probably a product of knowledge of the different ways of the rich in the hostland. While the former is believably flamboyant, the rich in the presently lived place is perhaps conservative. The exposure to different cultures increases the ability to differentiate. Reminding him of origin is an apparent benefit, but it goes further to demonstrate the power of the moving image, and their storylines on memories. The next participant introduces a generational dimension. She states:

---

[25] Hollywood denotes the US film industry, while Bollywood is Indian.

I watch the films a lot, particularly since I have been on maternity leave. My first son, who has never been to Nigeria, also finds them interesting. The little meaning he makes out of them tells him about home. He is beginning to develop a picture of what Nigeria looks like, through the films. Though my husband does not like them because he says they are easy to predict, but many are not. They keep you in suspense until you get to the end. **Iyabo, Female, 33, Leeds. Interview date: 20/03/2008**

According to this participant, the films help with long distance socialisation. The child, a nine year old, was obviously born abroad. He has never experienced the Nigerian environment, neither has he imbibed its ways in the manner in which the "home" born would. It is probably a worrisome issue for the mother. She is happy that the child's interest in the movies teaches him a few things about Nigeria. Besides, the films instruct the child about another culture, where the parents originated. He is learning that the inhabited place is not his. He is of another and a "double vision" (Bhabha, 1990), is developing. This may diminish the idealisation of parental origin, as images of the origin are regularly featured on screen. Absolute strangeness may not emerge in the face of a visit home, or in the usually difficult case of return. The exposure of the child to the films is helpful to the mother, to the extent in which socialisation at a distance can be virtually affected. This is because images and words are fragments of the imagination. The imagination can be an expansion or a contraction, depending on the skills, creativity and experiences of the producers and actors. It is also dependent on the extent of the child's exposure to a host society's ways. If the exposure were extensive, less meaning would come out of the films. Moreover, if not, more meanings could come of it. In this situation, what becomes overriding is the fact of the recognition of another culture, where a relationship occurs. It also confirms what one of the industry's analyst, Dr Akin Adesokan, means by noting that:

Nollywood is alive and well. The growth has only accelerated due to the phenomenal changes in the technology of filmmaking, the fact that there are many more Nigerians and other Africans living outside the continent than in, say, 1985. **Accessed at <u>www.indiana.edu/-/6fca/events/akininterview.</u> <u>html</u> on 30/02/2008**

ROLES OF RADIO, PRESS, POSTAL SERVICES AND "WORD OF MOUTH"

Other than the Internet, telephone and television, other media play significant roles in the mediation of migrants multiple relationships. These are radio, press, postal services and word of mouth. Reliance on the radio may not be as obvious, it helps remembrances, and fosters communal feelings when migrant groups come together to run programmes in native languages. There are broadcasts in the Yoruba language on a few migrant related radio stations. BEN TV station and the moribund *Radio Kudirat* own some of these. *Radio Kudirat* was particularly prominent in the fight against military dictatorship in the 1990's. Led by Nobel Prize winner, Wole Soyinka, it sensitised migrants to the ills of the ancestral home from an activist perspective, through negative reports about then military dictators. Its propaganda campaign was unsettling to the then Nigerian military dictators. The station provoked a crisis of confidence between the military leaders and some foreign governments in support of the campaigners. Some of these governments were those of the UK, Sweden, and Canada (Adebanwi, 2001). The station did not however outlive the fall of the military regime that led to its introduction; it went off air in 1998. Its exploits and those of others presently on air are a reflection of the migrant capacity to take risks in communication. The awareness they created and are still creating, is not only complementary to other media, but demonstrates the migrants' desire to explore the mediation potential inherent in respective media of international communications, whenever the need arises.

Many migrant magazines and newspapers exist. A lot are short lived. Notable ones in Nigerian and in minority stores are *Ovation International, Positive, Focus Magazine, Nigerians and Africans Abroad, and Highlife. African Today* published for a while, before it stopped, just as *Chic Magazine* did. There are several newsletters as well. Many have online versions. They focus mainly on reporting migrant activities, like birthdays, deaths, graduation parties, immigration issues, burials, scandals, fashion, jobs, weddings, local eateries, accommodation issues, business opportunities, romance, memorable day celebrations, and visits of Nigerian officials. They are mainly weeklies, monthlies, quarterlies, and periodicals. Cost and inconvenience, given the possible difficulties in running a business in a foreign country may determine publishing schedules. Essentially, their area of concern is the mediation of migrant activities. Newspapers and magazines from Nigeria complement their efforts in migration. The physical editions of publications from origin are hardly timely, because of the difficulty in circulating them at a distance. Regardless of this limitation in circulation capabilities, many migrants are happy to read them when possible.

Apart from posting letters, and documents, through the public and private postal services, "word of mouth" is also important. Migrants easily know who is travelling and who is not from their networks. They share rumours, and leads to stories. Through travellers, they send letters, cash and deliver unwritten messages to friends and families in origin. It does not really matter if the messages go through several parties, as the case could be. Of importance to them is its eventual delivery. Replies often come through the bearers, particularly in cases where visits are brief. It all highlights the relevance of other methods[26], even though the internet is the medium in focus.

---

[26] In the African context as well, dance, traditional music, art, and the age-old oral literature are some other forms of communication (Eribo and Jong-Ebot, 1997). The practical expression of these in the migrants' case is not overtly noted in contributions. This is because their manifestation are most likely through the modern channels of video, or audio tapes, as well as in discs, usually made available to them from the *homeland*.

CHAPTER FIVE:

TRANSNATIONAL NETWORKS OF THE NIGERIAN DIASPORA

Diasporic discourses reflect the sense of being part of an ongoing transnational network that includes the *homeland* not as something simply left behind but as a place of attachment in contraptual modernity **(Clifford, 1997: 256).**

The last chapter concentrated on the main dimensions of the Nigerian diaspora use of the Internet. The chapter revealed communication uses of the network and available alternatives. However, other matters arise through communication. Those identified in this study are transnationalism, nationalism and identity. I shall discuss transnationalism in this chapter, while the two chapters after this shall be on nationalism and identity. I shall argue in this section that in moving, seeking integration, trading across borders, acquiring properties abroad, and visiting the *homeland*, participants are active in transnational spaces. They are found in different locations, and they interrelate from those locations. Modern media like the Internet facilitates these interactions. This chapter maps how the Internet enhances the transnational activities of the migrants, by discussing how the migrants' cross border activities have become banal, and how the Internet makes this possible. In this context, transnationalism is discussed within the larger framework of globalisation, and the inevitable role of communication in its processes.

Destinations are determined on the promise it holds for economic improvement. The projection is also dependent on residency rules, popularity of a place, and the particular cause of dispersal. As shown earlier in this work, participants' inclination to move to the West is high. The relative economic prosperity of Western nations, because of the main economic reason for dispersal, remains a ready explanation for migration. George (accessed at www.eturbonews.com on 01/07/2008) adds, "It has become a matter of status symbol to have a family member living overseas". In situations where Western nations happen to be difficult to penetrate, many migrants have looked to the rising economies of Asia, or African economies like South Africa's. The desire to migrate is strong because of a controversial belief in Nigeria that migration automatically leads to prosperity. This belief at times makes migrants' consider some non-western destinations, classed as developing countries. Examples of these are Ukraine, Libya, Morocco and Egypt.

Importantly, the Internet has been helping the construction of imagined communities, as will be shown in this chapter. The dispersed people are either constructing websites, or contributing to those constructed by others. Networks of newsgroups also flourish amongst them, just as events feature online. The diaspora members exchange invitations to contemporaries in diverse locations. As will be shown, their transnational activities experience endless forward and backward movements, residency in a particular location before another; and a continuous search for currencies with higher value than the Nigerian Naira. There is a flurry of remittances or desire for it. The dense process of gathering and exchanging information on a daily basis, across distance matters as well. Other than remittances, transactions in material resources are high. I shall explain how these paths of transnationalism is commonplace in cyberspace. Then the way virtual space initiates physical manifestation of their cross border activities will feature.

Before looking at transnationalism in the present, I shall first examine how a historical link between cultures is represented online. I shall do this in a bid to demonstrate that while the Internet is important in fostering modern day transnational activities of the diaspora members, past relationships are also on display on the network. I am referring here to the case of a US group, which constructed a cultural narrative similar to that of a major ethnic group in Nigeria. They are important to this work because the Internet partly sustains their existence and their everyday imaginary connection. It is a significant case, as it gives a historical perspective to transnationalism through the viewpoint of culture. Apart from interviews, arguments made in this chapter are the result of observations of sampled websites, especially Types A, B, C, D, and H.

THE *OYO-TUNJI* VILLAGE IN SOUTH CAROLINA VERSUS THE YORUBAS IN NIGERIA

The participants' experience of transnationalism began long ago, through the slave trade, which was a regular activity across borders. The slave trade was of great consequence because of the high level of labour mobility that took place. If slavery carried traces of transnationalism, and partly began its present expression amongst participants, the succeeding colonialism, and post-colonialism are no less significant in originating it, because they also set off dislocations. Slavery has left significant traces in the West, through particularly the presence of blacks. And a few black groups in the place have common cultures with ethnic groups in continental Africa. Some black groups also deliberately come together to align themselves with the cultures of ancestral origin.

The case of "Oyo-tunji"-The African Village in South Carolina, founded in 1970, comprising about fifty residents (Clarke, 2004: 9), is unique in the expression of the multilocality of Nigerian migrant groups. The representation of the Yoruba group from Western Nigeria in the distant US is a reminder of the force of history, culture and agency in the creation of transnational communities. Their online portrayal at www.oyotunjiafrican village.org, goes further to show how the age of transnationalism and globalisation leads to the undermining of place as the root of culture and identity. In this age, our understanding of the self comes up in space through the development and modification of values and ideologies. Clarke (ibid.: 21) writes:

> With the power of religious ritual, Oyo-tunji Village awakens at night. Ritual and rhythmic drumming echo in the endless hours of the night as residents remake their ancestral *homeland* outside of the territory of Africa. If Africanness is defined as doing, rather than simply being, then *orisa* practitioners in South Carolina use ritual to produce a deterritorialised community in a US landscape through which they become "African" in their terms.

The author published an image that partly represents the culture of the parent Yoruba group in Nigeria. The image is *"atibaba"* in Yoruba. It loosely denotes a "sun cover". The cover protects assembling villagers who sit outside for drinks, discussions or consultations. This image protects the village town crier, who manipulates the contraption beneath to announce messages sent out by the village head to villagers. Its representation in the distant hostland of the US is again an instance of the attempt of participants to recreate practices in origin even away from it. The presence of the image online regularly sustains remembrance of the very distant compatriots. This peer exists in a different continent, but the distance dissolves in the Internet space because of continuous textual and pictorial representations.

Site of alert for drumming communication to villagers.

Figure 15: A Cover for Village Town Crier in Oyo-tunji

Kamari Clarke who did an ethnographic study of the village expands on the meaning of the above image by referring to aesthetics, traditionalism and history:

> This sign, posted outside the front gates to Oyotunji, introduces a community that resembles the popular US image of a quintessential African Village somewhere on a faraway shore, whose articulations of subjectivity lie in the enactment of the imaginary. For many visitors, its artistic presentation, coupled with the mementos of ritual, evoke nostalgic desires to see and experience ancient African village life. Named after the once powerful West African Oyo Empire of the sixteenth to eighteenth centuries, Oyotunji is a black nationalist community of African American religious converts to Yoruba practices who have reclaimed West Africa as there ancestral *homeland*. Most Oyotunji practitioners trace their origins to the descendants or the men and women taken from West African communities and exported to the Americas as slaves. Because of the belief that they have a right to control the African territory that was their *homeland* prior to European colonisation, residents of Oyotunji Village have reclassified their community as an African Kingdom outside of the territoriality of the Nigerian postcolonial state **(Clarke, 2004:41)**

Although it is not an online group, the Internet facilitates presentations across transnational spaces, as it "has promoted...online *Orisa* chatrooms and Internet based services" (Clarke, Ibid.:7)[27]. Besides, it helps to nourish the link with the parent Yoruba group in Nigeria. The process of doing this may foster a sense of belonging with the Yorubas in other locations, thus expanding the possibility of imagined communities. Transnationalism will possibly not be limited to cross border activities of nationals of a nation-state abroad, or to their activities between the *homeland* and hostland, but could include their cross border ethno-tribal relationships. More like a transnational cultural group, their experience is one forerunner to modern evidence of multinational actions, as the following reveals.

---

[27] Orisa is a religious system, which believes in the supremacy of God, as *Eledumare*, or *Olorun*-all meaning the Supreme Being. It is a practice common amongst many nations and nation-states, including the Yorubas of Nigeria, and their peers in the Republic of Benin, Brazil, Cuba, Domican Republic, Jamaica, Trinidad and Tobago, and the US, amongst others. (Accessed at http://www.wemba-music.org/orisha.htm, on 30/08/2008).

EVIDENCE OF TRANSNATIONALISM AMONGST THE NIGERIAN DIASPORA

MOVING WORKERS, CROSS-BORDER BUSINESSES AND FOREIGN ACQUISITION OF PROPERTIES

The Internet offers migrants a freedom that brings forward transnational belonging. The freedom enables the migrants to be active in a competitive global environment, which is not only representative of "a bottom-up experience of transnationalism" (Georgiou, 2002:1), but one that makes communicating spatially instantaneous, "everyday, virtual and visual" (Georgiou, ibid.; 1). The participants' transnational activities are mainly intra and inter migration. It is inter, when they relate with migrants of other nation-states and intra when the relationship is within fellow migrants in closer locations. It involves the *homeland* when the activity is between its space (the *homeland*) and hostland. The problem of the digital divide nevertheless limits the participation of Nigeria in the relationship. Participants are, however, able to reveal their cross border activities. The view below justifies this claim in the area of the development of epistemic associations online.

> Despite the existence of a digital divide, the transnationalisation of African diaspora communities has produced complex webs of relationships. These include social, political, economic and intellectual linkages that take the nature of epistemic communities. An epistemic community is one that has a network of colleagues who maintain close ties, have shared beliefs that influence the positions they take on social problems and issues, shared ideas on what is valid, use similar approaches and methods in their work, desire common policy outcomes, and exchange information. **Okome, Female, New York, online: 11/12/2006.**

As observed during the period of study, transnational activities feature in the conduct of many participants. In the first place, the trouble in Nigeria leads to dispersals and consequent settlement in hostlands for some. For others, those troubles simply lead to circular living. These people do not want to be too entrenched abroad, and neither do they want to lose touch with socio-economic and political developments in Nigeria. To live in both places, therefore, they move back and forth, exposing themselves to the supposedly secured environment of the West, and engaging in physical and psychological relationship with Nigeria. Economic or political engagement determines the length of stay in one part. The determination is to make the best of both worlds. Some of these people may resent a few things, including for example, a possible crisis of integration in the hostland. They do not want to fully experience the challenges and the assumptions on the limitations of personal development. At the same time, the better environment of the hostlands lures them. The compromise position is to live amid the borders of the two places. The Internet enables them to keep in touch, while circulating as Supo attests to here:

> I live in Lagos, but my family is here in London. I visit them as often as possible, say three times in a year. I left London to go and work, to establish my company some two years ago and it has been rewarding. When I was here, I did all sorts, and I never went beyond the ordinary. Now, I employ people in Nigeria, and I am proud of myself. My family can remain here (London); in the meantime, so that my children can get a better education. We communicate always, everyday with my wife and children on the telephone and on the Internet. That (communication) is not a problem at all. **Supo, Male, 41, London. Interview date: 05/06/2006.**

Splitting family members between Nigeria and Western countries is a common way of showing transnational belonging amongst participants. Many of them express fears that Nigeria will not remain a single political entity in the future. They predict war, ethnic nationalists' insurgency and many other forms of unrest. This state of mind comes from the seemingly fruitless efforts of some committed leaders to work towards development. The pains of watching the behaviour of many self-serving leaders is also frustrating. The statement of a former Nigerian government officer responsible for fighting financial crime, Nuhu Ribadu, stresses this feeling:

> Most of the public officers have several houses and concubines abroad, awaiting the total collapse of the nation and its economy for them to take off. We are trying to see if it is possible to change the people's stereotyped orientation towards corruption, we are trying to see if we can stop the people who have turned the economy of the state to their personal estate. **Accessed at www.thisdayonline.com on 23/03/2007**

Because of a lack of assurance in Nigeria's unstable economic and political system, the West becomes another home away from Nigeria. Any of the two places, Nigeria or abroad, may turn out to be a workplace, and then they travel back and forth. This practice is especially common amongst the rich, who often buy homes abroad. Their activities have led to booms in estate business amongst migrants, as many migrants have become emergency estate consultants, who compete with few experts. They consequently make the Internet a target place for advertisements. While they publicise for fellow migrants, those in Nigeria are also targets. The image below is from www.nigerian.com (Accessed 18/06/2007), which is typical of the usually exhaustive web pages of the property consultants.

Figure 16: Sample Web Advert of a Nigerian Migrant Estate Agency Site

Worthy of noting is that because a typical Nigerian elite desires house(s) in the West, a lot have had to do this through corrupt practices. They sometimes buy these houses with funds from suspicious sources. The drive is to create or sustain a picture of international mobility, which becomes easier if they own properties in more than one location. Online activism has however been exposing many of them, as will be seen in the next chapter.

As Supo, a participant says above, many trans-migrants do reside in the West. Several of them claim citizenship before a possible return, as citizenship or residency is an ultimate guarantee of unhindered back and forth travels. Moreover, a return to the hostland becomes an alternative, in case staying in Nigeria is no longer desired. Those who fall into this bracket usually leave their families behind, while they engage in other endeavours in Nigeria. Babalola (Male, 47, Leeds. Interview date: 12/03/2006) for instance was in the UK for five years. He came as an asylum seeker during the period of military dictatorship. He eventually acquired British citizenship for himself and his family before leaving family behind to return to Nigeria for an appointment in the presidential department. He visits relations as often as resources and time permit. Again, he says the process of living in the two worlds becomes easier through developments in communication technologies particularly the Internet and mobile telephony. "I call my wife anytime and I am able to send e-mails to my children, who are more disposed to it whenever the need arises", he adds.

There is a gender component to this transnationalism. For example, the nursing profession is in high demand in the UK (as at the time of this research). The hostland is, therefore, attractive to many nursing professionals. Observations reveal that the Nigerian nursing population which boasts of more women than men find the UK to be a worthy destination. While the women go abroad to work, their husbands and children often stay back in Nigeria to await the rewards of the wife and mother's sojourn. The telephone, the Internet and word of mouth mediate their affairs during these separations. Sometimes, those who stay back in Nigeria join the migrant nurse. Before they rejoin, and in many cases where immigration hitches prevent it, the migrant worker travels back and forth to keep in touch with the family.

Transnationalism is not however limited to this category of migrants. Literature and my observations reveal a preponderance of illegal workers in the West. A significant number are from Africa, while Nigerians form a great percentage. Many of these illegal workers are entering the country legally as tourists. Friends and family members eventually help them to "manipulate" the system to gain employment. Many do succeed. While some return when their visas are nearing expiration, others send it to acquaintances back home for processing and return. This is especially so in cases where the embassies do not require physical presence to issue visas. Those who return go backward and forward as tourists, or holidaymakers, but are actually migrant workers, even though illegal. Often, a lot of them are young, literate and are ready to take risks. They populate the newsgroups, and write opinions in websites in a quick bid to demonstrate their status as travelled people. A writer Halilu, 44, refers to them:

> How many Nigerians in London are legal? These people work and send money home without having genuine papers. Soon again, they travel and return. They can even be deported, but before long, they are back. I just wonder how they get these things done with little or no fear! **Halilu, Male, 44, Leeds. Interview date: 02/04/2006**

Whether documented or undocumented migrants, they invariably form the basis of what Cohen (1997:160, cited in Vertovec, 1999:9), implies as part of the details of family activities in transnationalism:

> Traders place order with cousins, siblings and kin back home; nieces and nephews from 'the old country', stay with uncles and aunts while acquiring their education or vocational training; loans are advanced and credit is extended to trusted intimates; and jobs and economically advantageous marriages are found for family members.

The numerous Nigerian local shop owners across the world are notable amongst those who shuttle back and forth. They sell Nigerian foods to fellow migrants. They also advertise in noticeable online spaces. Examples of these in Leeds are Adonai Foods, Anti *Pheby* Foods, and Bliss Continental (Advert at http://www.nigerialeeds.org/advert.htm. Accessed 01/07/08). London has a lot more. Amongst them are 805, Nigerian Kitchen, Presidential *Suya, Wazobia*, and *Mama* Calabar. (Available at http://www.cafe151.co.uk/notebook/nigerian-restaurants-in-london. Accessed 01/07/08). These shop owners travel between the hostland and Nigeria to restock. At other times, they place orders with relations as Cohen said above. To begin, they may have borrowed money from friends and relations. The ultimate objective is to break even in a business that is taking place in a far away location, but involving parties in the *homeland*, which reflects transnationalism. The question again is important: What is their residency status? Legal or illegal? Visitors who have a legal right of entry, and has never changed, or legal residents still physically attached to Nigeria? Discerning this is most likely complicated (and it is not my present pre-occupation), but trans-migration and an online agency, are evident.

For many participants, their economic affairs across nations are eased through speedy networking media like the Internet. Many profit for instance in businesses needing instant messaging. Such businesses include the establishment of courier companies, for the transference of cash and goods, from one location to another. With patronages mainly from migrants, the promoters further advertise themselves on Nigerian affairs' newsgroups, e-mail groups, lists and at migrants' meetings. It all seems to be a determined attempt to replicate for the migrants what global companies like Western Union, Money gram, DHL and others do at an advanced and universal level. A lot of businesses or diaspora members also find it convenient to establish branches of their businesses in migrant locations. Some profit from the advances in communication technologies to move goods from one hostland base to another, like this speaker:

> I sell cars. I have lived in London for ten years, but I always travel to Holland where I was formally based, to buy cars. I go to Germany too. Sometimes, I ship the cars home for sale. Other times, I dismantle them and sell them in parts. I have representatives in Holland and Germany and we communicate regularly. Details of cars including photographs are sent to me online, and if the price is right and I am interested, I provide the funds, or I simply go there to complete the deal. **Albert, Male, 40, London. Interview date: 10/06/2006.**

Other types of businesses involving migrants are importation and exportation of clothing, shoes, wristwatches, and other accessories. They also provide job advisory services, soliciting or legal representations, traffic wardens, taxi driving, publication of migrant related journals/magazines/newspapers, and construction and maintenance of Nigeria related websites. The rest are computer and communication equipment sales, counselling of fellow migrants, church leadership, child minding, and African style hair weaving, amongst many others. Several of these trades go on via online networking, advertising and sales. Some are performed without physical interactions, highlighting again the influence of electronic relationships.

The case of Soyinka (the Nobel Prize winner) can be used to illustrate transnational activities amongst participants. Apart from a regular teaching job at Emory University, Atlanta (as at the time of writing), he is a popular face in press conferences, demonstrations and other civil rights activities in Nigeria. More often than not, he is on the front pages of newspapers, and webpages, while cyberspace pundits regularly analyse his views. My main point is that the writer combines his role as a university teacher in the US, with that of a social critic in Nigeria, by frequently shuttling between the two places. It is why most of his acerbic press pronouncements (like the quotation below) against the Nigerian government are from interviews at International Airports:

> Obasanjo has openly endorsed violence as a means of governance, embraced and empowered individuals whose avowed declarations, confessions and acts are cynically contrary to the democratic mandate that alone upholds the legitimacy and dignity of his office. Let me repeat this: the contempt of President Obasanjo for the demands for a democratic self-realisation by the electorate is no longer in doubt, and can be proved, chapter and verse. **Accessed at http://www.usafricaonline.com/soyinka2objgo.html on 03/01/2007**

TRANSNATIONAL REMITTANCES

Though remittances are largely bank and financial institution transactions, diaspora members use online spaces for remittance related issues like advertising. This use makes it significant in the analysis of the Nigerian migrants' transnational activity. The flexible space of the Internet is inviting to all including the advertisers or marketers. Participants' favourite websites are those of the *homeland* based newspapers, the news inclined sites and those of ethnic groups. These are repeatedly targeted for advertising by the money transfer agencies. The result of this process is at three levels. First, the online financial activities show the public nature of the transnational space of the Internet. Second, the activities highlight the deregulated space of international migrants' financial affairs. Third, the Nigerian diaspora's participation in the transnational process is demonstrated through the activities.

From the point of view of participants, remittances occupy a prime place in their minds. To those in Nigeria, failure to remit funds is a sign of failure[28]. It is why plans for it are frequent in the calculations of migrants. The pressure for remittance also leads to its featuring in the decentralised space of the Internet. Remittance shows the regular transnational flow of participants' income and expenditure. The evidence of this is in their website and newsgroup discussions. While the websites feature adverts on different remittance agencies, the newsgroups sometimes mirror the feelings of migrants on the challenges of sharing income with those in the *homeland*. This is incidentally because of the constant quest to survive in the hostland. Here are some participants' comments on this:

---

[28] As Hernandez-Coss and Egwuogu Bun (2007:8) put it, "Nigerian culture in general requires the more fortunate family members *(as those abroad are believed to be)* to provide for the less fortunate, and parents to invest in their children, who in turn will take care of them in their old age. Since, there are limited formal welfare systems in Nigeria, senders often feel obligated to provide for immediate family members as well as for extended family, friends and orphans" (*Emphasis mine*).

Over $12 billion is estimated to be repatriated annually by Africans. Nigeria accounts for $2.5 to $3.0. Remittance in Nigeria for instance surpasses the total asset base of the banking industry. **Peterside, accessed at www.nigeriaworld.com on 01/01/2007**

What do you mean Nigerians abroad are not contributing anything to Nigeria? What about the 10 billion dollars that get sent home each year to help family and friends? What about homes being built in Nigeria by Nigerians abroad? What about businesses being funded to provide employment for people at home? **Oasis, accessed at www.nairaland.com on 02/01/2007**

The possibility of error in these estimates is high, but the central argument is that through remittances, migrants are playing key roles in Nigeria's financial affairs.

A TRANSNATIONAL ONLINE ORGANISATION: THE CASE OF NIDO

The growing Nigerian in Diaspora Organisation (NIDO) is relevant here because it reflects the experience of transnationalism amongst the Nigerian diaspora. Emerging long after the Association of Nigerians Abroad (ANA), it presently enjoys Nigeria's government support. NIDO seeks to stand as an umbrella body of all migrating Nigerians, and surpasses ethnic differences, occupation, year of migration, length of time abroad and residency status of migrants, amongst other things. NIDO's present operational space is cyberspace. Exceptions to cyberspace operations come when they organise meetings and gatherings in some instances. Even then, the Internet is always the medium of communication. NIDO recognises that Nigerian migrants are in different places, but desires an online aggregation. As the networked computer is its global assembly point, a use of the interactive potentials of the medium therefore emerges. It also confirms its influential scope. Shown below are sections of some of the migrants' homepages from different locations. While there are many more, the few here simply illustrate the broad picture of the mapping of the activities of the migrants.

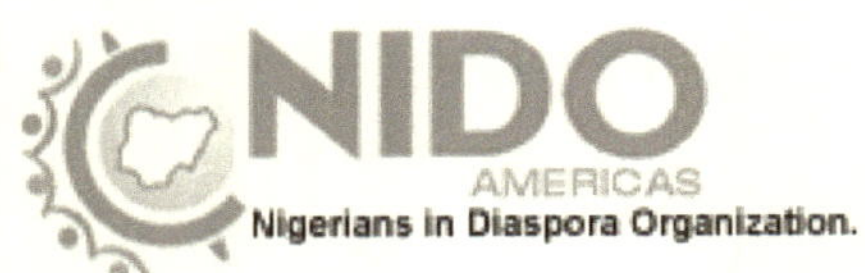

Figure 17: Masthead of a Transnational Organisation in America

The above is a site in the Americas. The site is huge, in what looks like a representation of the expansive American geography and economy. It translates into a visible and vibrant migrant activity therein. The European version is no less lively.

Figure 18: Masthead of the Same (Transnational) Organisation in Europe

Europe is, of course, another area of high migrant concentration. There are many reasons ranging from the historical to the cultural that account for this. Historical because of the earlier mentioned effect of colonialism and post-colonialism. It is cultural because of the prevailing influence of the English Language, a popular European language. The language link sustains a pull to hosts where the ability to speak it as given by colonialism is inviting. The Ukrainian chapter follows as a demonstration of the Internet's transnational space. The presence of a vibrant chapter in Ukraine is particularly instructive. Observations show that though the country is not a popular destination like western countries, it is an alternative for some desperate migrants. The popularity rating of their base somewhat disappears in the common transnational online space, which is why their site is filled with similar activities like those of the so-called popular destinations[29].

Figure 19: Masthead for the Ukrainian Chapter

---

[29] Some of the activities they are involved in as shown on their websites are request for ideas that can help develop the *homeland*; call for members to register online; and championing the cause of troubled members.

Links inviting the registration of members are common. Such sites also promote the *homeland*'s well being and progress. The line below summarises the mission of the transnational actors. Across the ocean is obviously figurative, as their dispersal is intercontinental. The separations make little or no meaning when they use Internet. Participants register an attendance, which other users are able to acknowledge across parts, divided by this ocean.

Figure 20: Another Masthead that Seeks to Invite Migrants

A NIDO leader indeed refers to the overall relevance of the Internet. He was clear on the need to bridge the gap in technological divides between the developed and the developing, through subsidies to the latter:

> The Internet is turning out to be a major facilitator of the globalisation process. Through the availability of the medium, the transfer and spread of expertise are being facilitated at an unprecedented rate. In addition to the spread of knowledge, the Internet is increasingly becoming a market place for all sorts of products and services for both rich and poor countries, as it offers equal opportunities for all to show case and present their products to the global market. **Edobor, accessed at <u>www.nidoeuope.com</u> on 10/07/2006. Speech was on 10/09/2005 at a UNIDO function.**

The NIDO recognises the transnational character of migration amongst its targeted members, hence its ownership of online branches in many migrant bases like those above. There are, in addition, online outlets in individual European countries like Italy, Greece, the Netherlands, Spain, Austria, Belgium, Luxemburg, Finland, France, Poland, Sweden, Switzerland, and Turkey amongst others. Its pride in having members across locations is a reminder of the widespread nature of movements amongst dislocated Nigerians. Recognition of settlement in the individual places also points to the different state of hostlands amongst the migrants. The expected interconnections between them indicate the active state of participants in transnationalism, which is a feature of the broader globalisation. Developments in communications' technologies, particularly the Internet, facilitate this process. The organisation defines its purpose, which literally sustains its life in cyberspace, as to:

Encourage contacts and networking amongst Nigerians living in Europe, the Americas and elsewhere and with community groups, voluntary organisations, government departments, statutory and non-statutory authorities, business individuals and all other organisations, and in particular based on pressing social, economic, democratic and cultural issues in Nigeria. **Accessed at <u>www.nidoeurope.com</u> on 12/12/2006.**

Observations reveal that possible resettlement in a host society sometimes indicates transnational acceptance. This character leads to an elevated sense of knowledge, which is good enough to help Nigeria. It probably leads to NIDO's homepage assumption that members are capable of providing "services or give advice on specific matters of social, economic, or cultural projects in the interest of Nigerians and Nigeria". (Accessed at <u>www.nidoeurope.org/nidoe/shtm/objectives.html/</u> on 15/12/2006). Though NIDO is only one amongst dozens of cyberspace organisations that underscore transnationalism amongst migrants, its quest to expand its chapters from the West through to South East Asia, the Pacific Rim and Oceania gives an idea of the wide physical paths of the migrants.

As an instance of a migrant group with connections to Nigeria, it stands as a reminder of multilocal online activities. The diaspora members are not in the multilocalities for adventure, but in pursuance of economic advantages. The pursuits should not hinder interactions with co-travellers, which is why NIDO is interested in networking. Networking indeed takes different cyberspace dimensions. One is the occasional signature drive amongst participants. The other is an endless call for participants to join discussion groups, or to be contributors to web pages with inclination for news and features articles. Yet another is through the organisation of conferences (as shown in the information below). The anticipated audience comes from different locations. The conference is an instance of several discussion events that they have organised. The Internet is therefore a forum where migrants are not only available through their sites, but where their offline activities begin, through online notices. Even though they are in different locations, they have a place of common presence and interaction. The situation makes the medium an everyday tool for the interface of diaspora members who are in different countries.

NIDO YOUTH FORUM
Reconnecting With & Rebuilding Nigeria Today, For Tomorrow

Conference Theme
â€œAwakening the Tiger in the Heart of Africaâ€
The Role of the Diaspora in the Socio-economic Development of Nigeria

Conference Location
Doubletree International Plaza Hotel
655 Dixon Road, Toronto, Canada M9W 1J3
Tel: 244-1711; Fax: (416)244-8031
www.doubletree.hilton.com

Youth Conference Theme
Reconnecting With & Rebuilding Nigeria Today, For Tomorrow
The Role of the Diaspora Youth in the Socio-economic Development of Nigeria
TORONTO, ONTARIO, CANADA
JANUARY 19 -20, 2007

Figure 21: A Web Invitation for Nigerian Migrants to an Event in Canada

WORSHIPING WITHOUT BORDERS

Religious networks in participants' transnational spaces of interaction use the Internet for expression. As observed, transacting activities across nations and ethnic groups is a difficult endeavour for participants because of the increasing competition in the complex global interactive environment. Divisions in the world across wealth, culture and class are also hurdles. Being largely on the disadvantaged side of the divisions sometimes diminishes chances of participation in the competition for relevance.

Many migrants attest to being on the weaker side of divides. "We may meet them (hosts) at individual level, but not at the corporate or collective level", a participant, Richard, Male, 39, says in Leeds, adding, "our problems are much in Africa, and it is why we have problems here (in hostland), because we are looked at with the eye of the African sufferer. But God knows best" (Interview date: 04/07/2006). The resort to God in Richard's comments is a sign of a general trend amongst migrants. God is seen as a last resort when difficulties appear. Participants consider God as always available to offer help when the many preventable problems and pains from poor image occur. God is omnipresent in their assumptions. This status gives Him a complementary abode in Cyberspace, as a globally available phenomenon. Participants therefore find networking for communion with God a worthy thing to do. Churches in Nigeria with branches abroad continuously expand online to reach dislocated members.

Many rely on the Internet to reach prospective and existing constituents in their local places. Some publicise through their websites neighbourhood branches abroad for the benefit of the migrants. Many believe their activities have been rewarding even to the hostland as this statement reveals:

Foreign mission operations have been positively affecting lives in their respective nations. Together with the church activities, they are positively affecting the spiritual and socio-cultural milieu of their host nations. Our networks of operations in the foreign field are listed below: Kenya, Ghana, Britain, USA, etc. **Accessed at www.worldmissionagency.org/ where2=missions on 28/03/2007**

Though evidence of nationalism will be discussed in detail in the next chapter, it is important to note here that it also features through participants' transnational religious activities. Nationalism can be religious when it becomes passionate in some cases. For the migrants, communion with God is a root to express concern. Migrants evidently seek God's help in the travails of Nigeria. Though individual communion is likely, the collective act is more noticeable. The belief system of respective migrants, including Christianity, Islam and traditional religions (the three major Nigeria religious groups), determine the mode of worship. Pentecostal Christians are more popular because of the relative regularity of gatherings and their constant use of the World Wide Web for the exhibition of their loyalty to God and country.

Some migrants admit to praying for Nigeria. In most cases, numerous Nigerian church founders, who have branches in foreign countries for tending to spiritual needs, preside over the sessions. Some of the churches that are popular for the publication of prayer sessions are The Redeemed Christian Church of God (RCCG); Living Faith Church; Mountain of Fire and Miracles Ministries (MFM); Christ Embassy (CE); the Cherubim and Seraphim Church (C&S); the Celestial Church of Christ (CCC); the Christ Apostolic Church (CAC); amongst others. Importantly, many of these churches boast of lively websites that encourage migrants to revive themselves spiritually, besides re-assessing the condition of their nation. In doing this, they create links between spiritualism and nationalism, and then spiritualism and dislocation. For the RCCG in the UK, it has this mission statement:

The vision of RCCG is reflected in a five-tier mandate: to get to heaven, to take as many people with us as possible, to live a life of holiness, to preach the gospel throughout the world and to plant churches.

The first branch in the UK started in 1989 at Baker Street, London, but officially from 1990 at Islington, North London (The Angel Parish). There are (now) nearly 100 parishes in the UK with more coming every month. **Online: accessed 28/02/2007**

The Living Faith Church has its site at http://www.winnerscanaanland. org/ (Accessed 21/12/2006), while the MFM also has its own, which is www.mfm.og (Accessed 21/12/2006). Importantly, notices and calendars of meetings are online, through mailing lists, or e-mail groups. Worshippers eventually meet in designated locations, usually rented halls in the hostland, where prayers for Nigeria feature as a matter of priority. One "prayer point" for the nation, at Alexandria palace in London exalted that: *Any power holding down Nigeria's development, die in the name of Jesus!"* (Prayer session held 12/01/2007).

They make spiritual attempts to reconstruct the Nigerian nation from a distance when groups cluster in churches sometimes after web announcements to fulfil spiritual needs. Examples include the estimated 15,000 worshippers in 50 different assemblies of the Christ Apostolic Church in London (Ajibewa and Akinrinade, 2003:6). Many more churches of the Pentecostal faith develop on a daily basis. Many are in London with branches in Leeds and other British towns. A majority are however churches with one branch in London. School, hotel and organisation buildings are rented for mid-weekly, night vigils, or Sunday meetings. They remind members of meetings via usenets, newsgroups, and group mails. They are also reminded through text messages or voice calls shortly before. Many of these churches buy television airtime. From there, they advertise their websites, and display telephone numbers. The church network plays its role in the routines of participants, as this respondent confirms:

I go to Church as often as I can. Christ is the armour I need because of my colour. The prejudice would always be there but with Christ, I am covered. I cannot fail to serve him, to pray for my self, my family and my country of origin. **Stella, Female, 37, Leeds. Interview date: 25/03/2006.**

Challenged by new realities, the last participant obviously remembers her Godly roots. To some, it determines their routes. Unlike Britain, Nigeria is more traditional. Religion plays a major part in its social and political life. As they profess, divine guidance conditions individual actions and inactions. The faithful turn to God seeking support when dealing with hardships associated with migration. It is why worship networks are common amongst them, and why contributors like to pray to God in instances of indecision. Many of the churches construct websites, from where they solicit prayer points on specific challenges. The migrant television network, *BEN Television* is moreover popular, both online and offline, but more so offline, for selling airtime to preachers and churches who in turn advertise their contact telephone numbers and addresses. Many migrants send e-mails to pastors in Nigeria for prayer points, while some telephone them for real time prayers or counselling. They support my online findings, from the testimonies of migrants, that memory and meanings about Nigeria evolve across distances, just as they negotiate belonging in the hostland.

From these transnational religious activity emerges a "Godly identity".
As shall be seen in Chapter Seven, the question of identity is obvious in the
migrants' engagements with the network. In this instance, they reflect this
through their pronouncements. "Man proposes, but God disposes", a
respondent Moji, (Female, 32, London. Interview date: 22/07/2006) says in
an instance, which reflects the Godly character of some migrants. She was
explaining her chances of return, eventually leaving the decision to God.
Another, Adaobi, (Female, 41, London Interview date: 16/06/2006) says: "I
will probably leave everything to God to decide", the return. For the
comfort, which is now realised in the UK, she gives all to the "glory to God".
She goes further and states, "I am not keen about events in Nigeria. I have
left them in the hands of God, so I cannot bother myself about Nigeria". The
submission to God in that last statement is not only a characteristic, but also
the entire country of origin is additionally committed to Him. Many others
leave the question of return to God. "I am not likely to return until God's
time", one person, Aisha (Female, 40, Leeds. Interview date: 16/06/2006)
says. Another sounds differently: "By the grace of God, I will return at some
point" (Masha, Male, age unknown, London. Interview date: 15/06/2006).
Then when things improve in the hostland, they express gratitude to God as
this respondent, Isa (Male, 31, Leeds. Interview date: 23/03/2006) shows:
"I thank God that things are getting better", while for all other plans, "God
will determine" them, he additionally remarks. The godly identity of some
of those studied is therefore evident. While natives in the hostland are
perhaps more secular, many Nigerian migrants as the above examples show
are more spiritual. It obviously works for them at the level of soothing or
even "practically", as a pastor, Dada, (Male, age unknown, Leeds. Interview
date: 29/05/2006) notes.

WEB PAGES AS MIRRORS ACROSS BORDERS

The box below exhibits the typical average range of commonplace
participation in Nigerian affairs' related websites. The box is a section of
the features page of the website www.nigeriaworld.com, as accessed on
01/01/2007, and carries articles from participants resident in different
locations including the Americas. Some of the writers are from the US and
Canada. Others are based in Europe, specifically UK, Germany and Italy. It
also includes writers from Africa, like one from South Africa. There is a
representative from Asia, and a participant from Japan. A look at the web
page on this day revealed that there were many more participants from the
Americas, with the US leading. To some extent, it may reflect the numerical
strength of the migrants' presence in the US. It could be a result of
contributors' desire to repeatedly participate. Regardless, participation is
not limited to the US based alone, as there are representations from other

locations. With the wide range of contributions, the network is showed as an intercontinental market place of ideas. This market place is not now a geographical place, but a spatial entity, pixels, and is available to many at the same time, in identical or different locations. The borderless marketplace, which works despite the intervening bounds of time, undermines the fact of distance. The reduction in the possible effect of distance therefore encourages transnational interactions amongst participants. The site, www.nigeriaworld.com is a modest space in the vast Internet space. That space is nevertheless large enough to accommodate the participation of people distributed throughout boundless global places.

Nigeria pipeline explosions: The wages of greed and "Instant Gratification"
RAYMOND T. BELLEH, Baden-Wurttemberg, Germany (Nigeria world) -

Madness ruling the land
STEVE U. NWABUZOR, Michigan, USA (Nigeria world) -

Grieving for Godwin Agbroko (1953-2006)
SUNNY C. OKENWA, Cape Town, South Africa (Nigeria world) -**BABS" MUSE**
Lagos fire disaster: The failure of leadership at all levels

SHILGBA: FROM MY HEART
Random talk on misplaced hype in Nigeria

Still waiting for Obasanjo

http://nigeriaworld.com/cgi-bin/axs/ax.pl?http://nigeriaworld.com/articles/2005/may/026.html***BENEDICT OKEREKE, Italy (Nigeria world) -***
Why Pope Benedict XVI is wrong about relativism

Figure 22: An Illustration of the Global Diversity of Contributions to a Website

DISPLACEMENTS AND REDEFINITIONS OF CLASSES AND FAMILY LIVES

NEW BEGINNING FOR MANY CLASSES OF WORKERS

Nigerian migrants' working lives often change as they come across new conditions of living and new value systems in the country of settlement. For the participants, the new differences are not only limited to realities of existence, but also include colour differences. Race and skin colour become more obvious in countries where the majority of the population is white. While some succeed in maintaining their working status while abroad, many are never able to do this. Some return earlier than expected, or they may carry on leaving things to chance. Several live between Nigeria and the hostland. It results in shades of disruptions. Careers could change with the impossibility of continuing to work in areas of expertise. Sometimes, the change could be drastic. Another interpretation of the data, which features in Chapter 4, will be helpful here. Boundaries in the graph below may not be rigid, but it is instructive that there is a prevalence of professionals, administrators and unskilled workers amongst the migrants. The lines between the vocations are flexible, meaning that a professional today might have been a menial worker yesterday, and vice-versa.

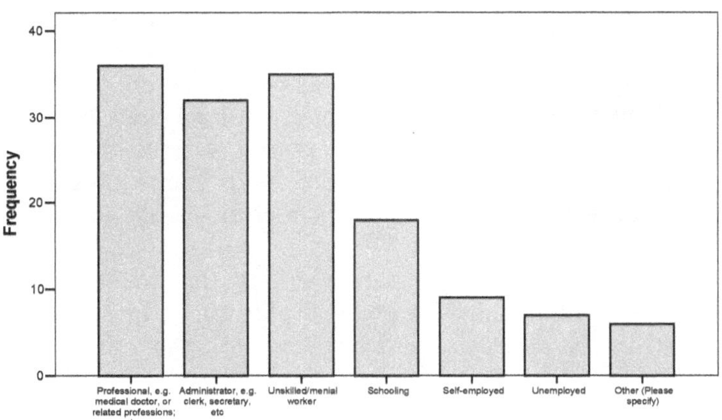

Figure 23: Occupation of Migrants in the UK

Additionally, observations show that a professional in Nigeria may become a security person in the hostland. A medical doctor could become a nursing assistant. A PhD holder may turn into a guard. They rationalise the changes as having been made based on necessity. A further argument is that the dignity of labour exists in the hostland. "So it does not matter what work you do. The wage is the most important thing. When you compare the wage with what I was earning in Nigeria, you discover I now earn more", an anonymous former banker in Nigeria, who now works in the London underground as cleaner remarks. A Leeds based political science PhD holder, Mike, who re-trained as a computer technician raises similar issues:

I had a first class in political science from Nigeria. I came here to do a Masters and a PhD but got disinterested in returning. Why should I return when my wage for two months is more than what I will earn in a year, if I return to Nigeria as a University teacher? It is a matter of choice and I am happy with what I am doing now. Very soon, I will start regular travels home, so I can work on something, may be building a house. **Mike, Male, 44, Leeds. Interview date: 05/08/2006**

A former food manager, Donald (Male, 51, Leeds. Interview date: 15/08/2006) in a reputable Nigeria based hotel is happy to relocate and team up with his wife to establish a Nigerian food restaurant. "People respected me for my position in Nigeria, but I struggled to make ends meet. Now, the respects are gone, but ends are being met.", he says. Those who are able to continue with their occupations abroad are usually professionals like medical doctors, lawyers, university teachers, engineers, and nurses. Even then, it requires some "humbling" processes. Medical doctors, nurses and pharmacists at times go through various programmes, which could include adaptation courses, re-training, or re-certification. The boss in Nigeria becomes a hostland servant whose choices are probably limited to return, transmigrating, or pauperisation. An exilic PhD who was a former Nigerian university lecturer anonymously reveals online how he had to work in the London underground, and then taught in a college before he got a job as a university teacher in London. Of course, still angered by reasons for dispersal, the migrants are happy to accept new realities in the hostland, to earn a living. The experience of accepting lower status job could even go with bearing the psychological cost of re-structuring their working and other identities.

The more common disruption to working life affects the status of migrants. The professional, who enjoyed high status in Nigeria and who now does menial work because it has become necessary to do so, is in the same category as the unskilled former worker in Nigeria, that continues her/his trade in the hostland. While the latter is happier, the former recalls the better working days at origin, and may hope for better opportunities in the UK. The unskilled worker may miss nothing in this context. If anything, s/he is glad to be doing it in the highly desired Western environment, where dignity in labour, it is assumed, reigns. In the hostland, there is a likelihood of an equal appreciation for persons regardless of job category. It could be skilled or unskilled. Occasionally, the unskilled worker heightens her/his job zeal, earns more and lives better as compared to the professional, who is weighed down by an inability to continue in his area of expertise. A more constant regret may take a better part of this migrant.

A diploma certificate holding female participant who works as a store assistant is happy to have a fellow migrant who holds a Masters degree as a colleague. Whereas she appreciates the hostland as a leveller, the Masters degree-holding colleague is dissatisfied. Though unable to get a suitable employment in the source country, he expects a better tomorrow in the hostland. The hoping is mostly endless. It delays the possible actualisation of return, and sometimes leads to immediate return or forward and backward movements. This is because the quest for a better life that led to dislocation is still to be realised. The myth of progress associated with living between the *homelands* and abroad sustains him. That myth continues online, through the networks, when loved ones at home encourage continuous perseverance and when he keeps giving the assurance of a better tomorrow. Stories of the few excelling, which are on the Internet and other media turn to beacons of hope, and are examples of the reward due to perseverance. Besides, there is a dominant black phenotype in origin. More varieties are now present in the hostland, because it is more multicultural. The former Nigerian professional and the unskilled worker are therefore presently the same before the host community. Influence and prestige are not immediately determined by type of job. The relative equal regard for everyone combine to weaken old classes, bringing up in its stead, identical opportunities for the migrants to begin.

PAINS AND PLEASURES OF FAMILY LIFE DURING MIGRATION, TRANS-MIGRATION

In the area of family lives and marriages, many migrants are married but live as singles away from the family while in the hostland. The economic advantage of working in the hostland propelled the migration in the first instance. Again, the divides cannot be rigid given problems of distant relationships as will be discussed. Cracks in family life are common. Determined to improve their economic or educational status, a spouse migrates. Husband, wife, or partner and children are left behind. Mediation of family life is now online or via telephone. A 39-year-old nurse who lives in London (Maria, Female, age unknown. Interview date: 19/06/2006), left her family six years ago and hopes to return in another two years. She notes, "I reach home mainly through the phone, while I keep in touch with Nigerian events through the Internet. I phone my husband on a daily basis, using international call cards." Another, John (Male, Leeds. Interview date: 24/08/2006), a 42 year old university teacher says he is "regularly online with relations and my fiancée. My fiancée that is happy to join me here any moment from now. We chat online, through the text or telephone, while she often sends cards to me online."

Yomi (Male, 34, Leeds. Interview date: 27/08/2006), below, is not concerned about distance, which separates him from his family. His reason: "My wife and children are doing well in Nigeria. I keep in touch with them through the phone. I am making plans to bring them to join me. For now, I have an English girlfriend who keeps my company". Here the respondent unites himself with hostland citizens through a relationship. The action sometimes further disrupts the stability of families, both at origin and at the hostland. It is the case when some relationships lead to marriages or child bearing and then creates different crises with parties in the distant origin. The Nigerian person could probably have heard of the development via a network. Many times, the re-marrying participant is not able to cope with the partner because of cultural disparities. Pain, separation and quarrels may result from them. The migrant questions her/his judgement, which further troubles the consciousness. The affairs may on occasions not even advance to marriages or childbearing, before legal, or "rightful" or "promised" parties become aware of them. This too, can be troubling, and often evokes memories of once stable relationships, besides questioning reasons for migration. Many of the migrants are however happy with the interactions. A lot of them do last, even for a lifetime. Disappointments may not occur in cases of faithful mediation, leading to re-unions, like this case: "My husband is at home in Nigeria, with my people (children). They are okay. I talk to them now and again on the telephone. I visit them too. They are due to join me any moment now" (Shola, female, age unknown, Leeds. Interview date: 14/03/2006). Sometimes the crisis of joint integration emerges when they do really come together. Re-adjusting to the new life in migration, in a new culture becomes complex as a collective experience. Difficulties often emerge as this nurse reveals:

> I joined my husband in this country after he had stayed for a while. It is not an easy place to stay. In Nigeria, we had house helps, a driver and a launderer. We lived well. However, my husband and I are now doing these things alone. The stress is too much. Our children are still too young to be of any assistance. Now and again, the stress causes unnecessary arguments and fighting. Threats of divorce have arisen several times. Even the police have had to intervene on few occasions. **Blessing, Female, 40, Leeds. Interview date: 01/05/2006**

The statement above is a clear case of social differences. In Nigeria, labour is cheap. It is easy to be a boss, with an average income. Disparities in comfort are wide, while state institutions are too weak to intervene. One form of labour is possibly superior to the other. Many of these are products of a poor economic state, which largely reflects a developing status. The case is nearly the reverse in the hostland. Inequalities in living standards are reduced. The economically disadvantaged often get assistance from authorities, through benefits. All jobs can be noble, whether skilled or unskilled. State institutions are stronger and can care for the needy through different "benefits". Unpaid house helps are illegal. Equal rights to life as a statutory provision are in evidence. Moving and integrating from the developing country to a developed one is always an overwhelming undertaking. It sometimes results in temporary or momentary problems as above, or permanent ones as below. When the situation is as below, a medium like the Internet is no longer an agent of good news, but is possibly a messenger of strains and stresses; or, may be discussions towards reconciliation:

My experience abroad is one of sadness and joy. I came here with my husband many years ago. We came with our children. We divorced and life became very difficult. He went back to Nigeria and wanted to go with the children. But I disagreed and thanks to the British government that took over my case. He sued and we are still in court. He has spent so much money pursuing the case now. My children are fine and the first child hardly wants to see the father again. The government actually asked me to leave London for Leeds and we have been here ever since. Often times, people have tried to settle us out of court, but maybe he just does not want the relationship again. Whenever arrangements are made for him to come, he will not turn up. I do not know if he has another woman in his life.....I am not bothered. My concerns are with my children and whatever I can offer them in life. **Nkechi, Female, 33, Leeds. Interview date: 28/04/2006.**

Nkechi's husband works for an international organisation. They have been moving from one country to the other, including Kenya, Indonesia, Austria and the UK. Their problems, according to her were building up, but came to a head in the UK, where things fell apart. Her experience and those of others again echo cultural conflicts. Woodward notes this much, adding, "in the West, traditional expectations about the nuclear family-defined as male breadwinner, dependent wife and children-have been challenged and new family forms and familial identities have emerged" (1997: 1). Patriarchal values are dominant in Nigeria. New experiences strain the bid to reproduce this trait in the hostland, which leads to many break-ups.

While Nkechi's story probably arose because of difficulties in jointly adjusting and readjusting to new locations, others have been because of living apart. It thus appears that distance weakens the bonds of relationships. Parties' sense of commitment achievable through everyday contact disappears when they are not together, as shown in the statement below:

I was in the USA for five years. I moved over here (the UK), seven years ago. My husband and two children were in Nigeria before I went to the US. The arrangement I had with my husband was to go, work, and make money in America for the sake of the family. They were to join me when I am able to pave the way. Soon after I travelled, I heard my husband had put another woman in family way. I am now thinking of bringing my children over, so another woman would not suffer them. **Cynthia, Female, 41, London. Interview date: 07/06/2006.**

Many families are engaged in a constant quest to beat challenges, which regularly leads to movements between diasporic locations. The statement below is the confirmation of a woman in this regard:

I came here as a nurse. I worked hard and succeeded in bringing my husband and three children over, and survival became more difficult especially with too many bills. Were we citizens, it could have been easier, but we cannot get it until after five years or so. I discovered America value nurses more, so I applied to an institution and got employed. Things then began happening after my green card was sent to my family and me. In a word, we are moving to America where things are likely to be better. **Rose, Female, 43, Leeds. Interview date: 18/02/2006.**

Integration problems once more come to the fore. Economic liberation or lack of it is dependent on the extent of integration. For the speaker above, the chance to have a US Green Card is a symbolic identity. It could initiate a sense of belonging and an easier route to an economic objective, more than the consideration of getting British citizenship after five years. What is overriding is the non-fixation of the participant to a particular hostland. It was why Durowaiye, (Male, age unknown. Interview date: 18/07/2006), says he re-migrated to Britain after three years in Germany. Therefore, his children can "grow up speaking English as against German, because English is Nigeria's official language." He adds, "Should they decide to return to Nigeria in the future, integration will not be hampered by language". So also is the case of a nurse, Peter, (Male, 46. Interview date: 22/08/2006), who relocated from Frankfurt to Leeds, so the two eldest of three children will begin schooling in an English setting.

The transnational people notably register their presence online. This is when contributions to newsgroups come from their locations in Singapore, China, US, Canada, UAE, Japan, South Africa, Germany, and elsewhere, as it appears in their signature lines. E-mails move backwards and forwards to those in their thoughts in other hostlands and to people with access in Nigeria. Webcams also relay distant images of close ones and places left behind. Telephones are busy, using the cost reducing impact of several international call cards. The sustenance of their relationships through the media across transnational environments is not limited to emotional needs alone. It helps the cross border interests of many of these migrants as well.

Individuals who grew up, or were born abroad are quick to dismiss Nigeria. The country is not important to them as an ancestral home. It seems faint in their remembrance, if present at all. Neither do they consider returning. The place of growing up is their natural home, which they would not ordinarily leave. Integration problems are rare in their considerations. Through the years, they have probably met and mixed with "host" community members. Many do speak, and perhaps think like the natives. Furthermore, they likely enjoy greater working opportunities than the Latter-Day migrants do, and are sometimes competing with the "original" inhabitants. The interviewee below, a second generation migrant represents this group of people:

Nigeria is not a place I can return to. Although, I have some of my dad's brothers over there, somewhere in the country, I do not know where they are, and I am not bothered. Once in a long while, I get e-mails from them and I reply promptly, but it takes so long to hear from them again. Its okay if they can visit me here (in Leeds), but I am not ready to go there. Otherwise, we keep talking online; you know what I mean? **Steve, Male, 28, Leeds. Interview date: 15/04/2006**

In living and communicating across borders, migrants acquire citizenship of some foreign countries- a topic to which I now turn.

DUAL CITIZENSHIP

The issue of transnational citizenship is also important. Over the years, many of the migrants gain citizenship of a host nation. Officially, therefore, they belong to two countries, and tend to make the most of the advantages possible. For them, it turns into a thing of pride, worthy of lifetime preservation. Through careful planning, they transfer the privileges in this status to their offspring. The transference is another source of pride, as they often believe it gives them an advantage over those in the developing origin. The statement below testifies to this:

> I miss Nigeria, no doubt, but life is about happiness. I have no regret whatsoever settling in the UK. With our British passport, we are able to travel to most places without visa, which is a privilege the Nigerian passport does not give. Just as we are Nigerians by birth, we are British by citizenship. We cherish the privilege to have the two identities. In addition, we believe it is wonderful to have stayed behind, especially for the future of our children, a future that is nearly absent in Nigeria, because of the way things are there. I am not saying home is not good. There is no place like it, but for now, we have to make the best opportunity of where we are. Like my husband said therefore, we may return in the future, but it is difficult to tell now. **Akinmade, Female, 44, London. Interview date: 02/06/2007.**

The problems of Nigeria create despair amongst the citizenry, which lead to a subtle craving for another nationality. Claiming citizenship of hostland often enhances transnational migration. The result is the presence of a high number of 'citizens' amongst respondents in the chart below, which also featured in Chapter 4. Sometimes, the quest for this citizenship lasts a lifetime, which does not really matter to the typical migrant. It may not however undermine the desire for longing and even trans-migration. This is because of the many challenges in the hostland as the research indicates. Acquiring citizenship improves their status in the estimation of the host community. It also signposts the likelihood that they have stayed relatively long enough to be so qualified. It further points out that return to origin will likely be continually idealised, rather than actualised. For many of the transnationalists, citizenship status is a source of pride whenever they are in Nigeria. Chances of outright return sometimes remain unpredictable because push conditions in Nigeria still exist, in the face of the improving pull factors of the hostland. Location now matters less with the existence of many on-the-spot media like the Internet, while they are enjoying citizenship rights.

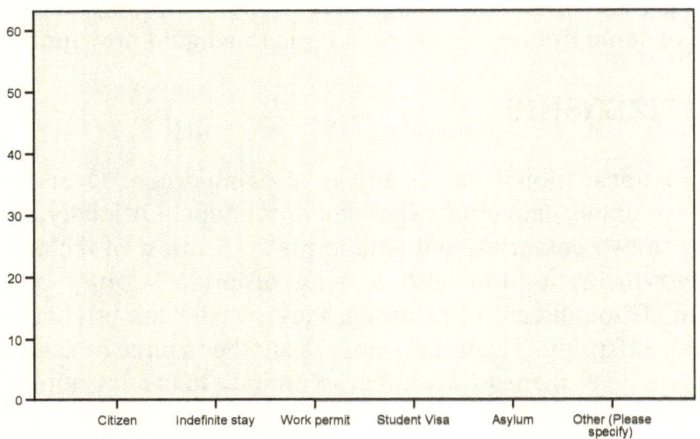

Figure 24: Residency Status in the UK

Imaginations of return, actual return and issues related to the controversial subject have featured in my analyses. They are also likely to be a continuing theme. I shall now discuss it within this context, given its close relation to forward and backward movements, and movements between diasporic locations, which are the focus of this chapter.

UNDERSTANDING RETURN AS AN ELUSIVE END

As with other diasporas, participants are in the hostland, from where transmigrancy takes place. The case in this research is not too different. My observations reveal that return is largely a mythologized aspiration as in the cases of other diasporas and migrant groups. As Tsagarousianou (2004:56-7) argues, globalisation flows affect diasporas as people at its centre. "In that sense, there is no going 'home' again. There is a detour and no return", and they are no longer "backward-looking". Modern media such as the Internet help to undermine thoughts of return as they "provide a sense of contemporaneity and synchronicity to the dispersed populations" (Tsagarousianou, ibid. 2004:62). For some, however, the plan is always to attain economic advantage and then return to Nigeria. Nonetheless, attaining that condition is rarely possible. The situation can forever be better. Nwaochei (2007:1) explains this:

> There is something unique about some Nigerians living abroad. They never regard themselves as emigrants. They always regard their stay in a foreign land as transient, or temporary. It is an age-honoured belief amongst Nigerians that a man should die and be buried in his fatherland

For many others, return is no longer a consideration. Those who give it serious consideration soon express fear of losing a better working environment and all other advantages in the hostland. The goal is to make remittances geared towards investments, or well-being of friends and families at home and then actualise it. It never really takes place in the end, though. Even then, it remains a consideration as this statement shows:

> It is an essential part of the Nigerian culture to want to return home, either to the village or the town of one's forebears. Generally, while a Nigerian could sojourn in search of work and employment in other parts of the country or abroad, he ultimately wants to return home some day. This may probably explain why Nigerians are not really established as entrenched communities abroad, as you will find with various European and Asian communities in this country for example. **Femi, accessed at <u>www.nigeriahcottawa.com/political/immig.htm</u> on 13/10/2007.**

The example below emphasises the perceived disdain of the migrants for endless stay abroad. The desire to return, which has roots in their culture, as Nwaochei and Femi above say, is further confirmed by what a majority of participants say. Quest for return sometimes takes them from one place to another, but rarely permanently, while the media mediates the dislocations. Yet again, and as seen in the above quotes, the influence of culture on online participants is implicit. They choose the hostland for economic gains, by conceiving it as a safeguard, and then leave after attaining the difficult economic objective. Nwaochei (2007:1) notes once more that:

> It can be said that any Nigerian who left in search of the Golden Fleece never consider the idea of staying abroad permanently. His principal aim was to go there, acquire necessary education, and contribute his quota, no matter how small it might be to the development of his country

While this submission could be doubtful, unpredictable and hardly empirical, it is a reminder of the elastic transnational space of interactions. It may be because participants are largely on the wrong side of divides in the third spaces. This eventually sustains nostalgia and longing, with expectations that a guarantee of dignity and security can only be provided in Nigeria. The quote below supports my argument. It is from a discussion at <u>www.nairaland.com</u> on the topic, *Nigerian Abroad Must Return* home:
Nigeria is made up of you and me and only we can effect change.

Complaining from across the ocean is not adding value. I have been back in Nigeria for about a year now after ten years in London. For a country like ours, change cannot be overnight and will probably not be evident in our generation, but you and I, the citizens, have to effect the change, in our personal lives and in our relationship with others. **Accessed on 01/01/2007**

Another commentator does not share the seemingly patriotic pronouncements of the person above. In his 70's, he paints return in the frightful analogy below. A columnist, Wale Adebanwi, in a Nigeria based magazine, *The News* [www.thenewsng.com], quotes the anonymous London retiree after a meeting:

I came here at 55 after retirement from the Federal Civil Service. It was a waste Young man. Life is too brief to spend it on an illusion. If you were doing well and celebrating in all that mess in Nigeria, I would have recommended that you have a ball while it lasts. Otherwise, take a decision, live a life, do not go back home. Nigeria is like having a witch for a mother. Whatever you do, in the end; she will give you up as a contribution for her mates' esoteric meal. (**Accessed at www.thenewsng.com on 21/03/2007**).

The speaker's remark reminds us of the pain with which some migrants associate thoughts of returning to Nigeria. It is not different from the trend of opinions that lately dominated interviewees' responses. Just as many hope for return, suggestions of return put off others. For one group, staying in the hostland is temporary, as they plan to leave sometime in the future. To the other, it is a new *homeland*, now constructed as a place to live in for a long time. Those who are indifferent about the positions share a similarity with the others through idealising. For a few others, criss-crossing borders, or building a transnational network is an answer to the question of return. Common but not definite to all the circumstances is that the subject of return remains an end that is desired, but which hardly comes.

CHAPTER SIX:

LONG DISTANCE NATIONALISTS OR LONG DISTANCE CRITICS? AMBIGUITIES IN THE NIGERIAN DIASPORA MEMBERS' PERCEPTIONS OF ORIGIN

The last chapter discussed how transnationalism is expressed and sometimes sustained through the Nigerian diaspora members' regular use of the Internet. While the reflected transnationalism demonstrates a simultaneous relationship with different nation-states, it is important to examine the degree of the members' engagement with a particular nation-state. The examination is because of the availability of data showing some evidence of nationalism. The chapter unearths the ambiguous processes that sometimes reveal nationalism in a transnational context, while in the process of communicating with origin. Other times, the revelations can possibly be a mitigation of longing mixed with anger. The indicated nationalism could be fastidious observations from the distance, which defies attachment. The complex relationship between diaspora and the *homeland*, raises questions regarding whether the migrants are long distance critics or long distance nationalists. Or could it be that they are simply enveloped in delusions about an ideal, unhelpful for the origin, or that they mitigate nostalgia through online exchanges? These questions arise given the operational definition of nationalism as the emotional and committed relationship between an individual, or a collective and the nation-state. The people in question, as one aspect of a binary are usually within the nation-state, but sometimes they live in a distant. The nation-state may express a top-down concern with the distant people, as it simultaneously relates with those within. How do we therefore consider the online relationship of Nigerian migrants with the *homeland*, within the framework of nationalism? This chapter discusses this based on data from participants' engagement with websites, sampled online groups, and their offline interview statements. Website typologies A to G on pages 87-88 are helpful in this analysis, just as my study of Naija-politics@yahoogroups.com, explained on page 85, section 3.3.1, helped in doing some of the analyses. I shall specify Types most useful for the analysis of each category, as the section proceeds.

As Alter and other theorists argue, nationalism often "conceals within itself extreme opposites and contradictions" (1985:2). In showing attachment to Nigeria, many of the migrants are positive about certain issues. However, others are negative on the same issues. The opposing standpoints reflect a relationship of a sort, which is necessary to understand nationalism. For this research, there is evidence to argue that a passion for virtual activities involving Nigeria exists. Furthermore, a definitive answer on the Nigerian diaspora variant of nationalism is out of place given the complexities involved in defining the term.

Consequently, online nationalism amongst the migrants, and the sometimes observed absence of it, shall be analysed according to groups. The groups are not defined based on class or status of the migrant, but because of online channels through which they express their ideas. These channels of expression can be, though inexclusively, ethnic or news inclined websites; or newsgroups and chatrooms. Participant in any group at a point in time may be in another group at some other time. The groupings help in understanding their feelings via different Internet functions. In a website for instance, the feelings may be expressed using the more permanent column, like "our profile", "who we are", or "our mission". But in the newsgroups and chatrooms, the stimulation of thoughts in the process of sending and receiving, can be livelier. The first category of users is those active in websites formed because of ethnic relationships. Each of this website is based on the original roots of parents, particularly that of the father in Nigeria[30]. Owners of these websites speak a common native language and share a common culture and heritage. Their root in Nigeria is either same or geographically close to each other. The pull of a common language makes them move closer to one another while abroad. The group converges online because of these affiliations. Sometimes, they set up utilities like e-mail lists to attend to their peculiar interests. The second group are the elites, who sound cultured, conversant and cosmopolitan in news/features stories inclined websites. They demonstrate a can-do spirit. Of course, these elites also belong to one ethnic group or the other as in the first classification, but this is concealed through their cosmopolitan posturing, when outside the ethnic online groups. These people are also often seen in sites of professional groups, individual sites, and sites of news media. The third group describes persons, who could be part of the previous two groups, but are now conversational. Members of this group can be called the polemicists, as they are often ready for prolonged exchanges, arguments, and controversies. They exhibit these traits in locations like newsgroups, listservs and in usenets. Though the categories may sometimes overlap[31], their online roles at different times distinguish them from each other. They are separated by the online facility in use. The simple diagram below illustrates these categories and the overlapping tendencies.

---

[30] In the country, legal paternity is for the man. Offsprings therefore inherit the status, and relate with the place as original or native roots.

[31] They overlap because a contributor in the elite group may become much more engaging in a newsgroup, thus making her/him polemicists. S/he may at the same time be associated with an ethnic website. This interconnection partly reflects human complexities, which manifests more in the interweaving Internet space.

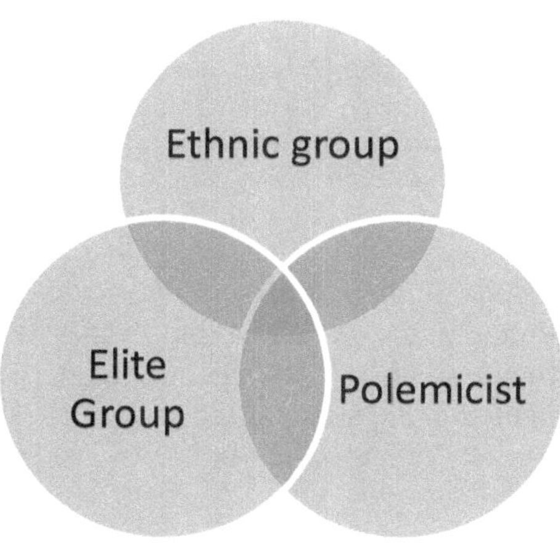

Figure 25: An illustration of groups and the overlapping tendencies

I shall first discuss the online context of nationalism or lack of it, within activities from ethnic groups. Then the chapter will examine the possible manifestation of nationalism through elite engagements with specified websites and the likely expression of fondness, or its non-appearance, amongst the third group-the polemicists. The chapter then discusses the gender dimension regarding possibilities of expressing nationalism.

ETHNIC ONLINE ASSOCIATIONS AND THE MITIGATION OF LONGING OR THE EXPRESSION OF NATIONALISM

The internet is rich with cultural and informational content and resources related to ethnic communities. A multiplicity of websites, servers and rings offer a variety of services to community members and cater for their online and offline needs (Chalaby, 2000: 20).

Ethnic online groups are useful for enacting the communion of the *homeland*. The associations reflect the multi-ethnic nature of Nigeria, and the numerical strengths of the groups. Dozens of these ethnic groups are online. However, the focus of analysis shall be on the three major groups, adjudged so because of their numerical strength and the expansive geography they occupy. They are of Type C in the typology on Page 88. I am focusing on these three groups for ease of examination, taking that there are over 250 ethnic groups in the country. Regardless, other smaller groups, usually called minorities are mentioned, so that diversities can be properly understood. There is, for instance, the Yoruba page-*Egbe Isokan* Yoruba, which loosely means the United Yoruba People. The ethnic group is one of the three major inhabitants in Nigeria. According to its mission statement, its goal is to:

Cherish, uphold, and project the honour and dignity of Yoruba culture, language and tradition in Africa and the diaspora; to promote the cultural, social, economic and political welfare of Yoruba; to work with other organisations inside and outside Nigeria to promote peace, stability, justice, and unity while working actively for the promotion of Yoruba interests. **(Accessed at http://www.yoruba.org/ on 10/18/2006).**

In what the website administrator describes as "keeping with its mission to promote the Yoruba culture in Africa and in diaspora", the webmaster made a trip to the *Oyotunji* African Village in South Carolina[32]. The sign of a Yoruba deity as sighted in the home of the head of the settlement is posted on the website to illustrate this association. It is reproduced below:

Figure 26: An Image of a Yoruba Deity: Yemoja, priestess of the ocean

Images like this, as well as others on the website, emotionally foster association to a nation from the prism of early ancestry (Accessed at www.africaguide.com on 19/05/2007). The recollection, which such image initiates, enables the imagination of a nation, and even a nation-state. An association with the Yoruba nation through this kind of image is evident. At the same time, in the website mission above, is a concern for the Nigerian nation-state that embodies the Yoruba language-speaking people. Although primary identification is with the Yorubas, loyalty to the larger political entity is part of the objectives of the site promoters, as seen in their mission statement. That loyalty is not only an evidence of nationalism as it is in the pledge to "promote peace, stability, justice and unity", but an indication of the complex character of Nigeria. Nigeria in this instance represents a political entity, while the ethnic group within the political entity represents the local place of origin. A duplication of the Yoruba page is "Oduduwa"

---

[32] I have also discussed this in Chapter 5 as an evidence of transnationalism.

(the Yorubanet). Smaller units of the Yoruba site also include, for example, those of Yoruba Community Association, Ontario; *Egba* Association of Florida; and *Egbe Omo Obokun* of Ijeshaland. Another is that of Oduduwa Heritage Organisation, which is in Oakland, San Francisco, and has a similar motive. It says on its website that:

> The Oduduwa Heritage Organisation (OHO) is of the Yoruba people. The Yoruba's originated from West Africa, and majority of Yoruba cities are located in the southwestern region of Nigeria. OHO seeks to preserve and promote the rich culture of the Yoruba nation among the Yorubas who live in San Francisco/Oakland. The mission of OHO is the promotion and encouragement of Yoruba tradition, cultural heritage and the education of the public to its benefits. (**Accessed** at http://www.oho.org/ **on 11/10/2006**)

The *Egbe Omo Obokun* of Ijeshaland is another instance of a smaller unit of the major Yoruba group, seeking union through its own Yoruba speaking town, Ijeshaland. Smaller sites appear when representation in the bigger group is viewed as marginal.

Like *Egbe Isokan* Yoruba, which represents a major Nigerian group in migration, the Igbo Community Association of Nigeria (ICAN) in Texas, represents another main group. A duplication of the site is www.Igbo-net. The website www.biafraland.com is also associated with the Igbos, and is more assertive in its commitment to the ethnic group. The word Biafra is a pseudonym for the Eastern part that attempted succession from the Federal Republic of Nigeria in 1967. This nation was known as *The Republic of Biafra*, and it reigned during their three-year agitation for a separate country. The name is still a reference point for the people, while its use in circumstances invokes memories of a fight for independence. The site shows its seriousness via statements like this:

> Biafra is a matter of survival of the Igbo Nation. The threat to Biafra comes from the politics of "one Nigeria," and most especially the Hausa-Fulani of Northern Nigeria. 2. The Biafran War of 1967-70 was a war of survival for … the Biafran side, and a war of genocide by Nigeria against the Biafran Nation. 3. While the war of 1967 (was) lost by Biafrans, the fact that Biafra and Biafrans are still alive today attests to the success of survival against all odds. (**Accessed at http://www.biafraland.com/ on 02/05/2006**)

Other websites by those in smaller groups, within the Igbo group are www.arochukwu.com; *Arondizuogu* Patriotic Union, New Jersey; Obosi Development Association and the Asaba group. While the *Arochukwu* people are proud of their population in Nigerian and abroad, the *Arondizuogu* feels the same. They (*Arondizuogu* people) are also concerned about expanding their membership, including through conferring honorary membership to females married to non-natives[33]. The Obosi group highlights their tradition and history, just as they invite members to contribute to community development projects in origin.

The www.asaba.com addresses migrant Asaba people. It represents a need to associate with a nation through ethnic affiliation, despite their minority status. Membership is for those "who share our desire to make Asaba a better place and have the concern and commitment to work towards achieving these goals". It was built in "1989 out of the need to unite all Asaba people and point them towards one goal of making Asaba better" (Accessed at www.asaba.com on 13/11/2006). The site is administered from Texas, and has many sections including those on its history, tradition, and festivals. A music section is also available for visitors to listen in, while Video clips are available for viewing. There is an Asaba discussion board where registered members are expected to "tell us what is on your mind". Some contributions monitored 31/07/2008 had the following headlines: "Think home, Asaba is the place", "Kindly look homeward, Asaba youths at home need you", and "Asaba youth and tomorrow". The theme of contributions was on the need for migrant natives to support their local community in Nigeria. Importantly, the Asaba group lives a lively virtual life, through registration, chatting, posting messages, announcements and the creation of mailing lists. Links to other relevant sites like the Nigerian government departments, newspapers and useful organisations are available. The Asaba group is a good example of the activity of minority groups online. Similar minority sites are www.warri.com; www.uromicommunity-ny.com; www.edonation.com; and www.rivnet.com.

The third major group, the Hausas, has one main site, called the Hausa main page. The Hausa language-speaking people are a dominant set occupying the Northern part of Nigeria. An influential Nigerian political group, they reflect the need to work for the "continued political and economic progress of Nigeria". They are pleased to invite website visitors to learn their language: a widely spoken language in the West African sub-region. This amounts to promoting an aspect of their culture in the bid to relate with their nation. Though a little more homogenous, they have splinter sites, like Arewa-online.com; Gumel (Hausa); the Hausa Culture Unit; the *Zumunta*, and that of the London based Arewa Union. Some of these have well defined objectives. The administration of the *Zumunta* Association site [www.zumunta.org], for instance, comes from the US. Its profile signed by Aliyu Mustapha seeks a distinction in its objective. In what shows a concern for its region in Nigeria, the association "aspires to help the North technologically, socially and economically, cater for its members, preserve the rich and diverse cultures of Nigeria, and improve the image of the

---

[33] The migrants are probably not bothered about males married to non-natives, because membership for women is automatic when they become married to the natives.

country in the global media" (accessed at www.zumunta.org on 06/05/2006). Gumel (Hausa) seeks to promote the cultures of its Northern Nigerian people through relating to each other in the native Hausa language.

These expressions of commitments to their culture, tradition and Nigerian, reveal an element of nationalism, as it aligns with a desire for progress of the nation. Again, it may simply be a desire to minimise longing, by virtually interacting with peers from the origin, rather than an interest in the well-being of a country, where economic needs are not met. An indication of nationalism, especially some of its ambiguities emerge in the circumstance. They display their ways in words and images that depict their lifestyle, as partly shown below.

Hausa is one of the most extensively researched of all sub-Saharan languages, and has a long tradition of song and poetry within a cosmopolitan Islamic culture that arose largely from the position of the old Hausa states astride the trans-Saharan and savannah trade routes. **(Accessed at www.zumunta.org on 18/10/2006)**

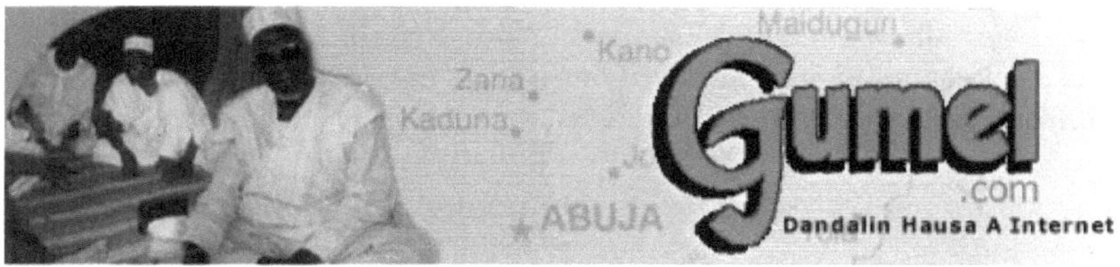

Figure 27: A Web Image Showing a Hausa Man Sitting on the Floor-A Preferred Way of Sitting amongst the Ethnic Group, While Eating, Discussing or Relaxing

Significantly, names like *Gumel*, *Egbe Isokan* and the *Arondizuogwu* are words from the native languages. Use of the word reflects a bond with the origin through language as a dimension of culture. It occurs despite possible exposure to other languages through dislocation.

The sites of minority groups often seek to popularise their own identity, to elevate it to prominence. It further reveals the ultimate desire of a small group to overcome insignificance through the creation of a definite online voice, and then have it influence the nation-state. Time and space are no limitations in the regular desire to relate with the nation. This desire is synonymous with the quest for emotional fulfilment, security and social inclusion. The drive for a union is associated with the majority, just as it is with the minority groups. Social categories like class, or numerical strength and spread of a group are not hindrance(s) for the individuals making up the groups. The process of associating in various forms amongst the migrants as it relates to the definition of a relationship with a bigger entity, a nation, reveals the multiple level of constructing nationalism, that involve very emotional and personal engagement with the *homeland*, as well as communal and political campaigns around the country of origin's affairs. Doubts may arise regarding the worth of this relationship. Clarification could come through the result of their actions and inactions towards Nigeria. But the outcome is still difficult to gauge, because studies of dislocations amongst Nigerians is relatively new, compared to many other diaspora and migration stories mentioned in Chapter one.

Apart from groups with websites, many others are active on the network through notices for meetings or announcements, via members' mailing lists[34]. Information that comes through the list initiates interactions that mark the beginning of recollections and reminiscing. It may lead to reviews of the state of Nigeria's affairs, given an apparent concern for it as this participant attests:

> I am a Yoruba man from Lagos State. I have been in London for ten years. I enjoy staying here, but I concern myself with my people. I do not miss home because my people are many here. We enjoy ourselves when we meet once a month. We communicate through the telephone, through the Internet, through reaching each other. When we finally get together, we drink, we party, we talk about Lagos, we talk about Nigeria...I really pity Nigeria because I cannot understand what our leaders are doing! **Ibukun, Male, 44, London. Interview date: 03/06/2006**

The participant's reference to communal interaction through fellow migrants indicates a way of belonging. A feeling of otherness may reappear when interaction returns to his migration world. A mitigation of the possibilities of lacking interaction in hostland takes place at monthly interactions with close friends from Nigeria. The cycle satisfies Ibukun and hence the confession of enjoying the hostland. However, Nigeria's growth and development remains a wish hence his regret regarding the inadequacies of Nigeria's leaders. The expression does not only show an attachment, but also reflects sympathy for the development crises in origin. The online ethnic unions further a sense of association in the face of possible integration challenges in hostland. The sense of association simultaneously goes on with a likely concern for native origin, and a worry for the nation-state (Nigeria), where this native origin is situated.

Overall, complexities abound in the definition of the majority versus minority groups. While the definitions of some perceived minorities are based on their geographical location, the mapping of others is because of

---

[34] Notable amongst these are some UK based migrants' ethnic groups like *Ekiti Parapo; Ogidi* Development Union (ODU); *Ose* Indigenes Associations (OIA); Oshogbo Progressives; and Ife Descendants Union (IDU). There are also *Egba* People's Association (EPA); *Owo* Descendants Union (ODU); Eko Club (EC); *Urhobo* Union (UU); *Itsekiri* People's Association (IPA); Arewa United Kingdom (AUK); *Ijaw* People's Association (IPA); *Igbomina* People's Association (IPA); Kwara Union (KU); and *Ilaje* Union (IU), besides others.

their linguistic peculiarity compared with the majority. Some supposed minority groups might not see themselves as such given the similarity of their language with the majority. Others will however be happy with the designation for political, social, religious, or other reasons (Achebe, 1983). For the sake of this study, however, while there are sites, which represent majority ethnic groups, there are also sites that represent the minorities. Sometimes, there are duplications of sites for majority groups. At other times, those of minorities also have duplication. Motivated individuals and groups within these ethnic bodies construct and administer these sites. The proliferation of the sites does not only represent the transference of the multi-ethnic nature of Nigeria to migrants' online space, but also denotes the interest of sections of the migrants to virtually reconnect with their roots. The sites of the minority group further symbolise resistance against the possibility of domination by the majority, despite similarities in language and culture. I have illustrated this with cases of the existence of numerous websites from minorities, like those of Asaba, Igbo-net, within the larger Igbo group; *Egbe Omo Obokun* of Ijeshaland and *Egba* Association of Florida, within the larger Yoruba group; and *Zumunta* and *Arewa* online, within the larger Hausa group. They are ethnically associated with the majority set and their websites, mailing lists, discussion groups are virtual outlets for identification, remembrance, and aspects of nationalism as seen above. Participants in this group possibly continue the portrayal of nationalism through other patterns, which are discussed in the next section. The pattern is illustrated mainly through their interests, and mode of socialisation. The analysis of this category appears below.

CONCERN FOR NIGERIA VIA "VIRTUAL ELITISM"

Sites of individuals and professionals represent the second major category of migrants' online activity. They are of Type B and D, and a bit of E in the typology on page 88. I have put these in one category because they are not necessarily based on ethnic cleavages like the sites discussed above. Their Interests, professions, self-assigned role and the need for ongoing survival in migration distinguish them. They are also differentiated by a marginal or deep attachment to Nigeria. Many of them see their sites as virtual routes to the *homeland*. The websites are additionally for representations in situations of exclusions from hostland media. In using this route, a semblance of loyalty to the departed nation-state becomes visible through the evolution of threads of thoughts on deficiencies of Nigeria.

Some of the sites focus on news and current affairs. They regularly try to outdo each other through the quality of items they upload. A few examples are www.nigeriaworld.com, which is a general interest site that uploads some topical stories from the home-based press. It has original contributors, as a leading migrant website. Www.amanaoline.com equally concentrates on news, while www.arewaonline.com is named after the notable word *Arewa:* an acronym for identifying people of Northern Nigerian origin. It uploads stories similar to www.nigeriaworld.com and features regular original contributors. Www.nigeriamasterweb.com does the same, but appears to be more detailed in its sections. It has links to numerous other websites including ethnic; those of activists; educational websites; websites of notable African and World newspapers, with notes on dead websites. Www.nigeriaweb.com is a part of www.nigeriaworld.com and was the first by the www.nigeriaworld.com, administrator Mr Chuck Odili, before its expansion. Www.nigeriavillagesqure.com is more interactive, because it encourages discussions of uploaded articles, besides publishing the latest news[35].

These sites typically provide detailed information particularly about Nigeria. They appeal to their users because of opportunities for cheery discussions and dialogues. They have several links to other sites, especially local newspapers. The sites welcome features and opinion articles from migrants. These readers take hold of the chance to express their thoughts on events in Nigeria. In a day, www.nigerianworld.com publishes articles from writers in different geographical locations[36]. Central to the headlines written by individuals in Canada, the US, UK, Russia and Germany is a supposed affection that is at once a sign of a disdain for Nigeria, and a wish for a better future. While some comments are critical and others are not, the inspirations behind the thoughts seem to be mostly reconfirming the authors' commitment to Nigeria. Their immediate impact may not be measurable because of their far location but contentment seems to be achieved because of the possession of a space for the expression of concern. The words of a participant based in Russia are revealing:

---

[35] Others performing the same role include www.dawodu.com (which is named after its administrator, Segun Dawodu); www.nigeria.com; www.nigeriaexchange.com; www.nigerianexus.com; www.nigerianation.com; www.nigeriadailynews.com; www.nigeriainforrnet.com; www.amebonews.com; www.gamjinews.com; www.wazobia.com; www.netnigerianews.com; www.worldskipnews.com; www.nigeriawatchnews.com; and www.naijamallnews.com.

[36] For instance, they once came up with the following articles with their authors: "AIDS 2006 Toronto: A Nigerian Perspective" by Ike Anya UK; "Time to deliver? Musings from the XVI International AIDS conference, Toronto" by Chikwe Ihekweazu, Canada, and "The Ordeal Blacks and Nigerians in particular go through in Russia" by Bode Eluyera, Moscow. Others were "Nigerian Courts, injunctions and the electoral process" by Akinwole Ogunlola, Chicago, IL, USA; "Transforming Nigeria, Igboland and blacks" by Emeka A. Njoku, London; "That Nigeria may be great, the Imbecility of an educated mind" by Kay Soyemi, London; and "Illegal Firearms and its menace to the Nigerian Society," by Raymond Beleh, Baden-Wurttemberg.

I came into the country officially as a Bureau for External AID (BEA) scholarship student. After living here for sometimes, I concluded that it is better to live at home and contribute to the development of our country. Why do we have to continue developing societies/countries that are more developed than ours are? I strongly believe that we hold a moral responsibility to our country. If we all live in America or Western Europe, then who is going to develop our country for us? As the saying goes, you cannot eat your cake and have it. **Eluyera, Moscow. Accessed at http://nigeriaworld.comárticles/2006/Oct/182.html on 19/10/2006**

Discussions take place in the sites, just as archives are kept. Updating is on a daily basis. A Nigerian in the US, Ekundayo, is one of the earliest administrators of a Nigerian issues based website (Bastian, 1999: 14), called www.naijanet.com. He began the network in 1991, leading thereafter to a proliferation of similar sites. More individual migrants' sites have since come into existence with the rise in the popularity of the Internet from the early 1990s, as this participant supports:

Internet use amongst Nigerians gained prominence during the fight against the military. Our compatriots in the US led the way and we followed from other parts. I remember Odili.net those days, and Nigeriaweb.com. They were very popular, and we posted many materials on there to fight the military. It was one of our main weapons. There are so many websites now anyway and you no longer know which is which! You cannot blame anyone: the Internet consciousness is now very high. **Ali, Male, 61, Leeds. Interview date: 18/05/2006.**

The question of agitating for a better Nigeria online introduces a new dimension to the discourse. Apart from being evidence that the Internet is an activist tool, it demonstrates the tendency of some migrants to correct the wrongs of the origin, if possible. A few websites are the products of activists' interests. They include those by Kudirat Institute for Nigeria Democracy, Movement for the Survival of Ogoni People (MOSOP) and Progress Action Movement[37]. The MOSOP site is for the interests of the minority Nigerian Niger-Delta Community, whose people suffer environmental degradation through oil exploration in their ancestral origin. Three recent news websites further fall into this category. They are www.elendureports.com, www.saharareports.com and www.thetimesofnigeria.com . The three are barely a year old at the time of writing. The popularity of the site is nevertheless shown in the number of references made to them in newspapers, and discussion groups. Moreover, the popularity surpasses many of the older websites. While a journalist, Jonathan Elendu administers www.elendureports, a former Nigerian student union activist, Omoyele Sowore, manages www.saharareports.com.

---

[37] Kudirat Abiola is the name of wife of late multi-millionaire politician, Moshood Abiola who died fighting for the validation of the annulled 1993 presidential election, which Abiola won.

Another journalist, Sunny Ofili, who is in the US, runs the last website. They often counter government pronouncements with facts, in manners the *homeland* press would not do. People with concerns also feed them with information. In this sense, an avenue for propaganda may have arisen in Internet space. This is more so because the government often responds through their own web pages, and on their transnational television network- the NTA. Various Nigerian leaders allegedly moving funds abroad hate the sites for publishing information about their activities. The reading migrants on the other hand celebrate the reports. With visual materials and vivid descriptions of the looting process, the sites sometimes publish the photographs of houses in foreign locations supposedly bought with public funds by these leaders. An instance from www.saharareports.com web page is reproduced below:

Figure 28: An Image of a Mansion Allegedly Bought With Public Funds

The strength of the three sites lies in their ability to report what mainstream, offline publications will not publish. Importantly, they take advantage of the immediacy of Internet production, to report breaking news faster than the sites of the local Nigerian press. They draw attention to such news by forwarding them to popular mailing lists like naija-politics@yahoogroups.com. While www.elendureports.comn did not publish a mission statement, www.saharareports.com whose administrator, Sowore was formerly with www.elendureports.com has one. It says, "We are citizens reporting the news and writing reports without barriers, oblivious of borders and regardless of frontiers"[38]. Nigerian newspaper sites occasionally adopt some of the stories with due references.

---

[38] Amongst some of its daring exclusive reports, in a country where equivocal reporting is still prevalent, are those with the headline: "Oil deal in Jamaica exposes OBJ (the president) and Carl Master; Obasanjo snatches kinsman's wife" and "El-Rufai (a federal minister) accused of homosexuality". There are also "Alhaji Aminu Dantata (a famous multi-millionaire) owes $194 million to the federal government in unpaid taxes and royalties; Trailing Babangida's (a former president) ill-gotten wealth; and Obasanjo plans to squander Nigeria's foreign Reserve".

The same applies to www.elendureports.com , which began the new wave of daring web reporting[39]. These activist reporters challenge the old order of evasive writing and reporting through an embrace of the new freedom that the Internet offers, from the distant migration space. Bolstered by unpleasant reasons for dispersal, and the new experience abroad, the zeal for change becomes a task. The zeal testifies yet again to the new online space as one of extensive possibilities, and in the case of the new wave citizen reporters, as a place for resistance against the failure of leadership in the *homeland*. The poor state had beforehand led to the likely ambivalent life in migration. The administrators, who are residing abroad, particularly the US and the UK, are frequent in Nigeria. They vow in several interviews to expose corrupt Nigerian leaders, in a bid to stop further abuse of power. For instance, Sowore notes in a web interview that:

> I am a pathological hater of oppressive power. If anybody exhibits such, I have no apologies (for going) after them. I am not paid to do that. I do it out of my conscience and out of my convictions as an activist. Nobody in my entire career as an activist has ever paid me to do anything. For your information, I cannot be bought. Nobody can buy me. **www.elendureports.com. Accessed on 20/05/2005**

Passion, determination and conviction against the problems in origin and the zeal to contribute towards alleviating it runs through the words above. Such commitment does not only come from a purportedly nationalistic mindset but one ready for sacrifices. Bade (Male, 39, Leeds. Interview date: 14/05/06) however argues that the likes of Sowore are extremists, who cause "confusion instead of helping development". However, while Sowore works through a site, which focuses on news/issues, other individual websites campaign for or against persons. An intriguing one, which became propaganda, is about the controversial former military president Babangida. This person was once in a campaign to return as Nigeria's democratic president. Two websites promoted his ambition. The administration of the sites notably came from Nigeria. Named www.Ibbheritageclub.com and www.Ibrahimbabangida.com, they projected the capabilities of the politician in the past, the present and his potential. Some migrants in the US challenged the moral right of the politician to return, via a website www.againstbabangida.com. Tayo Martins-Daniel, who is of the Ibbheritage, says of their mission:

---

[39] Some of its controversial exclusive reports include those with the headlines: "War on Corruption: Obasanjo's Oily hands; Olu Obasanjo's (the president's son) House: Lies, Half truths, and Threats; Atiku's (the vice-president) mansion and the war on Corruption; The sins of Gov. Orji Kalu (a state governor); Obasanjo, Young and Masters: What kind of Cabal?" amongst others.

We have set ourselves the selfless and patriotic task of democratically drafting IBB back into governance and national service.

We are calling on IBB to present himself for service to the nation at this critical moment so that he can move the nation from mere civilian rule to democracy and to a truly reformed market economy, which are the social engineering processes he inaugurated about 20 years ago. **Accessed at http://www.sunnewsonline.com/webpages/politics on 10/09/2006**

The opposition did not hide their displeasure for the candidate. And the Internet is available to them as well. So, their website administrator also notes:

Our mission is to wage a civilized battle against dangers to true and virile democratic development in Nigeria, symbolised by Ibrahim Babangida. This project is aimed at initiating action to stop Ibrahim Babangida from ever ruling Nigeria again. **Accessed at http://www.sunnewsonline.com/ webpages/politics on 11/09/2006.**

The site operators soon clashed online, reflecting conflict as a possible feature of web exchanges. This is likely in a free discussion space, where interests compete for attention. Martins-Daniel had written to those against his pro-Babangida crusade:

I am personally extending a nice hand of friendship and free membership of IBB Heritage Club to you all. IBB Heritage Club shall rehabilitate and train your members on sound morals on how to respect leaders. I know that you people are lay-about looking for cheap popularity and money. IBB Heritage Club shall keep you people busy productively. As you know, most of your members are crossing over to IBB Heritage Club. Please note that it is very unacceptable for some lay-about like you people to refer to some of our leaders as morons and evil. **Accessed at http://www.sunnewsonline.com/ webpages/politics on 10/09/2006.**

An immediate response came from his opponents. Their pronouncement here is a celebration of free speech that the web partly stands for. They are happy to use that space to further an interest. The group wonders why anyone would contest that right, even when they are not stopping others from exercising it. With a tinge of sarcasm, caustic jokes and abuse, they write anonymously:

Obviously, we are against Babangida. Therefore, if we are against him, we are not for him. Does that make sense to you? We have no doubt you are not brain-dead, just either brainwashed or hungry. Free speech is the inalienable right of every man, Nigerian or non-Nigerian. If we call anyone a moron, including yourself (and you seem to be), then that is exactly how we feel about you. Anyway, may your road be rough. Even if it is not rough, our job is to make it rough. **Accessed at http://www.sunnewsonline.com/ webpages/politics on 12/09/2006.**

Invariably, the US migrants are parties in the exchange of ideas. This is not only with fellow migrants, but also with people in Nigeria. The web as an expansive meeting point that traverses boundaries is a forum for this. An emotional link to the origin has driven the www.againstbabangida.com administrators to protest through the web (their unique available space of expression) the chances of returning a "bad leader". In doing this, they identify a place where they have a stake. The stake signifies a sense of association, and a sense of legitimacy and right to engage with political affairs: this connection and politics are not hampered by distance or dislocation. While they negotiate integration in the hostland, they are active in a campaign subjectively deemed necessary for the development of their origin.

Several other diaspora members in the "elite class" have personal websites. It seems to be a form of self-endorsement in a flourishing global entity. Notable sites in this group are those of career persons like Cardinal Francis Arinze, a Catholic clergy in Rome named as a possible successor to John Paul II, before the announcement of Pope Benedict XVI in 2005. Philip Emeagwali, a computer expert in the US who is famous for his work in supercomputer development, hosts many sites. Ben Okri also has his. So does Soyinka. In addition, Chika Nnigwe, an Afro-Belgian writer of Nigerian ancestry also has a site (accessed at http://library.stanford.edu/ africa/nigeria.html on 25/04/2007). *Weblogs* thrive amongst the migrants. Professor Aluko, who administers *Nigeriamuse*, is a case in point, amongst tens of others. *Blogging* on Nigeria events, owners invite discussions after providing leads from their individual point of view. This is even if the central focus of the blog is on personal stories. Important to them is the obvious emotional or less emotional concern for Nigerian affairs and a desire to lead topics for discussions.

A number of "virtual elites can also be found in a few relatively general sites. Notable here is the Association of Nigerians Abroad (ANA) and the Nigerian Diaspora Organisation, mentioned earlier. The ANA started in the early 1990s as an activist site. The site was constructed in the wake of the turbulent political climate of the period made worse by the controversial annulment of the June 12, 1993 presidential election. An earlier chapter already remarked that the former President Obasanjo administration encouraged the formation of the Nigerian in Diaspora Organisation (NIDO).

Its presence to date is mostly on the Internet. NIDO says in its mission that "Numerous societies and clubs of Nigerians (professional, ethnic, and family) already exist in many European countries, and it is not the intention that NIDO replaces them". The European branch introduces what seems as a commitment to Nigerian nationalism:

> NIDO provides the unique opportunity for Nigerians living in Europe to learn to work and collaborate with one another in the task of nation building, especially from outside the borders of our country. The main vision of NIDO is to bring Nigerians living in Europe together and to identify those willing to offer their skills (economic, education, information technology, science, arts, gender and youth empowerment, law, health, governance, management/ administration, building, etc to assist Nigeria's development process. **Accessed at http://www.nidoeurope.org/ on 10/03/2007**

The site has sections for migrants in different locations, while new members are invited. A website of Nigerian professional in Germany further signposts nationalism through the issues they raise in this category. The site, http://www.nidogermany.org/projects.htm notes that they are a non-profit group, which "provides a platform for Nigerians living in Germany to participate in the development of Nigeria". The clause "participate in the development of Nigeria" signifies a quest for involvement in supposed developmental efforts in origin. This concern also explains why they made further calls to members to come up with ideas that support projects like Agriculture, transportation, security, energy and education. They seek information on how to help the *homeland* on these areas, by calling on members, "friends and well wishers of Nigeria to forward proposals and suggestions on what you think can be done and what you can do in these areas".

Many other migrants express ideas as professionals. They interact at the level of common calling, eventually defining a path to relate with Nigeria and then try to contribute to its progress. A lot of them show specialist concerns for problem areas of Nigeria in which they have expertise. An example is the case of some Nigerian doctors who visit the country annually to help with medical care. Then Hernandez-Coss and Egwuogu Bun note:

> IT professionals in the diaspora on visits home (who) bring equipment and volunteer their expertise. Digital Aid, a US based diaspora-led initiative, collaborate with the Africa Leadership Forum (ALF) to facilitate technology transfer to Nigeria by collecting and transferring used personal computers to Nigerian schools (2007:54).

Some other similar gestures reported online are from groups like www.nigeria-arts.net, and www.nigerianexpertsabroad.com in the Americas. The Nigerian Experts Abroad is a "web based resource which allows Nigerian Professionals across the world to make contacts with each other and share valuable knowledge and information". The Association of Nigeria Physicians in the Americas says it has over "2,000 members" and "is a non-profit organisation of physicians and surgeons of Nigerian descent who are practising in the US and Canada".

Also important is that many in this category access online version of Nigeria newspapers. This assertion does not ignore the possibility of opportunities to read physical copies through transnational networks; it only emphasises the irregularity of this type of access. Unreliable and expensive offline supply systems across international borders cannot be practicable alternatives. The immediacy, low cost, and relative convenience of online versions make them a regular mediation mode. The comment below testifies to this:

> I get up to date information/news on Nigeria on the Internet. The Internet helps people greatly in reaching home. If you go anywhere, you hear people talking about Nigeria, saying I read this on the Internet or I read that. I visit websites of Nigerians abroad, like www.elendureports.com, www.saharareports.com, and sometimes I read the trends of discussions on naijapolitics@yahoogroups.com online. Using the Internet is one thing I usually do on a daily basis. **Dupe, Male, 43, London. Interview date: 02/06/2006.**

The commentator underneath attests to a very regular interaction with the Internet, in the bid to know about Nigeria, which a consistent access helps:

> If I am not writing to people online, I am surfing to be abreast of Nigerian issues. I go to many websites in a day, when I have the time. Note that I have a twenty-four hour access in my home, so I have the opportunity of reading papers online. The time I spend on it is limitless. **Emeka, Male, 46, London. Interview date: 02/06/2006.**

The next participant introduces an addictive dimension. It is possible when a routine becomes a necessary element of everyday life, eventually leading to a consciousness of long distance belonging. Engagement with the Internet could be addictive, when an inability to use it becomes worrisome. In the case of this person, the situation arises because he visits his favourite site at least once a day:

> I am an addict of www. nigeriaworld.com. I visit the site at least once a day, where I am able to navigate many newspapers' sites. This is apart from reading the stories they have on screen. I am well aware of goings on at home. In addition, I think I am even more informed than some of my friends at home. I read all the newspapers (online). **Adeyemi, Male, 37, London. Interview date: 02/06/2006.**

The Internet particularly mediates the interaction of members in the elitist sense in the noticeable quest for belonging. Diaspora members find a virtual space of connection through news and issue based sites. An expression of concerns manifests through professional and individual sites. The virtualised ties seen in the foregoing, supports the argument that longing and nostalgia for nation, and nation-state take place alongside a wish for its well-being (or a resentment for it), which most times take a nationalism turn.

THE POLEMICISTS AND THE LIKELY EXPRESSION OF NATIONALISM

The third category to which I classify virtual ways through which nationalism likely manifests is in the course of news/discussion groups. Some of these groups use popular portals like Yahoo, Hotmail, and Google. A few other discussion groups are located on ethnic, professional or individually maintained websites. It increases the possibility of this category to cross Types. Importantly, analysis in this category is based on the study of naijapolitics@yahoogroups.com, as explained on page 85, in section 3.3.1. Apart from reasons of purposive nonprobability sampling that led to the choice of naijapolitics@yahoogroups.com, it is also the most noted amongst participants from interviews' excerpts. These make it a good case study for the investigation of possible reflection of nationalism through a continuous flow of thoughts amongst participants.

Moderated by Martins Akindana, who is based in the US, the group somewhat shows the owner and participants' conversational dispositions. The discussant postures further translates into an interest in maximising the Internet network potentials for discussions on Nigeria and other issues of interest, like sports, and their love lives. The migrants are notably the most regular visitors to naijapolitics@yahoogroups.com, as shown from their signature lines. With about 1,900 members at the time of this study, it registers an average of 50,400 contributions monthly. A registration is required before participation, while participation cuts across ethnic and professional cleavages. At the time of writing this report, the group had nearly 2,000 members. Some of its competitors are talknigeria@yahoogroups.com; naijanet.com; and net-Nigeria. The word "Naija" is a popular pseudonym for Nigeria amongst nationals. Using it as part of the groups' username, deliberately make for an informal environment. A cordial atmosphere comes forth with the slogan. It eventually leads to the informal tones of discussions. Against this background, some discussants can become trivial, unduly jocular and possibly unserious. It all shows another character of the Internet as a domain that is prone to trivialities. Frivolities are possible because of minimal or non-existent control, which sometimes allows participants to indulge in unproductive activities. The so-called freedom therefore becomes a liberty to reflect weaknesses, poverty of thoughts and probable overindulgence. Nevertheless, Naijapolitics has this disclaimer:

> Forum members (should know) that NaijaPolitics is a moderated forum for gavel-to-gavel discussion of political developments in Nigeria, Africa's largest democracy. There is freedom of expression in NaijaPolitics. Views and opposing views expressed in NaijaPolitics forum are the rights of individual contributors. Mutual respect for people's views is the cornerstone of our forum. **Accessed at naijapolitics@yahoogroups.com on 02/04/2006.**

On naijapolitics@yahoogroups.com, administrators of news' sites post notices of breaking news on their sites, for visitors to follow[40]. As mentioned before, some participants, like London based solicitor Emetulu and US based Professor Aluko, are popular on naijapolitics@yahoogroups.com because of their regular participation. Others get tired after a while, leaving the space to new entrants. Being on the relative "right" side of the digital divide, as settlers in the developed Western world, where there is a higher Internet connectivity, interactions in naijapolitics@yahoogroups.com, represent a forum, where the absent people relate with virtual others in Nigeria, and mainly in migration. Meetings regularly occur and there are no breaks or closing time. Participants have to decide this, as the network is readily available. Moreover, as Jordan says, in this space, there is a levelling; it is possible to hear everyone despite the volume of her/his voice, or strength of her/his wallet (1999:3, 87). While barriers disappear on naijapolitics@ yahoogroups.com, some others may appear in the quality of contributions, and in the frequency of involvement. A few ideas are more committed or formal than others. Some are abusive, and some respectful, while a number of participants pop in for one or two contributions and then disappear. Yet others are regular, regardless of the topic. The quote below is an instance of a posting, which is abusive of Obasanjo, whose pseudonym is OBJ:

> OBJ needs psychiatric evaluation and treatment. It is a tale of unfortunate event that OBJ is the president of Nigeria and not a roadside mechanic as he rightly claims he would have, if not for the God that just wanted to punish Nigeria. Accessed at **naijapolitics@ yahoogroups.com on 03/03/2006.**

---

[40] News' sites that do this are mainly www.elendureports.com, www.saharareports.com, and www.thetimesofnigeria.com.

The example beneath illustrates a sober moment amongst participants. It appeared the same day as the one above. Bolaji Aluko who is a regular contributor writes:

Compatriots,
India's land area is just above 3 times that of Nigeria. Its rail length is about 20 times that of Nigeria, and highway length is 13 times that of Nigeria. Therefore, we need roughly 6 times the present rail length of Nigeria and 4 times the present highway length to begin to compare with India. Accessed at **naijapolitics@yahoogroups.com 02/04/2006.**

Another participant joins him. This one, obviously an issue oriented person, sees in his (Aluko's) contribution a chance to do something that can be meaningful for Nigeria:

I like your take on the terrible state of our transportation sector. It is a refreshing departure from the tribal rant of other posts on the same subject. I will join you, anytime, to pursue a public policy that would establish a comprehensive rail system that encompasses all parts of Nigeria. **Reggie Akpata, USA, accessed at naijapolitics@yahoogroups.com on 02/04/2006.**

Response fatigue (Bastian, 2004:4), disinterest, work distractions and holidays are some likely issues that determine duration and how habitual a participant is, on this newsgroup. The popular group is one of over 50,000 newsgroups online (accessed at www.Yahoo.com on 22/10/2006). The newsgroup can have at least ten contributions in an hour, as previously said. This rises with breaking stories in Nigeria and decreases when stories become routine. Participants are free to raise issues to provoke discussions. As above, individual news site operators promote their lead stories on there, prompting users to explore their sites. For instance, www.elendureports.com once prompted newsgroup visitors to its report on the death of a prominent politician, noting:

Veteran politician and perennial candidate for the office of Governor of Lagos State, Funso Williams, was assassinated today. Sources at the office of the Lagos State Governor confirmed this to Elendureports.com. According to sources in Lagos and London, the late Funsho Williams was alone in the house in the early hours of the morning when some gunmen entered his residence. **Accessed on 01/05/2006.**

Because the death was expectedly mournful, as it was one of the many in Nigeria, which causes security concerns for the migrants, responses to the report were rapid. Some were short, and some long. A few examples are contained here:

Who killed Funso Williams? Why was this man killed? For what purpose and for what reason? There is a terrible thing happening right before us. Is power very important that a man had to be killed because someone out there perceived him as an obstacle? **Accessed at** naijapolitica@yahoogroups.com **on 01/05/2006.**

Then there is a short and sharp one, which says "a shame: may God have mercy on Nigeria". Furthermore, announcements are regular. Participants using pseudonyms are mostly informal with language, sometimes sounding crude and rude.

It was soon time to remember the death of a popular activist. A contributor posts a remembrance message, stimulating responses. Two appear underneath:

Yes! Tai Solarin was a great man. I will never forget him. A few months after the war in "Biafra" zone, most schools had no classrooms or supplies. Classes were under trees and bombed out schoolhouses. Tai Solarin showed up at St Catherine's Nkwerre with lorry loads of school supplies, bags of rice, (and) beans for the students. I remember the lanky man in shorts and matching shirt addressing us in the school chapel. **Accessed at** naijapolitica@ yahoogroups.com **on 01/05/2006**

My first encounter with Dr. Tai Solarin, the education icon, human rights activist and humanist was sometime in the early 1980s during my primary school days where he was invited to our third term prize-giving day ceremony to present a paper. I was surprised that an adult could wear a short *khaki*, and top with a *khaki* cap to match to such ceremony. Innocently, the question that ran through my mind was who was this strange man? **Accessed at** naijapolitica@yahoogroups.com **on 01/05/2006**

The discussion of Solarin's death came from the initiative of a participant who feels the personality should be borne in mind, even in death. The individual uses a celebrity revered in the *homeland* as a reminder of the need for progress, a theme that dominated the lifetime campaigns of the dead activist. For the participant, he approaches the discussion group in the network via an individual, with legendary ideals. Doing this means associating with a symbol of progress, something with which many migrants often want to be associated. The Internet permits choice of self-assigned roles. The way these take place in the discussion group, and in relation to the state of the *homeland*, unfolds shades of nationalism.

The interests of some migrants in the newsgroup are periodic. To these few, it is never viewed as a priority. Most of them do so when the opportunity arises. Alternatively, when they have nothing else to do, they then resort to the Internet, and particularly the newsgroup. A respondent notes:

The above comment suggests the relativity of time spent online. The
comments show that participants are selective in virtual relationships with
each other. Determining the suitability of a fellow discussant is probably
dependent on ethnic grouping or elitist representation, and the topic in focus,
like when Aluko and Akpata discussed transportation problems of Nigeria
above. Volunteer moderators, administrators and/webmasters might interact
with the technology much more than some others, who would need idle time
to probably express nationalism on the group. Though the network
condenses an otherwise diverse global time, the individual user however
needs to create periods to go online, and onto the newsgroup. The network
is probably ready for habitual and continuous use, but it is subject to
interruptions. For many Nigerian migrants, interruptions are caused by their
busy work schedules, arising from working long hours, or combining jobs,
as Mohammed (Male, age unknown. Leeds. Interview date 07/04/2008)
notes: "I do shifts: one in the afternoon and in the night. In between, I sleep;
wake; and try to say my prayers. My state of mind determines if I will
remember my laptop". Surfing, or perhaps, participating in discussions, is
therefore dependent on interest, and occupational responsibilities, which
eventually determines the degree to which attachment to origin may be
expressed.

The newsgroup activity nevertheless helps the migrants feel more at
ease. This takes their status further away from the traditional perception of
migrants as a fragile group, endangered species or an unsettled people.
Through a virtual life, they are able to share experiences, express pains and
joys while discussing Nigeria, probably making them to cope better with
their troubled everyday. Consequently, with naijapolitics@
yahoogroups.com, participants are brought together, "through the mind,
through artefacts, and through shared imagination" (Cohen, 1997: 26),
while it revives national belonging. Virtual reconnections at naija-
politics@yahoogroups.com, replace the physical absence from Nigeria.
Possibly unable to find representation in the media of the settlement society,
naijapolitics@yahoogroups.com provides a forum for the exploration of
innovative possibilities towards national identification. It soon becomes a
"habit for these modern sojourners" (Anyanwu, 2004).

Karim (2004: 18) adds that with new communication technologies,
"diasporas are able to obtain cultural materials with growing ease from other
parts of the world". Besides, he says, "Governments are finding it
increasingly difficult to compel them to assimilate minorities into the

dominant national culture in the face of globalisation-from-below" (Karim, 2004: 18). From another viewpoint, the Internet saturates everyday life including those of diasporas (Georgiou, 2002). The Nigerian diaspora members are obviously involved in this saturation, especially as it offers a new avenue for connection with peers and with origin, pursuance to the demonstration of attachment. naijapolitics@yahoogroups.com is therefore round-table where virtual discussions, mainly on the *homeland* affairs, go on without conclusion.

THE GENDER FACET

The gender element of online nationalism activity is worth discussing. Bastian records Lola as starting a female network from the University of Pennsylvania in the early 1990's (1999: 5). The writer continues: "Naijanetters to whom I have appealed for information on this question suggest that the male to female ratio is in the area of 60:40 or 70:30". Foregoing discussions might have revealed a leading male participation in online nationalistic activities, female interactions are also complementary. This is even if patriarchy still predominates in Nigeria. In the countryside, people see men as heads, breadwinners, or natural leaders. Below is a writer's description of discrimination against women in Nigeria:

Discrimination against women continues in both physical and structural forms. Women empowerment is still treated with suspicion by the Nigerian male, as well as the social system, and no matter how highly placed or successful a woman may be, men are more likely to relate to her as someone's daughter, or wife, or girlfriend or mistress, in other words as chattel belonging to a man. Whatever successes (that they) may have ... achieved can be easily found in the areas of education, economic power, and the relatively increased representation of women in public life. But this success is gravely circumscribed, rendered almost ineffectual, by the resilience of traditions and customs that are entirely patriarchal in orientation, obnoxious, and chauvinistic in application. **Abati, accessed online at www.nigeriavillagesquare.com on 11/05/2008**

The description becomes more fitting towards the hinterlands than in the cities. It suggests that the concentration of the trend is proportional to the degree of cosmopolitanism, the people are experiencing. Exposures to modern civilisations make them more open-minded, while the opposite encourages being narrow-minded. Those in the hinterland are more conservative. Though many women achievers are present in various places, the popular thinking is that home affairs should be their forte. This believe however experiences alterations amongst migrants, because they are now part of a culture, with a stronger tendency towards visible gender equality. Female migrants imbibe an orientation of independence, equal rights, or are averse to semblances of discrimination against them. They are less concerned about feminists', or similar labels (Azikiwe, 1996; Sarikakis and Leslie, 2008), they may afterwards earn. The action of Lola above represents the transference of this re-orientation to the virtual world. Apart from the Kudirat site, there are some other sites, which are specific to female affairs or have women as a primary reference point. Examples of these are those of Nigerian women organisation; Nigerian Business Women; Nigerian Women Association of Georgia and Motherland Nigeria. The last has sections on healthcare; food and drinks; cultures and customs; and home management, all fundamentally from the Nigerian perspective. Some female interviewees' however confess to leaving the business of Internet use to their husbands or partners. The instances are below:

> Some new sites are now very daring. In reporting what newspapers would not report, they have attracted me to their websites and then the Internet the more in terms of current affairs. My husband had earlier called my attention to them. Some of these sites are www.elendureports.com and www.saharareports.com **Angela, Female, 39, London. Interview date: 16/02/2006.**
>
> My husband reads the Internet and briefs me on goings-on in Nigeria. I hardly have time for all that. **Ronke, Female, 44, London. Interview date: 09/06/2006.**
>
> I use the Internet for many things really…but sometimes too when I am occupied with feminine things, which I cannot reel out now, I rely on my husband to read the papers online and brief me. **Ilori, Female, 34, London. Interview date: 09/06/2006.**

While the delegation of Internet use does not provide sufficient evidence to conclude that there is a prevalence of one gender over the other in Internet use, it nevertheless reveals how Internet use by proxy often occur. Direct engagement with the network takes place when Internet use is between the person and a network terminal. A third party comes in when the person relies on another for the performance of the network function. The go-between briefs the waiting party of deserving information. The distance created between the concerned party and the network through the agency of the third party, may (or may not) impact on the value of nationalism. It nevertheless introduces one alternative to Internet access, which is browsing it by surrogating[41]. This reinforces some reasoning that males lead in use (Snow, cited in Manzrui, 2006: 11).

From another perspective, the women who use the Internet through proxies may be doing so for other unstated reasons. The three contributors

---

[41] Chances are that the use of the option can affect originality, because messages eventually received will be coloured by the perspective of the mediator, as it is a characteristics of gate keeping.

above are between ages 34 and 44. They are therefore mature, and could probably be mothers, preoccupied with childminding. Their responsibility may affect their chances of giving a high priority to browsing, even if they would ordinarily be interested in it. In their position, they could make do with the husband or partners' help in that regard. On the other hand, they may belong to the class of traditional Nigerian woman that believes in allowing the man take the initiative, including Internet use. In other words, they are the hesitant set, who believes in total reliance on the man in the house. Some other women are however different. They are educated, and are initiators themselves, despite their marital or partnership status. They are often enterprising, modern, sometimes taking the leadership role in the home. The character blossoms when marriage or childbearing are not hindrances. It may not be different when they are. A contributor describes the new space, through blogs thus:

> Suddenly, more Nigerian women are blogging and making the Nigerian blogosphere sizzling with hot posts. And they are attracting hundreds of thousands of visitors. Most of the blogs are what I call scuttlebutt blogs or daily social gist and titbits blogs. And <u>Bella Naija</u> leads the pack, followed by <u>Linda Ikeji</u> and company. <u>Adaure</u> is still in a world of her own, because she is like the Oprah Winfrey of the Nigerian blogosphere in her subject matters. <u>Queen Ebong</u> and others are still exciting and thrilling. The most profiled Nigerian female bloggers remains Sokari Ekime of <u>Black looks</u>. And <u>Funmi Iyanda</u> would be more enlightened if she spends some quality time with Sokari. **Orikinla Osinachi, accessed at www.Nigeriantimes. blogspots on 04/06/2008.**

As expected, women like men have varied interests. While some focus on beauty, a lot are concerned with career matters. Several are blogging in first-person, whereas many literally detach themselves from their contributions. A Norway based woman, blogging under the title "Nigerian woman in Norway", says that she is looking to live life to the fullest. She intends to "seek and grab all opportunities in life and contribute to humanity in my very little way" (accessed at www.blogger.com/profile on 04/06/2008). Iyanda sometimes operates from the lenses of her profession as a journalist, by publishing current issues on her blog, *Nigeriantimes*. Links with the name Nigeria, particularly in the case of the migrant women, could well mean a desire for attachment with an origin. This is happening even when they have the option of doing otherwise, or even using the name of their respective hostlands. The women are therefore active participants in the expression of a relationship with ancestry, whether for good, ill, or indifference.

Other than this is the tendency of mothers amongst the Nigerian diaspora members to cherish living in the west for the sake of their children, in what further raises questions on the quality of attachment to Nigeria. However, this desire is often common amongst other categories of people including fathers, but many mothers significantly confess to preferring the relative predictability of life in the west, than in Nigeria. They are concerned about the provision of better health facilities, availability of good roads and better educational institutions. To them, their children would rather take advantage of these facilities, and live a better future than what was available to them when parents were growing up in Nigeria. Some, as would be seen in the statements below, are happy to be left behind abroad while the husband may return, or shuttle between abroad and the *homeland* in search of means of livelihood. To others, living abroad, either is fulfilling a life dream, or complying with what appear reputable to many people in Nigeria.

> I have 3 boys, 19, 15 and 10. It was not initially easy bringing the eldest because of his age, but I succeeded two years ago. They have all started school…the eldest, Harry, is due for the university. We applied online to Bradford and told he is not qualified for local rate. We are still working on that, because my husband will not want him to school in Nigeria anymore, where schools are regularly closed down because of strikes. In just a year after the two others began schooling, the difference is already showing. **Tani, Female, Age Unknown, London. (Interview date: 16/03/2008**
>
> Bashi (Husband's name) hopes to go back to Nigeria, in another two years when we would have qualified for indefinite stay. I am prepared to stay behind for the sake of my children. He can go and continue the struggle, but for me to return to fuel scarcity, religious riots and power failures is unreasonable. **Florence, accessed at** www.nigeriaworld.com **on 20/05/2008**
>
> I regard it as wickedness to take my children to Sokoto (a Northern Nigerian city), from London. I have committed myself to making the sacrifice and living in Grantham (England) for the sake of my children's future. I know that they would miss Nigeria's culture, but it is a matter of priority…better education is more important to us. **Grace, Female, 41, Leeds. (Interview date: 30/03/2008)**

The preference for hostland amongst women continues the ambiguity about migrants' perception of origin. To the women, priority is given to the future of the children, basic needs of life and a better ability to plan than sheer appreciation of Nigeria. If Nigeria has to be appreciated, it must be able to fulfil basic expectations; otherwise, the inclination will be for the hostland, where they could be available. Then concern for Nigeria would simply be as a place of original belonging. Would these female diaspora members then be said to be nationalistic? To the extent that some form of concern and relationship exist with Nigeria, it can be argued that nationalism is inferred. A counterargument could arise that because fondness is for another country, then they are not interested in Nigeria. This does not also indicate an absence of nationalism, as nationalism is laden with contradictions. The position of the women above can be seen as a more realistic, conditional form of nationalism, shaped in the meeting of the personal, the familial and the communal needs and priorities. Core to the debates is that nationalism is ambiguous. This ambiguity sometimes makes it flexible, as long as a relationship between the nation and nation-state on the one hand; and the individual, and/or the collective on the other hand is established.

CHAPTER SEVEN:

ONLINE CONSTRUCTION OF THE NIGERIAN DIASPORA MEMBERS' IDENTITIES

The movement of large masses of people across national boundaries, technologies that deliver modern instantaneous communication, the culture of simulation, and globalisation in all its forms are some of the forces determining the contemporary context of identity (**Paul Gilroy, 1997: 303**).

Having examined the activities of the diaspora members in relation to transnationalism and nationalism, which represent some of the core areas related to their online activities, I shall now analyse my data concerning how the Internet affects them as individuals. I shall focus on their changing individual and collective identities, by revealing the different identities that result from the migrants' use of the Internet. The chapter situates the transformation of the Nigerian diaspora members' identities within the context of the growth of the Internet and its role as a tool for a people experiencing new political and economic challenges. The relative freedom and limitlessness of cyberspace encourages equally boundless online activities of diaspora members. The boundlessness combines with its low cost and easy access to help form new identities[42], or the firming up of old ones. From there, cultured or enlightened participants, "public advocates" and those with self-defined reformation abilities, amongst other characterisations emerge. The initial advantage of the Internet, which continues to date, is identified within the framework of self-representation in multiple forms. The migrant, as I will show, has become not only a wiser person, but also a possible agent of political, social and economic change. This takes place via their new roles as network activists, moralists, defenders of principles, and ideas. The chapter locates the migrants' virtual self-representation as individuals, groups or collectives and reveals personae that evolve via simulations and the limits of representation in an alternative space. The section essentially reveals how some migrants are compelled to "rethink their identities", after "they move to the west" (Nesbitt, 2002:78).

---

[42] Some of the new identities may simply be limited to life online, as they could have little or no offline relevance. These may therefore be online identities. Online identities can occur where, for instance, the many online debaters do not find corresponding roles offline. The construction assume a new dimension, as is more common, where participants online roles are recognised offline, like in the case of those, as shall be shown, who have become popular as webmasters, and newsgroup moderators.

Though the Internet is still maturing, its benefit to sections of societies particularly marginal and fragile communities like migrants is apparent. The evidence comes through the multiple manner of expression for which participants use it. Questions regarding possible manners of self-representation may arise (Wood, 2001:47), but it does not mean that representations cannot be self-influenced. A "complex personal and social construct" (Wood, ibid.: 47), identity is constructed by migrants online, in manners that shift opinions about them in the eyes of people in Nigeria and those in the hostland. Analyses in this section however note that virtual identities are short-lived. This is because the Internet user would sooner rather than later retire to the original, natural self, after online activities (Robins and Webster, 1999). The chapter proposes that the brief periods of change, could be beneficial for the dispersed people in the light of their often challenging experience. Many times as well, the changes are reflected in life offline, when their online engagements determine their characterisations offline. I shall now evaluate this process from the period of the rise of the network to present times. Interpretations from this section come from literature, texts, interviews, sampled newsgroups/mailing lists' discussions, and websites typologies A and D on pages 87-88, while taking bits from the rest.

SOCIAL AND POLITICAL SPACE OF IDENTITY CONSTRUCTION

VIRTUAL CAMPAIGNS FROM A DISTANCE

In this section, I focus on virtual political identity from 1993. This year marks the beginning of the rise of the Internet, which coincided with a complicated political development in Nigeria. The then Nigerian military regime annulled a presidential election were candidate Moshood Abiola led. This was on June 12 of that year. The election was the fairest and freest in Nigeria's unstable political history, going by the judgements of local and foreign observers. The cancellation of the results by the military President Babangida angered sections of the country. It nearly led to another civil war-after the one of between 1967 and 1970. Despite the might of a military regime, there was resistance in various forms. Its internationalisation, as encouraged by the positive commentaries of international observers on the success of the polls, came shortly after[43]. British Scientist, Tim Berners-Lee, had only two years earlier invented the World Wide Web (WWW). This initiated Uniform Resource Identifiers (URLS), which expanded the

---

[43] International observers at the polls were from the United Nations (UN), the European Union (EU), the National Democratic Institute (NDI), and some Non-Governmental Organisations (NGO), with political inclinations from Western nations.

frontiers of the Internet.

Still emotionally attached to Nigeria, sections of its diaspora, including those who at that time were escaping from the military enclave, cashed-in on the free network to regroup. They shared ideas, initiated sets of connections and sought critical perspectives to the state of Nigeria. These activities had become dangerous in many Nigerian spaces of public expression and media. Those who were escaping began joining other categories of migrants including older settlers, first or second generation migrants who still associate with Nigeria. They challenged with vigour the then military government's controversial decision.

The Internet eventually became a new place for political propaganda for the migrants. Besides, as Chalaby (2000:20) argues, the network enabled them to "coordinate their political lobbying, construct their collective identity and share information and resources". It became, and still is, a place for the re-negotiation of a real or imagined Nigerian identity (in the face of the political crisis). The network also became a place to study their relationship with the identity of Nigeria as a nation-state. The dialectical interplay of the process has ultimately gone beyond temporal and spatial dimensions. It has continued overtime, resulting in other facets of social relations in the course of migrancy. One of the very first notable Nigerian oriented migrant websites that came in the wake of the protracted campaigns for the de-annulment of the polls was www.nigeriaweb.com. Constructed in 1996 by Chuck E. Odili in the US, Adebanwi (2001:15) quotes him on the rationale behind the development of the website: "Nigerian community lacked an organised, coherent voice in their host countries to effect tangible change in the government in Nigeria". The site, he adds, therefore "came into existence to facilitate the empowerment of Nigerians in the diaspora by collating information on events in Nigeria". The administrator emphasised that he was interested in ensuring that migrants knew about events in Nigeria. Apart from helping the displaced population to have a "common front" or a "coherent voice" to "effect change", the administrator's motive also lay in helping the development of knowledgeable migrants. That last desire became realisable through the regular uploading of information on to the website. The website intended many roles for the migrants. Noteworthy roles are those of a political lobbyist, activist, agitator, and the epistemic.

However, while migrants may have carried all or some of these identities before the creation of www.nigeriaweb.com in 1996, use of this website re-enforced them, as I will show this in this chapter. The website also introduced others to those roles, which arose from engaging with the network. A few visitors, who until then did not have those traits, perhaps acquired some of them through visiting the site and gaining access to information and opinions previously not available to them. Adebanwi again quotes Odili as testifying to the initial success of the websites' aims and objectives as follows:

Individuals and interest groups from around the world that used Nigeriaweb
as primary source of information on actions (of) the Abacha government and
developments in Nigeria, contacted (the webmaster) with ideas for enhancing
the website, for greater interaction amongst Nigerians and pressure groups.
(Adebanwi, 2001:4).

The comment below is also another testimony. It explains the reason
behind the success of the site, as it notes the rise in the modern medium. It
also hints at the readiness of the Nigerian user to be involved for the
realisation of their objectives:

(There is also) www.nigeriaworld.com where thousands of Nigerians from
all over the world engage in discussions of political and social issues on an
hourly basis. The site, formerly called Odili.net, is the creation of Chuck
Odili, a Nigerian based in North Carolina. It is a phenomenal success, an
exceedingly vibrant site owing to a conjunction of several factors, the most
immediate being advances in communication and the extreme radicalisation
of Nigerians in the aftermath of the annulment of June 12 polls. **Adesokan,
accessed at www.nigeriainsamerica.com on 01/10/2001**

As of 2001, the site reportedly hosted 28,000 visitors on a daily basis. Of
this number, 83% were in the US; 6% in the UK; 4% in other European
countries; 3% in Canada; 1% in Asia; 1% in South America; and 1% for
others. Less than 0.5% of visitors came from Nigeria. For contributors 75%
were US based; 15% were based in Europe; and 10% were in Nigeria, while
less than 1% were in the rest of the world (Adebanwi, ibid.:16). The
dominance of contributions from migrants further suggests their desire to be
involved in mediation with the *homeland*. It signifies a resistance against
exclusion, which is intensified by distance. Physical distance often hinders
participation in the *homeland* affairs. The www.nigerianweb.com provides
a place where involvement is possible despite absence, as well as being a
venue for psychological re-integration.

As at 2006, the website was reputedly one of the most popular amongst
migrants', partly because it has constructed additional sites including
www.odili.net;   www.naijapages.com;   and   the   all-embracing
www.nigeriaworld.com. The site is constantly changing probably to remain
relevant in the dynamic Internet space. However, its general focus gives it
a continuous edge, in the proliferating world of websites. Andrew (Male
42), who has lived in Leeds for seven years, says of the website:

I do not read Nigerian newspapers, as they do not contain much. I read
www.nigeriaworld.com, where you not only have the papers summarised,
with most important news reproduced, but where you also have links to their
sites. The articles published are very informative. They keep me busy when
I want. **Interview date: 13/03/2006.**

Beyond information dissemination which is a key role of the media, and for which Andrew finds the website useful, an evolving power of knowledge leads some others to further an activist identity[44]. They find the online space as a path to agitate. Their activities revolve around the purposeful expression of desires; mobilisation of co-travellers; and in general, propaganda activities. One of their methods is the creation of websites, which are usually more emotional, and more incisive in the analysis of Nigerian issues. Many more are forceful in the expression of viewpoints, and less welcoming of arguments. While the informed self subsists in the circumstance, they have now added the activist facet to the self. As a demonstration of this, some participants have had grounds to mobilise others towards a cause online. An example was when discussants on naija-politics@yahoogroups.com in 2005 asked group users to sign-up to reject the plan of former military ruler, Ibrahim Babangida to return to power. London solicitor, Kenneth Emetulu who initiated the cause justifies it on the grounds of the politicians' anti-democratic tendencies while once in power. His role in this instance as an online mobiliser shows how the network can transform a character.

If the mobilisation were to be offline, it would have involved traditional activists' means. This could include distribution of leaflets, posters, announcements in electronic and newspaper press, and perhaps word of mouth campaigns. Compatriots are most likely living in diverse places, with different densities in the hostland, which will make these traditional methods difficult. The different locations can be complex to cover in the physical. On the Internet, the newsgroups, usenets, networking locations, websites and e-mail lists, replace roads, streets, crescents, terraces, boulevard, avenues, and closes of the city. The computer terminal becomes a narrow gate to reach many in different places. Offline mobilisation may also be unwieldy, costly, and perhaps ineffective. The online variant is nevertheless cheaper, doable and potentially more effective. Though the migrants' influence as voters is still absent, because they are yet to be part of the voting population during elections. Nevertheless, many silently pride themselves as being influential in the voting process, given an ability to persuade family members and friends on the choice of candidates. The thinking is that their views are likely to be respected because of their travels and because they are breadwinners due to remittances.

Emetulu is prominent in many online discussion groups, like naijapolitics@yahoogroups.com and talknigeria@yahoogroups.com. He sensitises migrant users to issues that relate to Nigeria and then urge them to discuss it. This reflects a virtual commitment to actualising a cause. Segun Dawodu in the US, who administers www.dawodu.com, also poises

---

[44] The activist here means those who consciously push for social and political changes in the *homeland*.

to instruct, inform and create awareness amongst visitors. It is another case of a migrant's commitment to effecting social change through the Internet. Bolaji Aluko also pre-occupies himself with www.nigeriamuse.com, through "sharing insight and information". He goes further to say that he writes "always to inform, to teach, to provoke, to amuse, to inspire, to express a point-of-view, and to inquire, whereupon to learn!" (Accessed at www.nigeriamuse.com on 12/02/2007). The professor of chemical engineering is not only a scholar but also a virtual activist, by his own construction. His regular participation in the naija-politics@yahoogroup.com is another evidence of this. Martins Akindana's other website www.chitafrik.com is yet another instance of an effort to create awareness. These participants online locations reputedly admits different migrant contributors, where the freedom to be heard is of prime importance[45]. In maintaining the online locations, Dawodu, Aluko and Akindana become key persons in the settler's virtual activities. Sometimes, the virtual activist identity evokes pride. By publicising information on Nigerian political troubles in an open space, the activists cause concern and unease among Nigerian politicians and even more so, among potential future dictators.

A WEB BASED MIGRANT ORGANISATION, SEARCH FOR A NIGERIAN IDENTITY

For now, the Internet is one of the ways through which Nigerian migrants identify members of groups and organisations. This is especially applicable to the notable Nigerian in Diaspora Organisation (NIDO). A Canadian based medical practitioner, Dr Ola Kasim, leads it. As discussed in section 5.3.3, its formation was encouraged by the previous President Obasanjo administration, as a link between the Nigerian government and the many Nigerians abroad. Other than this, participants deliberately attempt to sustain a connection with the name Nigeria. This manifests through symbolic identifications, names and practices. In the US, many immigrant groups are identified in a fusion, first because of their origin and then when they add their American status. Examples include, Chinese-Americans, Indian-Americans, Greek-Americans, Spanish-Americans, Jewish-Americans, Irish-Americans, Iranian-Americans, and African-Americans. Participants have started to identify themselves as *Nigerian-Americans*.

---

[45] It is significant to note that the multiple function of the Internet affects users. In what appears an imitation of real-life, participants in their virtual life can fit into roles. The participants are able to reveal their hidden self because of the absence of prosodic signs and other gestural and facial cues.

Though the name seems transnational in appearance, the redefinition of identity on an ethno-national basis shows an attempt to negotiate recognition away from the identity of African-Americans. Previously, they had presumably been phenotypically members of this group. It is also a development in line with positioning themselves in a similar trend to the abovementioned more established migrants in America. References to Nigerian-American are present in many cases of participants' work. Examples are "Nigerian-Americans should decide whether they want to be part of the charade going on in Nigeria or not", by Benbe (accessed at www.nigeriansinamerican.com on 22/10/2006). "We Nigeria-Americans should not fail to be supportive of the democrats as they are more peace loving and friendlier to Africans", by Daniel (accessed at www.nigeriansinamerican.com on 23/10/2006). There is yet another:

> Nigerians still have some depressing tales to tell about their sojourn in a foreign land. Apart from the usual exposure to prejudices and stereotypes that every Black person has to face in God's own country, these Nigerian-Americans also have the daunting tasks of raising their children in a land well known for its absolute freedom and liberty. **Olawole, accessed at www.nigeriansinamerica.com on 01/12/2006**

The quote above is another reminder of the challenge of migration. Life on the move is sometimes risky. This is because of uncertainties of strangeness, which can make a migrant anxious and unsettled. Though comfort may be achieved at some point, the travails of dislocation and the absence of a sense of permanence constantly challenge likely routes to the gains of migration. This is why the above speaker talks about "depressing tales", arising from trying to integrate in the hostland. The tales are often reminders of an original self, the Nigerian origin and the need to seek association with it, even via its name. More directly, how is the individual identity affected in this mediation processes? I shall turn to this in the next section.

CYBERSPACE AND INDIVIDUAL DEVELOPMENT

THE SELF AND THE INTERNET

The Internet allows some of the migrants to assume multiple or fictional identities. Easier access and the absence of editorial policies of offline media aid them in possible self-representation. Issues of quality may arise from the act, but the short-lived satisfactions from the self-representation can be soothing. Though some sites have rules, the fact of marginal implementation and difficulty in sanctioning breaches encourages participants' undiluted thoughts. Some real identities in the form of the "real" self may appear. And from these real ones, new identities, like being contributors, virtual opinion moulders, webmasters, bloggers, online publishers, editors-in-chief, and list-owners reshape their self-conception. It initiates individualism and the chance of self-projection, leading to a possible increase in self-worth. When the words "I", "we", "us", "my", are also present in blogs, sites and in contributions, the subjects freely mirror themselves. Self-satisfaction could come through the expression of their individual identity. The occurrence is probably a contrast to migrant experience in real life, where identity is probably still a matter for negotiation. The statement below shows for instance, how participants feel free to write from the first-person angle:

I have just been demoralised by Nigerian Football Association's ineptitude and lackadaisical attitude to duty.I woke up this morning and tuned the TV to SKY news and on the sport news segment, I saw the Ghanaian National
Team scoring an equaliser in a friendly game against Australia. The game ended 1-1. **Parke, accessed at http://blog.onlinenigeria.com on 18/11/2006.**

Talking about themselves online enables their discovery and identification in an ever-shifting social formation. The opportunity to construct a site, to link up with one reduces the sense of loss in migration. They canvass relevance and recognition for the self in what is believably fulfilling in an ambivalent migration life. Another example follows:

I am proud to be a Nigerian. We have one and only one identity, which is our nation-state (Nigeria) not our ethnicity. That is what brings us all together and we should be proud of that. **Dantata, Egypt, accessed at www.nigeriaworld.com on 18/11/2006**

Migrants are more conversational than they probably were in origin. They are prone to backward and forward gazes, and combined with a new epistemic outlook, there is always the temptation to engage with issues related to Nigeria. Dispersion is perhaps a beginning of a divided perspective, one for the *homeland* left behind and the other for the inhabited hostland. Trials of dislocation force the migrant to reminisce and to idealise return. It leads to thoughts about life "then", and the embrace of media like the Internet, which can make this occur:

Before I came to live abroad five years ago, I could not be bothered about the Internet, but not anymore. I am a columnist on www.nigeriaworld.com and I use the Internet many times a day, to be abreast of issues in Nigeria and provide proper perspectives on developments. **Dupe, Male, 44, London. Interview date: 02/06/2006.**

This person points to a main attribute of migrants. Before migration, Internet use was minimal. It increases after travel, due to a range of reasons. To Dupe, use was probably limited in Nigeria because of access problems, or because offline contacts and relationships are easier because of proximity. Abroad, physical relationships with many other Nigerians have become limited, hence its substitution with virtual interaction. The interactions are not simply with websites, or on discussion groups, but through sending and receiving e-mails, photographs and other documents. The Internet as a channel of re-integration fosters a remembrance of the *homeland*, and its people. The network then helps the sense of discovery and identification in the face of the inconveniences of dislocation. The process of sending and receiving e-mails for instance implies a variant of contact, which moderates the sense of absence in migration. They see the self as not only important but as one with promise, given their position as parties in exchanges across distances.

Engaging with more people, in what exemplifies the Internet, as a network of many to many, appears to have eased the everyday networking desire amongst participants. Invitations to join newsgroups, discussion lists and to be contributors to websites are a regular feature. They also relax rules for the admission of prospective contributors. Contributors have the opportunity of relating with individuals, instead of groups, through posting of personalised emails to single addresses. Websites often have links to "contact us". The chances of networking are open to a regular user of the web. It is often a feature of the migrants' interaction as they meet each other online. With the Internet becoming a mandatory technology[46] rather than choice for the migrants, they become available to other users, who in turn see them as companions in virtual social interaction. Eventually, many participants become people with a high sense of association. The interviewee below supports this point:

> I use the Internet for sending e-mails, and for reading about Nigerian events. In terms of relating with Nigeria, I can say it is through the Internet. I also meet people online. The meeting once became physical when I discovered the person lives on the same street as mine. We are now good friends. I like to network so I can succeed in the business I am working on. I am relying on the Internet to help me reach out to potential patrons. **Awal, Male, 48, London. Interview date: 27/02/2006.**

In reaching friends via email, the participant minimises the possibility of loneliness that dwelling in a new environment could cause. S/he becomes an agent behind a node in a network. This gives a sense of being active, just as it enables remembrances, through relating with fellow travellers and in reading about Nigeria.

---

[46] The network turns out to be mandatory because of a growing number of new users, out of a need to embrace a modern technology, and to be in the virtual network with peers.

Through their contributions to discussion groups, in chatrooms and on newsgroups, the migrants turn into public commentators, analysts and opinion moulders. The simulation of real life online is characterised with chances of greater anonymity, which gives the participant far more vocal and opinionated contributions. The representation may not have been possible for a shy person, or those with any form of inhibition. The likely quiet self is by-passed through the depersonalised opportunity, which the Internet offers. A desired or undesired public character in real life is then additionally realisable in the migrants' virtual life. This public identity arises in the process of unrestricted advocacy. In itself, it emerges via continuous idealisation of how life could be better in Nigeria. An identity of people canvassing for the "public interest" emerges in the course of discussing social and political issues in the *homeland* and on ways of improving them. The virtual agents of change come up with an online representation of the public-spirited, the public commentator, or the "public intellectual". This new virtual identity improves with an ongoing exposure to other cultures. It expands their worldview, eventually opening them to new perspectives on life and other issues.

Many virtual public interest campaigners appear on the web[47]. The website, www.nigeriansinamerica.com features scores of participants from the US and the UK. They contribute to issues in columns like life abroad; Nigerian matters; and Africa and the world[48]. These participants became online celebrities because of their regular contributions, references to their thoughts by others and for expressing controversial opinions. As shown earlier, Seyi Oduyela provokes reactions many times, so does Uche Nworah and Bolaji Aluko.

Many use pseudonyms[49]. Some writers in Nigeria like Abati of www.ngrguardiannews.com regularly have their contributions reposted on web addresses like www.nigeriavillagesquare.com and www.nigeriaworld.com. This is typically for the attention of the migrant audience. Although, some of the contributions of the migrants are limited to one website, many others cross-post contributions, which broadens the scope, and likelihood of identification. Ajayi for instance maintains a column in www.nigeriaworld.com and contributes to www.zumunta.com. Okey Ndibe also writes for

---

[47] Some of those with names that look real are Sunny Ofili, Okey Ndibe, and Femi Ajayi, who are all in the US. There are also Uche Nworah, and Greg Obong Oshotse in the UK.

[48] Listed as its popular authors are Sola Osofisan, Sabella Ogbobode, Ike Anya; Tokunbo Awoshakin, Wunmi Akintide; Uche Nworah, amongst others.

[49] Examples are NOK1, *Otito Koro*, (Truth is bitter), YKO, Imodoye 05, Adaoma_o, and Lil Joe, amongst others. A few like Akindana also has an identifiable pseudonym, which, as previously noted, is "Matto".

www.nigerianvillagesquare.com and then www.ngrguardiannews.com, before he went to www.thesunnewsonline.com. Uche Nworah is a regular in www.saharareports.com, www.nanka.com, www.nigeriavillage.com, and www.nigeriansinamerica.com, besides contributions on his own site, www.uchenworah.com. The major claim of the contributors on migrants' consciousness stems from the virtual world. In this world, their sense of presence is immense and their identity as public policy analysts grows. A few instances of their commitment to fostering better public order in Nigeria are below:

> Besides their military career, the comparison is no more than garbage that someone tries to sell on Internet. Otherwise, how can an intelligent person compare a world-renowned dictator with no single achievement in eight years to an elected president? Even career propagandists have some respect for the intelligence of people and will not use such comparison to sell their candidate. **YKO, accessed at naija-politics@yahoogroups.com on 22/11/2006**

This contributor, a regular one, was participating in a debate on which the better leader is, between two former Presidents, Obasanjo and Babangida. A section of Abati's write-up, reposted in www.nigeriavillagesquare.com also states:

> Festus Oguhebe stands trial and faces sentencing after pleading guilty to charges of child abuse. He may go to jail. He also faces the risk of losing his job. The Alcorn State University's spokesperson, Christopher Cason has been quoted as saying: 'Alcorn State University employees are expected to be of good moral character'. **Originally published in www.ngrguardiannews.com on 19/11/2006, accessed at** www.nigeriavillagesquare.com **on 22/11/2006**

The court handed Oguhebe a two-year sentence[50]. His fate caught the attention of the public advocates. It resulted in many commentaries, nearly one hundred at the time of writing. Many appeared after Abati's analysis. They were in www.nigeriavillagesquare.com (Accessed 22/11/2006.) All were with pseudonyms. The virtual commentators are more concerned with

---

[50] Festus Oguhebe, a Nigerian born, Alcorn State University lecturer, in the US, was tried November 2006 for using pepper juice and ants to punish one of his sons. This is an acceptable disciplinary method to a very few parents in Nigeria. The method is however illegal in the US and perhaps many other Western countries. His attempt to apply the disciplinary process in another country obviously put him against the laws of an inhabited country. He was jailed for five years by Hinds County Circuit Judge L. Breland Hilburn, but with "three years suspended on his no-contest plea to one count of child abuse". (Accessed at http://www.nigeriavillagesquare.com?option=com_content&do_pdf=1&id=4142, on 24/08/2008)

Oguhebe's experience because he is a fellow Nigerian migrant. Oguhebe exhibited a cultural particularity in a culture that regarded his actions as a criminal offence. The clash of cultures and the consequence for the victim is a rude reminder of their fragile condition as "outsiders", needing to negotiate their way. Debating this development means a continuous assessment of their ambiguous condition in the hostland. A few comments are here:

> In Africa, Oguhebe will receive praise for his strictness. It will in fact be in his favour, that because he is divorced, he would not want to be a failed parent turning out failed children. **Exxcuzme, accessed at** www.nigeriavillagesquare.com **on 22/11/2006.**

The contributor above looks at what he regards as the essence of Oguhebe's controversial action. He reasons that he was justified in trying to instil discipline in his child in a way he deems right, without looking at the efficacy, or lack of it of the action as the participant below do:

> I do not think this Oguhebe person is disciplining his children, the African way. Rather, he is either sadistic or crazy, but more of the latter. Who in Africa would add pepper to a child genital if not critically insane? The person needs to have a psychiatric evaluation for these abnormal acts on his children. **Demo, accessed at** www.nigeriavillagesquare.com **on 22/11/2006.**

The next participant points to the crisis of mixing with other cultures. With a sense of perspective, the participant notes the challenges of integration through the outlook of a particular way of life. He adds that Oguhebe's experience represents a test case in the difficulties migrants face by living between two cultures:

> I am unable to understand why Nigerians find it hard to adopt the culture of their resident countries. Is it a question of having your cake and eating it? There are pains to living in a new country, and this involves adoption of the new culture and shedding of old cultural practices. **Katampe, accessed at** www.nigeriavillagesquare.com **on 22/11/2006.**

While another person below justifies the need for punishment, and the need to bring up children in cultures that are suitable for family cohesion, s/he raises questions on the rationality behind the use of the "extreme" methods that Oguhebe used:

> Look at all the cultures around the world, you find strong family ties based on rules and discipline; whether Chinese, Indian or Japanese or African villages; RESPECT is maintained in the family so most of the children are not wayward. Respect in children is by discipline, including corporal punishment. If it was wrong, God could not have STRONGLY recommended it. **Ula Lisa accessed at** www.nigeriavillagesquare.com **on 22/11/2006.** (*Emphases in original*)

The above discussion shows how participants air their opinions on issues of the day, which further clarifies the position that they have now assumed identities of public commentators and personae.

A WIDE RANGE OF INTEREST IN IDEAS, DIFFERENT IDENTITIES

Some migrants' websites are regularly interested in the contributions of writers in Nigeria. This indicates a commitment to public ideas and their cross-fertilisation. It is also a sign of a deterritorialised web union. The coming together takes little or no notice of barriers, and makes a maximum gain from the variability of the Internet space. The initiative of the webmasters and administrators in reproducing contributions that they consider relevant to their context resembles such exchanges in real life. The difference lies in the more expanded web, as against the limited offline element. The migration context of these instances additionally shows their emotional attachment to the place of Nigeria in terms of longing. The processes of proving this importantly bring out the identity of the "public advocate".

Web activists' online development of the self is one instance of many Internet possibilities. They represent virtual vistas of liberty. The vista enables the pursuance of the participants' desire for rights. The rights may however become a license for overacting via, for instance, indecent use of language. It may be positive via conscientious contributions. In any case, the fact of self-actualisation with little hindrance is central. Overall, the new vista suggests a latest scenery for self-expression and representation. The continuous identification of the wrongs of Nigeria could lead to a critical participant through this vista. Helped by the opportunity of interacting with a wider range of people in the hostland, the participant may rightly point at areas of change. It then increases the usefulness of the Internet as a platform for this course. This is because the liberty inherent within the network allows for limitless experimentations. It is through these shades of experimenting ideas that those engaged with it unburden themselves. Fulfilments emerge, which again confirm the permissive character of the network. A continuation of an engagement with the Internet develops the consciousness of participants towards the *homeland*, the world at large, just as it helps with the discovery of online spaces. The interrelationships construct and reconstruct identities, resulting to transformations. However, not all these result from a simple administration or ownership of websites. Neither is it limited to a few forms of online roles. There are those who do not have a website for instance, but feature regularly in many. They dissect the Nigerian situation with an emotional zeal, through well thought out pieces[51].

The identity of the "purist" also comes out, when participants show little or no patience for imperfections. It is possible that seeming drive for perfections in hostland, through their ability to make things work leads to this posture. They are consequently incapable of taking excuses for observed lapses, neither are they able to understand why Nigeria cannot do things properly. Many participants see issues from the ideal perspective, and are easily angered by fellow migrants, sympathetic to Nigeria's troubles. This writer, Oduyela for instance, notes:

> Journalism in Nigeria has shifted from mirroring society to protecting rogues in power. It has moved from its position as the watchdog to collaborator in the killing of a nation through mis-information and covering-up for dishonest public office holders. It is no more news that editors and publishers call Ministers, Governors to inform them of stories about them and the possibility of killing it. **Accessed** at www.nigeriavillagesquare.com **on 09/11/2006**

A fellow migrant, Uche Nworah, thought the above submission amounts to a generalisation. He writes a rejoinder:

> Why do I think that this is the season of professional bashing, or better still media bashing even from members and non-members of the media constituency. Have things really degenerated to such alarming proportions to warrant the sweeping comments of concerned observers, most especially Seyi Oduyela in his media-bashing article? **Accessed at www.nigeriavillagesquare.com on 18/11/2006.**

For impatience with moderation, Nworah was himself not spared. Another commentator argues as shown below that he was doing something ominous. He points at alleged deceptions that have been obstacles to Nigeria's growth as being evident:

---

[51] Some notable writers like Okey Ndibe, and Seyi Oduyela post articles at different times, on different topics, in websites like www.nigeriaworld.com, www.nigeriavillagesquare.com, www.nanka.com, and www.ngrguardiannews.com, which amounts to using the license of freedom offered by the Internet to reach a wide audience.

This is a well-written thrash! I am simply tired of this constant resort to philosophers and clichés to justify the rot in our society-Nigeria. Maybe you too are trying to prepare our minds for your next misadventure (as a press secretary or corporate affairs manager somewhere) good luck! We are confronted with a media that is going down the drain, yet they stand on the back of our people to make their name and wealth, you are simply saying just accept them-good or bad! A shameful article. **Accessed at** www.nigeriavillagesquare.com **on 30/08/2005**

Puritanical postures may flow from discussions in the distant. The distance prevents the appreciation of realities on the ground, which Nworah minimally sympathises with, but which other commentators do not like. Some of the migrants, as in Nesbitt's (2002:72) criticism, become "conduits of Eurocentric thought for African consumption through the adaptation of the latest trend in European American perspectives to 'explain' the African experience". But, it would rather be definitive to take a position on which group is right or wrong, but what is clear from some viewpoints like those above is that many are finicky about Nigerian issues.

Related to the above is that the migrants can be more critical about Nigeria than even non-Nigerians can. The poor state of the country, which is causing emigration, often leads to controversial perceptions of migrants by some hostland people. They are perceived as dishonest, with a potential to commit crime. The grounds for this position towards some migrants may be justified, but the vast majority are responsible individuals. This responsible lot nevertheless carry on with the burden to establish themselves as trusted individuals, different from the deviant group. Because of the burden, many blame Nigerian leaders for not creating the enabling environment for a positive international image. The Internet as a space of expression is not limited to Nigerians alone. Every interested person across nations is a potential consumer of the condemning discussions. This actually angers some participants. Olawole, contributing in www.nigerian sinamerica.com senses an exaggeration of the negative as against the positive about Nigeria. He argues that participants write as if they were outsiders, without any real or imagined stake in the origin. The process shows the flexibility of identities as it either pinpoints participants as constructive or acerbic critics. He alludes to these puritanical postures as follows:

Nigerian Internet columnists are falling over themselves to outshine biased commentators in Western media in casting aspersions on Nigeria. Any interested foreigner can log on to this website to read about a country that is described as being comparable only to hell and a people whose president is described as a bastard, a moron and a crazy man fit only for a mental hospital-all in the name of criticism. **Accessed at www.nigeriansinamerica.com on 11/13/2003**

Many of these participants also identify themselves as middle-class. The harsh economic realities at origin make it difficult for this class to be identified. The reality arguably produces the very rich and the very poor, with no group in between. Migration helps the re-discovery of the alienated middle-class, following their possibly new ability to act as elites, partly through an engagement with a modern technology like the Internet. It is also through a subdued glee in being identified as professionals, enlightened enough to proffer solutions to the travails of the origin. The comment below highlights this observation:

If the world is not going to swallow our story, why not woo our own people in the diaspora, a vibrant middle-class, making waves in nearly every area of human endeavour and in countries that gave them a break. A lot of them are intellectuals who ran away mostly because some of our leaders regarded their brains as sawdust. Some ran away because the government in power chased them. For others, the enabling circumstance for productivity was just not there. The thinking in government today is that the thinking and orientation of the brethren in the diaspora is the thinking of the white man with whom they rub shoulders daily. **Oghene Bob, accessed www.nigeriansinamerica. com on 10/31/2006**

The above excerpt is a narrative of how some migrants believe the *homeland* people perceive them. It can be illusory, but it points at a historical trend. This trend is one of admiration for migration to the West. The migrant is correctly or incorrectly urbane, cultured or civilised in the mould in which many regard the white host. Some settlers behave similar to what Fanon (1967) called the "artificial white man", in a bid to feign superiority. To some thinkers however, the description is justified, as they are "white black people", because colonialism "led them to be far too willing to please, mimic and uncritically adopt practices of 'white people'" (Clarke, 2004:14). In some other cases of exposures, the migrant gains an edge in competition with the *homeland* peers. The middle class, which is absent in Nigeria subsequently beckons because of cosmopolitanism through migration. Many migrants are truly confident of this new status, especially when they engage in skilled work in the hostland. It confers a great deal of confidence both in the hostland and in the *homeland*, which erases the thoughts of degrading themselves by doing unsuitable jobs as the participant immediately below attests:

The percentage of Nigerians living below the middle class level in Western countries is achingly miniscule. Nigerians remain the most educated ethnic group in America, much sought after and well compensated by employers because of their focus and dedication to work. **Osofisan, USA, accessed in www.nigeriansinamerica.com on 12/4/2000**

Besides, they enjoy greater comfort in Western institutions, which often function better. Many become used to it, frequently leading to "western struckness" (Naficy, 1999), which ultimately make returning difficult. Living in the west amounts to a departure from the state of origin where only the rich and government officials can meet the basic needs of life, whether legitimately or otherwise. This does not mean that all migrants were poor before migration. A small percentage of migrants were not. This set probably relocated for other reasons other than economic[52]. However, a majority of are from the lower economic group. Some of this majority frequently talk about their new advantages. The testimony of the participant below is an attestation:

> Nothing the rich in Nigeria has that I cannot afford. Credit facilities are there for me, if I cannot afford the cash. The way I live here is miles better than what it was at home. As a university teacher, I could not maintain a car; neither could I send my children to good schools. My doctorate degree should have entitled me to an above average, or middle class life, if not the life of a rich man. However, not in Nigeria, where the middle class has been wiped off...you are either rich or poor. Rather ironically, I found my feet after migration to the West. I was first in the US before I moved to the UK and I have God, to thank for His mercies, which has transformed my life and that of my family. **Balogun, Male, 38, Leeds. Interview date: 20/04/2006.**

Being free, the Internet enables a proliferation of post migration pundits. These self-acclaimed experts and analysts proclaim superior opinion on Nigerian matters. Saying they are right or wrong in this regard is perhaps improper. They find the act a useful one, through projecting themselves creditably or otherwise, as people with authoritative views about the origin. They project themselves because a lot have one or two ideas on what the problems with the *homeland* are. Countless also claim to have solutions. All participants carry on with a self-righteous fury, which when added to the purist identity, produces the character of "distant redeemers". The ideas may or may not be realistic as they are from the experiences of the different hostland cultures, but they carry on sounding off, satisfied that they are representation of solutions to Nigeria's problems. Nworah notes this, in a piece entitled, "Fear and loathing on the Internet:

---

[52] Some of these reasons already identified in Chapters one and two are need to invest in the more stable Western societies, and escape from military repression. Many are as well escaping from the shock of being victims of crime, or from allegations of bewitchment. A lot also try to avoid family troubles, especially those from polygamous background. Yet, some like to stay away from over commitments that happen where there is an excessive dependence on them for financial assistance, by friends and family members. A few are also fleeing from prosecution after allegations of crimes have been made, or when they are soon to be made.

We thrive on the Internet. Welcome to the 21st century baby, your worst nightmare if you are a Nigerian politician. Nigerians all over the world now have a new and favourite pass time-punditry. **Accessed at www.nigeriansinamerica.com on 06/30/2006.**

These pundits are unpaid. However, a few who manage popular websites welcome advertisements where earnings may come. The majority contribute for the sake of satisfying a passion to discuss. On the other hand, it could be to show that they like joining issues. Internet seems easiest to express these views and hence their punditry identity.

In addition, migrants like to use peculiar expressions. The words appear in the naming of websites, newsgroups and in conversations. The uniqueness of some of these words could confuse the uninitiated. Using the words helps socialisation of the stranger, the stimulation of interaction, and perhaps, the continuation of their "Nigerian" identity through language. The *homeland* location becomes a shared interest, when they use their languages, as a heritage, and as a variant of culture. Some of these words are *Baba Iyabo*, (Iyabo's father), which refers to the former president, because the first daughter's name is Iyabo, and *Carry go,* which is Pidgin English[53] synonym for go-ahead. Yet again is *settlement*, usually used for bribing, and *ajebutter*, which they use to describe those born into comfort. Naija-politics@yahoogroups.com is named after the *Naija* representation of Nigeria, as seen in the first half of the username.

Migrants are equally concerned with their original culture, either as imagined or practiced. Many wish that their offspring were able to imbibe it, instead of a wholesale adoption of the Western culture, which to them is not good for their future. They believe that total Westernisation is a downside to migration, and could be a problem for identification. This bothers a contributor, Simi Abohwo who thinks migrants are worried about the future of their children abroad. He offers some solutions:

I am a 38-year-old Nigerian living in the UK and bringing up two sons (aged 10 and 7). My sons were both born in the UK and one of the issues that I have to deal with is whether my children will grow up being able to identify with Nigeria and its culture. In other words, will they see themselves as Nigerian first and British second? Will they appreciate Nigerian/African values? Alternatively, will they, sadly, become culturally and morally "lost" to Nigeria? **Accessed at www.nigeriansinamerica.com on 10/06/2005**

---

[53] Pidgin English is a corruption of the English language that is common to some people along the West coast of Africa.

To make the children know Nigeria as an ancestral origin therefore, the writer recommends a few things including annual visits to Nigeria and reading literature on Nigeria and Africa. He also proposes the reading of African and Nigerian born authors. Other suggestions are the practising of common Nigerian courtesies, and ensuring that they have some traditional Nigerian dress. In addition, playing Nigerian music like *juju, Fuji, afro-beat, high-life,* and Nigerian *hip-hop* in their residences; eating Nigerian dishes; and the need to send children back to the *homeland* for a few years in secondary school are important. In contrast to this, some parents prefer to have "Westernised" children. This mother states:

> My children, ages 5 and 3, were not born here. I brought them from Nigeria. They are not going back until their accent change. They have to speak like *Oyibo* (a Nigerian parlance for the whites). That is my aim. It puts them in a class. I met a woman, a Nigerian born, with the Nigerian nametag, Dupe, in a supermarket. I was happy seeing somebody like that in that big shop. Her accent was British. She told me her parents were Nigerians, but she has never being there. She dismissed Nigeria…that is how I want my children to grow! **Tinuke, Female, 39, London. Interview date: 22/07/2006**

In growing up like that, many of the migrants' also lose a connection with some cultural trait they previously shared. Their accents are affected, just as their manners could become artificial. In some cases, they have not wholly imbibed their hosts' ways, just as they are not properly in touch with the ancestral the *homeland*. They seem misplaced in terms of identity. A message to an e-mail list describes this sort of migrant:

> They speak with a strong Nigerian accent but mess the whole language up by *slanging.* They sound like a Canadian born Chinese living in Germany and studying French. **Forwarded from haliluhamma@yahoo.com to witswords@yahoo.co.uk on 01/04/2008.**

Children's issues, which Abohwo refers to, are a reminder of their circumstance in the hostland. More often, they play a role in the parental or family decisions on migration. Because of dislocation, offspring regularly have problems of rootedness in cultures. Questions are asked about which culture should be imbibed and how? Is it that of the *homeland* or the culture of the hostland? Can they imbibe the *homelands'* when they inhabit hostland? Moreover, if it is the hostlands', what becomes of ancestral roots? Disorganisation invariably occurs in offline family life, as "scattered living". This implies where the husband is apart from the wife and children, or the wife is apart from the husband and children. The three could also be apart, and in the worst-case scenario, everyone is apart, including sibling from sibling. Reunion may occur online, particularly when love is still alive. It may be when maturity comes, or when they are Internet users. Physical bonding, and socialisation may be absent, but virtual union rouses recollections. Sometimes however, it leads to identity problems for the distant person[54], probably translating into transnational or societal crisis in the longer run. The next section will give a further empirical insight into the reshaping of the self through virtual engagements.

VOICES OF VICTORY IN AN ONLINE VILLAGE SQUARE AT WWW.NIGERIAVILLAGESQURE.COM: IDENTITY (RE) CONSTRUCTION AT WORK

This website is an example of migrants' exchanging ideas. With the catchphrase "the market place of ideas", the forum seeks to virtually represent the traditional African village setting where consultations go on in designated venues (the square), while the King or traditional head presides. Conclusions at such places are binding on villagers. In the web version, the moderator represents the king. His assumption of the role of the King is self-promoting, representing again, some form of redefinition. In the virtual version of the village square, as in the www.nigeriavillagesquare.com, there is a main place, which is the "The Square", where discussions go on. The moderator (king) says it is where "you will find a rich interchange of ideas, stimulating discussions, and intellectual debates about our country and the world at large". Moreover, in this main square, there are sections including those on business, literature, health, the information age, entertainment, careers, jokes and stories. The sections in the main square represent divisions in traditional village affairs. Titleholders, who report to the King, head those sections in real village settings. In this virtual imitation however, only the King (moderator) takes charge of everything. While the virtual world enables a remoulding of his identity, it might as well have made him a person with multiple talents, much more competent than the native traditional village head that he sought to virtually represent.

On www.nigeriavillagesquare.com, regular visitors are "villagers". Many contributors use pseudonyms. The hidden identity is at times a license for fearless and sometimes careless contributions. The contributions underneath were made around November 2006, specifically from the seventh, shortly after the story of a presidential aide, Andy Uba who allegedly smuggled dollars into the US, broke. This contributor, Big K, who says, "Threatening court case against websites (as threatened by those exposed) is an unwise move", is mindful of the relative lack of litigation against web postings. He assumes that issues on the Internet do not deserve any challenge, as it is a different space. He adduces no reason for this, other than a desire to enjoy a new freedom. Litigations should therefore not affect this freedom, as is possible with mainstream physical media. He desires an

---

[54] This is because mutual support in real life is likely to be more effective than simulation.

insulation of the virtual space from legal challenges, even without reason. The participant celebrates virtual journalism, concluding that its overall objective is for the benefit of the "ordinary" people:

> This is saharareports.com moment of glory and I am happy to identify with their very effective style of journalism. At least, it is yielding great results. Finally, the emperor is getting the message of ordinary Nigerians. *Hasta la Victoria Sempre* to www.saharareporters.com . **Labaran, accessed at** www.nigeriavillagesquare.com **on 08/11/2006**

The exclusive reporting of fresh stories online excites Labaran. He sees it as a good development, as it was hitherto difficult in offline media. The Internet to Labaran is rightly or wrongly a space for the powerless. While it is true to the extent that accessibility is cheaper, and can reach many, it is wrong when its possible relevance to the powerful, is also in consideration. In between the possibilities is a satisfaction from sourcing information as implicit in the statement of Labaran. It also reflects the identity of a knowledgeable person arising from the power of information. That characterisation is further evident in the comments of the next speaker, who is not only glad at the activity of the site but thinks the case could have been different if the owners were in Nigeria:

> Great thanks for doing your generation proud. I see if you were in Nigeria, you will possibly be before some high court judge answering to "sedition" charges for embarrassing the president of Nigeria. **Mamaput, accessed at** www.nigeriavillagesquare.com **on 08/11/2006**

The thinking is that were it a physical Nigeria based medium, state apparatus may sanction the web reporters. Because the Internet space is complex and convergent, besides the fact of distance, locating the reporters for a local sanction is difficult. The nearly indeterminate extent of the Internet again comes to the fore. This extent protects online agents, just as it leaves further allowances for the display of virtual potentials. The next person further notes how ridiculous a challenge of Internet freedom can be. This freedom releases the users' capacities with little or no hindrance. It broadens the scope for the construction and the reconstruction of their identities, through exposing previously hidden abilities:

> I do not think that *Baba Iyabo* (the president) is that stupid to think he can stifle the freedom of speech, personal expression and opinions of people that are not in his country, let alone on the Internet. **Abamieda Wanderer, accessed at** www.nigeriavillagesquare.com **on 09/11/2006**

Another participant shows the meaning from varieties of virtual media. The contributor notes the popularity of other media as a basis for the better appreciation of patterns of activities. The Internet alternative therefore represents a variation, which broadens its scope. Any attempt at preventing the new and expanding form amounts to stopping options:

Finally, notice of the fact that the stories on the www now make a lot of difference to how people view his style of government and lifestyle (is taken). **Anonymous, accessed at** www.nigeriavillagesquare.com **on 09/11/2006.**

The participants are nevertheless aware of the possibilities of disrupting the flows of the web as the next discussant indicates. Delighted at the newsbreak, he fears the possibility of an attack on the website through "virus, worm, and Trojan Horse invasion":

Thank God! Now, we know, they are allergic to the seamlessness of cyberspace, which is quite intimidating to them to control, as they usually would have done, without qualms…employ professional web hackers and IT consultants to attack (via a cocktail of virus, worm, and Trojan Horse invasion), and ultimately , demobilise and bring down the saharareporters.com website. **Abraxas, accessed at** www.nigeriavillage square.com **on 09/11/2006**

These are some of the illegitimate means of limiting information flow on the Internet. A handy weapon in the hands of "hackers" and "phishers", the methods are virtual synonyms for arrests, detentions, suits, and outright closure of media houses in Nigeria. These could occur when authorities become intolerant of the critical offline media. While evidence of online reproduction of this is yet scanty, there are possibilities that it can happen. The celebrated website www.saharareports.com suspects this when it sent e-mails to subscribers to the effect that their site is down. Excerpts:

Our dear websites: www.saharareporters.com has been shut down. Since we published the story linking President Obasanjo to the Any Uba money laundering fraud, he has used every means available to get back at us. Our web hosting company complained to us that our website was 'abusing their server and using their CPU at 100%' and as such had to shut down SAHARA REPORTERS because it was rendering other sites on their server 'inoperable'. Again, these technical jargons show a conspiracy to put our site out of existence. However, this will not happen, as such we will be working round the clock to resume our activities online ASAP. **Email read on 14/11/2006 at witsword@yahoo.co.uk**. (*Emphasis in original*)

They probably succeeded as they returned two weeks later, before going offline again. The site returned shortly afterwards though. Whether or not the allegation is true, it reveals that disruptions can take place in virtual space. It shows that processes of identity moulding, and re-moulding can be fluid and unpredictable. Importantly, while the commentators may not be able to prevent some offline development, their new freedom to know may remain. The euphoria of freedom is also empowering through information. It transforms into power, even if emotionally. The resulting awareness that is on the rise refreshes the migrant, particularly via the development of a new identity of a distant purifier. This logic of freedom is important to them, as it relieves them from the problematic image of country and continent in the hostland.

As the freedom of virtual life brings shades of creativity, transformation could take place when it leads to a reassurance of worth when offline. Online activity minimises possible inactivity in hostland. The confidence derivable from the individuality of virtual life can credibly go onto life offline and then a high sense of importance, which again leads to a productive identity. This participant confirms the standpoint through sarcastic writing:

> We are constantly (writing) essays, opinions and commentaries. Nobody pays us: we are just a bunch of boomers suffering from midlife crises, tired of our miserable good lives in the West and advocating for best practices. **Nworah, accessed at www.nigeriasinamerica.com on 30/06/2006**

CONCLUSION

The Nigerian diaspora members re-conceive the Nigerian identity, not only individually, but also through communal life. The reconstruction is filtered through experiences that relate to identifiers like gender, education and class. The shaping and the re-shaping of the self evolve in a temporal and spatial context, essentially through the mediative possibilities of the Internet. The network helps the migrants to rediscover who they are, and who they can be. Though physically away from their origin, the *homeland* is re-imagined via cyber activities that cut across the reading of Nigerian newspapers online; Nigerian-related news sites; sending and receiving e-mails to loved ones with access in the *homeland*; and networking with fellow migrants. The online mediation of affairs with Nigeria may re-create logic of alliance, absent through the dominance of the "others" in the hostland. Participants therefore find a place in the virtual space, for the invention of a union with the source country. The invention is continual, while distance reduces upon connection.

The practice of engaging with the Internet remoulds identities at different levels, including individual, social, and religious. It also includes gender, education, class, marital and professional status. Though the phases could conflict, shaping occurs when they mediate affairs with the origin, with the hostland and with fellow migrants. The relationship evolves through "sameness and difference" (Gilroy, 1997:302), and then helps the location of a balance within.

Apart from playing a role in constructing identities, the Internet provides migrants with more space for claiming rights, and a greater right to place (Georgiou, 2002:4), in everyday life, where activity transpires even in passivity (Silverstone, 2001:13). The new technology additionally influences the visualisation of origin; interactions and cross-cultural exchanges; and the alteration of identities (Gillespie, 1995:7; Appadurai, 1996). The changing identities reflect online via their viewpoints on their *homeland* and on their host community emphasising the fluctuation in the context of globalisation.

CHAPTER EIGHT:

CONCLUSIONS

This research investigates the connection abilities of the Internet with a focus on the case of the Nigerian diaspora. It examines the Internet's capabilities and potentials for long distance communication within the context of international communications and the complementary roles of preceding media, which includes the press, telephone, television, and word of mouth. The Internet is in focus because it possesses a great ability to reach many, simultaneously across different spaces, with less cost, while giving users the chance to be both producers and consumers of media messages. These advantages make it more appealing for mediation, particularly in the case of migrants and diasporas usually affected by deterritorialisation, forced mobility and resettlement. For the Nigerian diaspora, regular online connections are widespread, even though the country of origin does not always enjoy the same level of connectivity. In connecting, the network becomes an attractive option for crossing physical distance and reaching some people in the *homeland*, including family, friends, with consequences for the sense of longing and belonging. Investigating the migrants helps in the interpretation of some intersecting subjects around communication, like nationalism, transnationalism, and identity, through an examination of how the migrants' activities aid the analysis of the issues. I shall now proceed to explain the implications of the research for issues and themes that featured in its course. These issues are the Nigerian diaspora case; the possibilities and limitations of the Internet; transnationalism; nationalism; and identity. The section will then analyse the implications of the research for policy, alongside suggestions for future research, before noting its limitations.

DECONSTRUCTING THE AFRICAN DIASPORA: THE NEW CASE OF THE NIGERIAN

This research shifts emphasis from previous overriding references to the African diaspora by examining the important case of the Nigerian diaspora. It argues that the Nigerian case deserves a detailed, independent examination (even through the realm of communication), because of its huge domestic and migrant population. The migrant population are especially growing, and are becoming more visible in many destination countries, particularly because of their presence in many hostlands' labour force (Stalker, 2001). Besides, many of the migrants have spent several years in these destinations, in what could qualify them as a diaspora given the sometimes flexible, but often contested use of the word. The Nigerian case is also important because of the absence of literature on its dispersing peoples. Analyses of Nigerian migrants are seen as part of the larger African migrant and diaspora. The present research deconstructs the analyses by looking at the specific case of a remarkable country, therefore, making it a reference point for the understanding of migration and the gradual emergence of a diaspora in a particular African country. While the Internet is relatively new, the Nigerian diaspora case is also a relatively new phenomenon. On this note, the paths of the subject matters meet, which explain the choices. Additionally, the investigation of the Nigerian case in this work is not only another case study, but also one that reminds us of the need to evaluate a medium of communication, not essentially from limited geographically specific cases, but to many others outside the dominant Western nation framework.

The research does not only add the case of Nigerian migrants to the literature on migrants and Internet use, but distinctly contributes to the global understanding of social and economic crises and how they relate to mediated representation and identity. It then goes beyond a Nigerian representation of studies like Miller and Slater (2000) on the Internet and the Trinidadian diaspora; Myria Georgiou's work (2000) on technologies of communication and the Greek Cypriot community in London; Ien Ang's work (2001) on the Chinese diaspora; Schulz and Hammer's study (2003) on the Palestinian diaspora and Kadend-Kaiser's (2007) work on the Haitian diaspora, as it is situated between a historical and present day experience. This is because despite the similarity to the above works, the Nigeria case is unique because its diaspora is not only new in the sense of its recent emergence, but it is different from the old black diaspora, dispersed through enslavement. The present sets are voluntary, even though their forebears were enslaved. Therefore, the research identifies the Nigerian diaspora, out of the old black and African diaspora in a "tertiary…and the circulatory stage (of movement, which) involves movements among the several areas abroad and may include Africa", as described by Harris (1993: 8-9, cited in Akyeampong, 2000: 187).

Deconstructing the African diaspora through the Nigerian case is significant because they carry a special character, in addition to the constant challenge of integration amongst migrant communities. The bases for this challenge are on two grounds. First, there is the racial discourse, where as blacks, they contend with the vagaries of their troubled history and the need to negotiate existence away from evolving perceptions of the downtrodden. The ground may again stem from their witness to slavery, colonialism and post-colonialism. These occurrences produce binaries involving a powerful and a powerless; a "master" and a "servant"; and the "weak" and the "strong", which did not only stunt the physical growth of the "weak", but perhaps inbuilt a dependency complex. The complex partly leads to Westward movements, with dogged zeal. Though there are few cases of successes in migration, many seem to be mere satisfaction with the admiration of 'images of wealth' (Seabrook, 2003) in the West, or simply staying because returning without fulfilling economic objective could be shameful (Parnwell, 1993:124).

Second, there is the modern day true or erroneous perception of the Nigerian as a representative of dubiousness. As I wrote this conclusion, two Nigerians were sentenced to jail in London for financial crime involving the use of the identity of some frontline soldiers' cheques to collect money totalling £120,000 over a period of years (*Metro* Newspaper, of 02/07/2007). That kind of story may not be peculiar to Nigerians, but it is nevertheless common with them. Just as it represents a bad case, those of good conducts are not absent. The case of Chimamanda Ngozi Adichie awarded the 2007 Orange Broadband Prize for Fiction for the novel, *Half of a Yellow Sun*, is one instance of the good. While their ongoing interest in dislocation and relocation seem unconcerned about the negative representations that come as challenges, the dawning of difference in migrancy prompts and maintains migrants' imaginations. The interplay of the subjects partly finds a template in modern media predominantly the Internet, which is the focus of this research. Online life for the Nigerian migrants therefore, is a new way to suspend offline stereotypes. This is because vagaries of offline life as participants confirm, eases off online. It represents a late modernity's way of adaptation and re-adaptation. Some stability therefore comes via virtual reconstruction of identity; the possible exposure of nationalism; and the abating of longing through the sustenance of some contacts online.

Moreover, though Nigerians are associated with the loneliness and trials of migration, an unusual drive to beat the odds is propelling for participants. Many still cherish origin, especially with the possible presence of families and friends therein. The discouraging state of Nigeria combines with the regular nudge of loved ones behind to continue the struggle in migration, enable the drive to beat odds. This compelling situation brings in a sense of urgency. The urgency is one for professional or financial success, as a forerunner of sustenance and remittance. The objectives become strong enough to ward off the crisis of dislocation. The presence of the media, with the Internet playing a key role is helpful, as it supplies information, both on the country of origin and on the country of settlement. The sense of freedom in life online also sometimes reduces challenges of life offline to nothing, through the provision of a sense of an alternative existence. Migrant online activity eventually leads to the shaping of characters, at the political, social and economic sphere, with the development of confident public personae, restructured gendered roles, multi-positional everyday existence, that can simultaneously be here, there and possibly in a never-ending in between: an irreversible transnational condition. I shall give further details of issues revealed in the research in the section that follows.

POSSIBILITIES, LIMITATIONS OF A MULTI-SIDED NETWORK

This research identifies the role of the Internet as helping a simultaneous and constant connection, exchange of information, participation in public spheres, national and transnational belonging amongst peoples, particularly those at the margin of development. It is a new forum for engagements that are helpful for a recollection of the past amongst migrants and diasporas (the subject of this work), and for limitless interactions amongst many stable communities. However, the study indicates that the

Internet is still not a routine medium like the telephone or television. It remains what I regard as a *detached* network. This is because of the "distance" that exists between a bid to use it and the negotiation of convenience for its use. Though cheap, timeless and borderless, it requires a settled position most times to go online. Some level of concentration is necessary for its use. Utilisation of the mobile phone as a variant of the telephone can be on the go, sometimes with the cost reduction advantage of numerous international call cards, but the Internet may not. Even if surfing is to take place on the mobile, in line with advancements in Internet technologies, it needs more concentration than the simple, regular act of mobile phone calls and conversations. This limitation therefore reduces the credentials of the Internet as an instantaneous communication network between migrants, their *homeland* and with hostland. The observation thus affects celebrations of the Internet as a liberating, overarching and democratic technology. Even so, it is still very relevant in a number of other ways. In the case of the Nigerian diaspora, it helps in being updated about events in the *homeland*, through the reading of online editions of the *homeland* newspapers, and through a patronage of news inclined websites, usually managed by fellow members of the diaspora. The network is useful for networking amongst fellow diasporas, and for connecting with hostland, through information sourcing and exchange. Its relevance for one-on-one communication with many people in Nigeria is still hampered by low connectivity in Nigeria, which is why other media, like the telephone leads in this regard.

In basic terms, the Internet is a tool and a social space of interaction in the sphere of communication, which is core in this investigation. It enables the sending and receiving of e-mails, e-mail attachments, between some migrants and a marginal e-literate people in Nigeria, with access to the network. It importantly helps them to be abreast of developments in Nigeria, and in networking on possible ways of assisting the *homeland*. The last case is common amongst the professionals. There are also the benefits of distributing information to mailing lists amongst migrants, with those in Nigeria and even with the host community. In making online contributions, the migrants deliberate on the problems of origin. The thoughts are possibly realistic, or unrealistic, given distance and the position of the migrant, but the fact of an imaginary or real participation in the evolutionary process of origin manifests in the process. Online mediation may also contribute to resolving the likely crisis of belonging, sometimes shortly, and other times for a longer time, through a soothing interaction with fellow travellers. Remembrances and recollections of the *homeland* come through contacts, networking and the consumption and appropriation of online resources. The commonness of an addiction to the Internet manifests through the exposure of those who make it a regular affair, everyday and through long commitment. As some migrants become addicted, so are other kinds of users (particularly women), who sometimes surf through proxies, usually partners or husbands. Then there are also women who are directly engaged in online activities as a mark of self-fulfilment. There are, as well, irregular surfers involving those who go online, only when the time permits. Some others also note its social networking roles, while others focus on its educational relevance. It is through these divergent functions that intersecting issues like transnationalism emerge. These divergent roles importantly implicate the Internet as a space, which is subject to any individual control and use. I shall now explain the importance of the research for transnational belonging.

THE STIMULATION OF TRANSNATIONAL BELONGING

As a transnational technology, for instance, the Internet enables the thriving of migrants' cross-border activities. This happens when the people simultaneously relate between nation-states, that could be the *homeland* and hostland, or between one hostland and the other. The activities take place through trading, and participation in migrant political activities between countries, with the Internet remaining a tool and space for the expression of the actions. Transnationalism is also expressed via the construction of websites, which particularly target the Nigerian diaspora visitor in different countries and continents, in a bid to seek a likely everyday relationship with them. An example of this is the NIDO website, which seeks a virtual integration of Nigerian migrants across different places. The increasing participation of the members in online advertisement, particularly those targeted at prospective investors in estates (a passion of the Nigerian rich in hostland), is another example. Transnationalism is, as well, culturally expressed through activities like those of the *Oyo-tunji* village in South Carolina, which seeks an imaginary link with an historic peer in the *homeland*-the Yoruba's of Nigeria. This community, which worships *Orisha* (like some members of the parent Yoruba community in Nigeria), uses the Internet as one place of expression apart from promoting a transnational imagined community with their Nigerian counterparts. With these activities, the migrants eventually make the Internet space an everyday media for the crossing of distant physical spaces, while being involved in a simultaneous real time relationship with peers, with the *homeland*, and many times, between hostlands. The commonplace state of these activities also enables them to lay claim to the membership of a transnational imagined community, despite a relative unequal participation in the circumstance. Overall, the Internet sets them on platform greater than preceding communication technologies like the television and the telephone. While the television visually represents them, with an additional bit of audio effect, interaction is minimal if not absent. Radio representation is essentially auditory and one-way. In both situations, their inputs are nominal, if at all present. The Internet however combines all the abilities of the television and the radio to enhance the migrants' transnational agency. Through online activities, they display their cross-cultural links, their interest in the sharing and the expression of this, while also exhibiting potentials within the context of nations. The Internet space subsequently bridges living between places. Other than this is the implication of the research for nationalism.

AMBIGUITIES IN THE INTERPRETATION OF NATIONALISM

Perspectives for the interpretation of nationalism keep expanding in an age of innovations in media and communications' technologies. This has to do, first with the ambiguities in the definition of the term and the exposure of new trends through the technologies that further opens up new spaces for the interpretation of the term. As communication technologies mediate relationships of absent nationals, they (the technologies) enable the revelation of the deep recesses of interacting parties in freer conditions, through expressing opinions and ideas, about the *homeland*, their experiences in migration and about hostland. This activity sustains a sense of worth and association that continuously defines a group, and possibly, in part, the departed nation. In the process, nationalism may be revealed, as the migrants positively or negatively visualise the departed distant origin. In a sense, the network becomes an alternative place to negotiate association from afar. Association is fostered because a likely crisis of distance, and a presence in the midst of others, reduces the chance for a physical show of associations. They may experience companionship at migrant gatherings, but the sense of the minority, which may occur in hostland, is likely restrictive. The restriction reduces online when the people meet in chat rooms, on listservs, on websites and on mailing lists that are common to them, to remember the origin left behind. This shapes nationalism, given evidences of concerns for the well-being of the country of origin (Cohen, 1997). In another sense, it is criticisms and anger for origin, which sometimes become deep seated, resulting in statements like the anonymous speaker on page 167, who describes Nigeria "as being like having a witch for a mother", and "whatever you do in the end, she will give you up as a contribution for her mates esoteric meal". Critical as the statement is, it yet shows a sense of a relationship with an origin, which the contradictory conceptualisation of nationalism sometimes implies. Yet another side to the ambiguity comes when propositions on projects that could be helpful to the *homeland* government officials materialise, like in the case of Nigerian professionals in Germany, seeking ideas on the *homeland* projects. (See page 185). To the migrants, the Internet is a place to extend an attachment to places-the *homeland*, hostland, and in between locations. The present place (the hostland) is fragile for them (Dayan, 1999), sometimes contested and needs negotiation for the attainment of some degree of permanence. The past place (origin) exists as an optional place to relate. Discarding it may not come about because of a possible continuing intricacy of living as an outsider in hostland. Therefore, there is a conscious or unconscious pressure to reminisce. The Internet presents an opportunity for this. Evident in the circumstance, is a multiple sense of place. Nevertheless, the sense made out of the *homeland*, through mediation, which may though be evolutionary, reflects some form of rootedness in a nation, and nation-state, (even if departed) and the seeming highlighting of nationalism. Equally important is the question of identity, which comes next.

THE CONSTRUCTION, (RE) CONSTRUCTION OF IDENTITIES, AND/OR ONLINE IDENTITIES

The Internet is also a mediation space for Nigerian migrants to construct their identities. Acting in the main through narratives in blogs, webpages, newsgroups, and networking locations, the migrants define their personae through philosophical or descriptive accounts of the self, by feeling free to tell personal or group stories, sharing ideas on issues of concern, and deliberately identifying themselves with some Internet roles. Such roles include webmasters, moderators, and list owners. In being identified with these roles, many also appear puritanical, apart from being interested in joining issues at the slightest nudge. The image of the knowledgeable person may as well emerge, because of a readiness to sound off on any the *homeland* issue. The self consequently becomes a bastion of potentials, whether real or imaginary. All these are possible because the Internet space allows for creativity. An ability to use the Internet with little let or hindrance, probably helps to release some burdens. For instance, the possibly shy migrant with limited drive for offline interaction has a space. The "secretive" person needing advice from people other than close friends and family members can disguise and achieve her/his aim. The physically challenged could cross-fertilise ideas with others without attracting wanted or unwanted sympathy, praise or snide comments. While the Internet may conceal locations, participants' contributions in many groups are also independent of their different classes or categories, because job category, age, riches, and other identities are obscured during contributions. Though some difference may emerge in the quality, or design of a diasporic website, this does not diminish the status of the network as a relatively level playing field. The research highlights these facts particularly in the manner in which the web space helps migrants to change the self, within the confines of a stable Western environment as against the anxieties of living in the underdeveloped world of the *homeland.*

The process of online construction of identity is evident in multiple and complex forms through individual or group activity, in a shifting and endless process. The shaping of identities also reveals Internet capacities, because the network experiences further developments via feedbacks from complex uses. The mutual interaction may make the concerned to gain more experience. While the migrant redefines identities online, it also alters the Internet state through a regular manipulation. Sometimes, it could be in the negative sense through criminal perversion of online spaces. The act of redefining identity in the largely liberated network often leads to a continual renewal of the diasporic being. When this combines with becoming (Hall, 1996; Ang, 2001), which in this case implies new experiences and challenges, in addition to the pre-migration person, the migrants append to their sense of value in a dynamic, competitive and contested space (Brah, 1996). As a constructed experience (Hall, ibid.; Gilroy, 1993; Giddens, 1991; Castells, 2000), identity structuring emerges in virtuality, which eventually powers life in migration when it gets offline. For some however, like administrators of less known Nigerian related websites, identities constructed online may simply remain on there (online identities), as it changes nearly nothing in the way they are characterised offline. For the notable ones, they are easily recognised as bloggers and activists, like Sowore and Elendu, in Section 6.3, even while offline. Many Nigerian migrants therefore derive strength from using the Internet. The strength comes from a power to be more expressive, to be conversational and to air their views on Nigerian matters in an environment with fewer controls. The new power, through virtuality, constitutes a new experience that aids remembrances, mitigates nostalgias and longings.

FURTHER QUESTIONS, FUTURE FOCAL POINTS

The Internet's considerable level of freedom leads to its celebration by many of its users and by academics and policy makers. This arises because of its relative low cost, its interactivity, transnational nature, possibilities given for citizens and consumers to turn producers and journalists to become publishers. The fact that use can be individualistic, involving a person and a connected computer reaching places behind a screen (Gibson, 1984), is also a reason why it is qualified as pioneering. Though regulation is minimal, the space can still be a source of high quality views, as different views are available online on an everyday, or even an hourly basis. These can get value through a systematic grouping of the views. Because the views are varied, the process would be engaging. However, can these different views not be systematised into groups, themes, resources, and other forms of classifications? For instance, can migrants' ideas on the *homeland* projects like road construction and maintenance, health care delivery, portable water supply, provision of regular electricity and the building of stable political institutions not be structured for the development requirements of the *homeland*? In addition, if this occurs, can it not be useful for policymaking individuals, agencies, groups, governments, non-governmental organisations, (NGO's), and Nigeria constituent state and federal governments, still concerned about progress? More specifically, this implies that the diverse opinions of the Nigerian diaspora online can be influential to Nigerian groups, agencies and government. This is more likely in light of the people's exposure to other cultures, particularly Western societies. Those exposures constitute new experiences, some of which are possibly valuable for perspectives on the *homeland* policies. Systematising online views may not have had attention, partly because of issues of online credibility. The volume and pace of exchanges may also be discouraging. Nevertheless, it does not wipe out the fact that many views are those of educated or informed migrants who interact with diverse societies and are much more confident on how things work. Just like traditional real life media like television, radio and the printed press set agendas, Internet postings may also do so. This thinking comes from the lessons from concerned migrants as this research reveals. Putting together the views of participants as proposals for policies may seem strange and time consuming, but it stands as an effort in a bid to integrate the views of a wider spectrum of people,(including migrants) in the decision making process. This is also in line with the popular preference of cultures and societies for freedom, increased participation in governance and the people-centric ideals of democracy. The Nigerian state and indeed any likely interested parties can become concerned about modes of harnessing online migrant opinions, as a potentially influential strand of views to the complicated process of administration, organisation and development.

Other than this is the need to further understand the relationship between media and migration. Should the media facilitate or discourage migration, through its analysis and reports, or should it be indifferent to it? If any of the above is to be done, how would it be situated in the process of global changes, where the media helps participants, including migrants and diasporas to cross distant physical spaces, through reports and the production of images? Also important is the need to contextualise these issues within peoples and places, and the reason why experiences would always remain different. For instance, the African migrant, who regards migration as a likely solution to continued existence, is probably different from a migrant from a Western country, who is relocating for adventure or professional reasons. What form of disposition should the media maintain in these circumstances? Is it one of sympathy or condemnation for the African; and praise or disapproval for the Western migrant? The media attempt to necessarily do this would, as well, further help in the continued understanding of the rewards and shortcomings of migration, to different peoples in different places, and at different times.

Also important for more examination is the nexus between nationalism and transnationalism. As earlier noted, the complexities of nationalism keeps growing in present times, and this growth leads to a connection to transnational relationship, through the manner in which participants interpret their activities, within and between nation-states. The processes often challenge degrees of attachments to nation-states, because of the regular, and often irresistible pulls to other nation-states, and an evolving desire to maximise opportunities in diverse places. How should the transnational space, which is fast becoming an alternative space for many, be defined in terms of relevance to the continuing need to understand participants' relationship within the nation-state? Given the stated role of the media in facilitating transnational relationships in present times, what other role can it also play in the interpretation of this emerging link between nationalism and transnationalism? An attempt to do this would, as well, be better through specifics, like particular peoples, their nation-states and their transnational activities.

Besides its speed, the Internet is frequently celebrated for its convergence, which implies its ability to combine the functions of television, telephone, radio, print and post. This capacity may though be unique; it has not however discouraged the independent use of these media, whose functions the Internet has aggregated. Rather, many of these media, like the television are also growing, through the rising influence of satellite broadcasting; and telephone, through the increasing sophistication of mobile telephony. This therefore invites us to continuously examine its significance as a convergent technology. The need for a regular examination is also important because even when its many to many quality is highlighted, the attribute is not exactly unique to it. Other technologies, like television, (especially digital services), and the telephone, (particularly the mobile variation) are also becoming convergent. Would technologies of communication eventually become less individualistic through convergence; or shall we have a "convergence of convergence"? The interpretation of the Internet convergence therefore requires frequent examinations, even as the growth of the technology continues.

Then there is the question of a multicultural society. As people in dispersion, the Nigerian diaspora represent a specific ethnic group in a host society. In a place like Britain, the migrants are players in the construction of a community of multi-cultures, as expressed online, and offline. Against this background, they bear a culture with Nigeria as its foundation. They share this in distant places of settlement. The sharing and understanding of cultures in multicultural settings can be important for cultural and public diplomacy (Taylor, 1997), which the Nigerian groups, states or governments may use as experiences of living with diversity.

There is still the need to investigate further reasons behind a rigid belief in Westward migration. While economic reasons remain central for migration, studies show that many such journeys fail in the realisation of these objectives (Portes, et al, 1996; Stalker, 2001). Many people in Nigeria are aware of these failure stories. They however often do not put off the journey. They would rather want to experience it, even at the risk of falling, in a new location in the West. The circle continues, despite occasional Nigerian governments' campaigns against improper migration, to avoid the travails of some past travellers. However, could the reason for this be simply colonial, post-colonial or the expansion of capitalist consumerism (Portes, et al, 1996), which has created not only economically dependent peoples and societies, but a mentally dependent one as well? Finding a complete answer to the near unbending interest in migration still lingers as a question. It could be because of the international communications' framework of this work. The difficulty in finding a complete answer thus keeps it as an ongoing problem requiring investigation for future researchers, not only in communication but also in the areas of sociology, history, political science, economics and other related subjects. Focusing on a specific question of why migration is seen as synonymous with progress, despite some practical evidence of failures and wasted journeys, would be appropriate. This is just as trying to know why it will be better to "die trying" to reach the West (as the BBC quotes a prospective migrant as saying) instead of seeking to die trying to survive in the *homeland*. The economic motives behind most movements often times shrink in the face of excessive passion for the movement. Many migrants also do not consider returning even in the face of failure to achieve original economic objectives, because remaining in hostland is perhaps sufficient as a status symbol (George accessed at www.eturbonews.com on 01/07/2008). Besides, many documented migrants are relatively contented lots in Nigeria, who can afford to meet basic needs of life relative to their society. Portes (1996) describes this set of ordinarily contented migrants as the consumers of capitalist products. In clearer terms, their ability to afford international flight tickets puts them ahead of hundreds of others in the impoverished state of the *homeland*. Many also sell their properties and other belongings preparatory to relocation. Through these, they again inflame the question of passion and the reason(s) behind it, despite the popular economic reasons for migration.

In doing this research, my methodology includes survey, which helped to put the migrants into categories; participant observation, which was useful for the closer examination of their activities online; and interviews that helped in recording the views of migrants on their experiences. The methods therefore bestrode qualitative and quantitative research methods. While participant observation and interviews represented the qualitative interviews, surveys was quantitative. The study took place in Britain, specifically in London and Leeds. Cost, time and considerations for convenience partly influenced the decision to concentrate on these locations. This was despite the expansive physical bases of online participants. The limitation to the UK was as well in the interest of manageability. In the future, it may even be better to meet the migrants in their diverse locations, other than the chosen but understandable restriction, which the choice of one country could post. Moving across countries for the study could be revealing given the differences in cultures and societies, leading therefore to variations in adaptation styles.

BIBLIOGRAPHY

- Achebe, Chinua. 1983, <u>The Trouble with Nigeria</u>. London: Heinemann.
- Achebe, Chinua. 2003, <u>Home and Exile.</u> Edinburgh: Cannongate.
- Adebanwi, Wale. 2001, "Techno-Politics and the Production of Knowledge: Democratic Activism and the Nigeria Exile", Research Paper of the First Claude Ake fellowships, submitted to the <u>African Institute</u> (AA1), Washington D.C., December 2001.
- Adeniyi, Abiodun. 2006, "Questions on Nigerian diaspora remittances" article published in *The Guardian* Newspapers (of Nigeria) opinion page at www.ngrguardiannews.com on 15/08/2006.
- Adeniyi, Abiodun. 2007, <u>No Tomorrow</u>. Oxford: Trafford Publishing.
- Adeyanju, C. 2004, "Hegemony and Transnational Practices of Nigerian Yorubas in Toronto", accessed at http://www.africanmigration.com/articles/c_adeyanju.htm on 17/03/2004.
- Agger, Ben. 2004, <u>The Virtual Self A Contemporary Sociology</u>. MA, USA: Blackwell Publishing.
- Ahmed, S. 1999, "Home and Away: Narrative of migration and Estrangement", in <u>International Journal of Cultural Studies</u>, Vol. 2, No.3. Pages 329-347.
- Ajibewa, Aderemi and Akinrinade, Sola. 2003, "Globalization, Migration and the New African Diasporas: Towards a framework of understanding". Paper presented at <u>International Workshop on Migration and Poverty in West Africa</u>, March 13-14, 2003, University of Sussex.
- Aksoy, Asu and Robins, Kevin. 2003, "Banal Transnationalism: The difference that Television makes", in Karim H. Karim, 2003, <u>The Media of Diaspora.</u> London: Routledge. Pages 89-104.
- Aksoy, Asu and Robins, Kevin. 2003, "The Enlargement of Meaning: Social Demand in a Transnational Context", in <u>International Communication Gazette</u>, Vol. 65, No. 365. Accessed online on 15/02/2008.
- Akyeampong, Emmanuel. 2000, "Africans in the diaspora: the diaspora and Africa" in <u>African Affairs,</u> Vol. 99. No. 1. Pages 183-215.
- Albrow, Martin. 1998, "Frames and Transformations in Transnational Studies" WPTC-98-02. Paper delivered to the ESRC Transnational Communities Programme Seminar in the Faculty of Anthropology and Geography, University of Oxford, 8th May 1998.
- Alpers, E. 2001, "Defining the African Diaspora". Paper Presented to the Centre for Comparative Social Analysis Workshop, October 25, 2001.

- Alter, Peter. 1989, <u>Nationalism: Second edition</u>. London: Arnold.
- Amin, Samir. 2000, "The Political Economy of the Twentieth Century". Translated by Pascale Ghazaleh. Accessed at http://www.monthlyreview.org/600amin.htm on 20/04/2007.
- Amin, Samir. 2004, "U.S. Imperialism, Europe, and the Middle East". Accessed at http://www.monthlyreview.org/1104amin.htm on 20/04/2007.
- Amin, Samir. 2005, "A Note on the Death of André Gunder Frank (1929-2005)". Accessed at http://www.monthlyreview.org/0405amin.htm on 20/04/2007.
- Anderson, Benedict. 1983, <u>Imagined Communities: Reflections on the origins and spread of Nationalism.</u> London: VERSO.
- Ang, Ien. 2000, "Identity Blues" in Gilroy, Paul. Grossberg, Lawrence. McRobbie, Angela. (eds.) 2000, <u>Without Guarantees in Honour of Stuart Hall</u>. London: Verso. Pages 1-13.
- Ang, Ien. 2001, <u>Living between Asia and the West</u>. London: Routledge.
- Anthias, Floya. 1998, "Evaluating diaspora: Beyond ethnicity", in <u>Sociology</u>, Vol. 32, No. 3. Pages. 495-542.
- Anyanwu, Chika. 2004, "Virtual Africans and New Diasporic Discourse"-IAMCR Porto Alegre, 2004, University of Adelaide, South Australia. Accessed online 26/06/2005.
- Anyanwu, Chika. 2005, "Virtual Citizenship and diasporic discourse" Paper presented at the annual meeting of the <u>Australian and New Zealand Communication Association</u>, Christ Church, New Zealand. Accessed online 26/06/2005.
- Appadurai, Arjun. 1996, <u>Modernity at large: Cultural Dimensions of Globalization</u>. Minneapolis and London: University of Minnesota Press.
- Appadurai, Arjun. 1999, "GLOBAL ETHNOSCAPES: Notes and Queries for a Transnational Anthropology" in Vertovec, S. and Cohen R., (eds.) 1999, <u>Migration, Diaspora and Transnationalism.</u> Cheltenham: Edward Elgar Publishing Limited. Pages 463-483.
- Appiah, Kwame Anthony. 2005, <u>The Ethics of Identity</u>. New Jersey: Princeton University Press.
- Asante, M. K. 2002, ''Afrocentricity and the decline of Western hegemonic thought: A critique of Eurocentric theory and practice'', in Mark Christian, (ed.) 2002, <u>Black Identity in the 20th Century: Expressions of the US and UK African Diaspora</u>. London: Hansib Publications Limited.
- Ashcroft, Bill. Griffiths, Gareth. Tiffin, Helen. (eds.) 1995, <u>The Post-Colonial Studies Reader, 2nd Edition.</u> London and New York: Routledge.

- Azeez, Adesina. 2008, <u>The Representation of Women in Nigerian's Home Video</u>. PhD Thesis, Institute of Communication Studies, University of Leeds. May 2008.
- Azikiwe, Uche. 1996, <u>Women in Nigeria: An Annotated Bibliography</u>. Connecticut: Greenwood Press.
- Barbour, S. Rosaline and Schostak, John. 2005, "Interviewing and Focus Groups" in Bridget, Somekh and Lewin, Cathy, (eds.) 2005, <u>Research Methods in the Social Sciences.</u> London: Sage Publications. Pages 41-48.
- Barker, Chris. 2004, <u>The Sage Dictionary of Cultural Studies</u>. London: Sage Publications Limited.
- Barney, Darin. 2004, <u>The Network Society</u>. Cambridge: Polity press.
- Bastian, L. Misty. 2004, "Nationalism in a Virtual Space: Immigrant Nigerians on the Internet". Accessed at http://www.WestAfricanreview.com/war/vol1.1/bastian.html on 22/03/2004.
- Bauman, M. 2004, "That Word Diaspora", in The Irish Diaspora Studies Scholarly Network, accessed at <u>http://www.irishdiaspora.net/vp01.cfm?</u> <u>Outfit=ids&requesttimeout=500&folder=46&</u> on 01/11/2004.
- Bauman, Zygmunt. 1996, "From Pilgrim to Tourist-or a Short History of Identity", in Hall, S., and Du Gay, Paul. (eds.) 1996, <u>Questions of Cultural Identity</u>. London: Sage publications. Pages 18-36.
- Bauman, Zygmunt. 2001, <u>Community: Seeking Safety in an Insecure World</u>. Cambridge: Polity Press.
- Bauman, Zygmunt. 2004, <u>Identity</u>. Cambridge: Polity Press.
- Baxandall, P. 2004, "Good Capital, Bad Capital: Dangers and Development in Digital Diasporas". Accessed at http://www.nautilus.org/gps/virtual-diasporas/paper/Baxandall.html on 27/10/2004.
- Baym, Nancy. 1998, "The Emergence of On-line Community" in Jones, Steven. (ed.) 1998, <u>Cybersociety 2.0 Revising Computer-Mediated Communication and Community</u>. London: Sage Publications. Pages 35-68.
- Beaulieu, Anne. 2005, "Sociable Hyperlinks: an Ethnographic Approach to Connectivity", in Hine, Christian, (ed.) 2005, <u>Virtual Methods Issues in Social Research on the Internet.</u> Oxford: Berg. Pages 183-197.
- Bell, Daniel. 1973. <u>The Coming of Post-Industrial Society</u>. New York: Basic Books.
- Benesch, Klaus and Fabre, Genevieve. 2004, <u>African Diasporas in the old and the new world: consciousness and imagination.</u> Amsterdam: Rodopi.

- Berger, Arthur Asa. 1998, <u>Media Analysis Techniques. Second Edition</u>. London: Sage Publications.
- Berger, Arthur Asa. 2000, <u>Media and Communication Research Methods an Introduction to Qualitative and Quantitative Approaches</u>. London: Sage Publications.
- Bhabha, Homi. 1990, "Dissemination: Time, Narrative and the Margins of the modern nation", in Homi K. Bhabha. (ed.) <u>Nation and Narration</u>. New York: Routledge.
- Bhabha, Homi. 1990, <u>Nation and Narration.</u> London: Routledge.
- Bhabha, Homi. 1994, <u>The Location of Culture.</u> London: Routledge.
- Billig, Michael. 1995, Banal Nationalism. London: Sage Publications.
- Bilton, Bonneth. P., Jones, D., Skinner, M., Stanworth, T., Lawson, A., Webster, L., Bradbury, J., Stanyer and Stephens, P. 1996, <u>Introductory Sociology. Third Edition</u>. London: Palgrave, Macmillan.
- Blaxter, L., Hughes, C., and Tight, M. 1996, <u>How to Research</u>. Philadelphia: Open University Press.
- Bonchek, Seth Mark. 1997, <u>From Broadcast to Netcast: The Internet and the flow of political information.</u> PhD Thesis, Harvard University, Cambridge, Massachusetts.
- Boyd-Barrett, Oliver and Rantanen, Terhi. (eds.) 1998, <u>The Globalization of News.</u> London: Sage Publications.
- Braakman, Marijie. 2005, <u>Roots and routes: Questions of Home, Belonging and return in an Afghan diaspora.</u> M. A. Thesis. Submitted August 2005, Department of Cultural Anthropology and Sociology of non-Western societies, The Netherlands. Accessed at http://www.ag-afghanistan.de/files/braakman_roots_a_routes.pdf on 15/04/2008.
- Brah, Avtar.1996, <u>Cartographies of Diaspora</u>. London: Routledge.
- Brass, Paul. 1991, <u>Ethnicity and Nationalism: Theory and Comparison</u>. Newbury Park, CA: Sage publications.
- Braziel, J.E., and Mannur, A. (eds.) 2003. <u>Theorizing Diaspora</u> London: Blackwell publishing.
- Brennan, Timothy. 1995, "The National Longing for form" in Ashcroft, Bill. Griffiths, Gareth. Tiffin, Helen. (eds.) 1995, <u>The Post Colonial Studies Reader</u> London and New York: Routledge. Pages 128-131.
- Breuilly, John. 1985, Nationalism and the State. Chicago: University of Chicago Press.
- Bridget, Somekh and Lewin, Cathy. (eds.) 2005, <u>Research Methods in the Social Sciences</u>. London: Sage Publications.
- Brown, David. 2000, Contemporary Nationalism: Civic, Ethnocultural, and Multicultural Politics. London: Routledge.
- Brown, Joanne. 2006, "Reflexivity in the research process: psychoanalytic observations", in <u>International. Journal of Social Research Methodology</u> Vol. 9, No.3, July 2006. Pages 181-197.

- Brubaker, Rogers. 1996, Nationalism Reframed Nationhood and the National Question in the New Europe. Cambridge: Cambridge University Press.
- Brubaker, Rogers. 2005, "The 'diaspora' diaspora" in Ethnic and Racial Studies Vol. 28 No1. January 2005. Pages 1-19.
- Buckley, Peter and Clark, Duncan. 2004, The Rough Guide to the Internet. London: Rough Guide Limited.
- Bulmer, Martin and Co. 1999, Racism. Oxford: Oxford University Press.
- Burnett, Robert and Marshall, David. 2003, Web Theory An Introduction. London: Routledge.
- Burns, R. 2000, Introduction to Research Methods. London: Sage Publications.
- Caincross, Frances. 2001, The Death of Distance: How the Communication Revolution is changing our lives. Harvard: Harvard Business School Press.
- Calhoun, Craig. 1994, Social Theory and the Politics of Identity. Oxford: Blackwell Publishing.
- Calhoun, Craig. 1997, Nationalism. Minneapolis: University of Minnesota Press.
- Callon, Michael. 1986, "Some elements of a sociology of translation: domestication of the scallops and the fishermen of St. Brieuc Bay", in John Law, (ed.) 1986, Power, Action and belief: A new sociology of knowledge. London: Routledge.
- Castells, Manuel. 1996, The Rise of the Network Society. Oxford: Blackwell Publishing.
- Castells, Manuel. 1998, 2000, End of Millennium. Oxford: Blackwell Publishing.
- Castells, Manuel. 2000, The Power of Identity. Oxford: Blackwell Publishing.
- Castells, Manuel.2001, The Internet Galaxy; Reflections on the Internet, Business, and Society. Oxford: Oxford University Press.
- Castles, S. & Davidson, A. 2000, Citizenship and Migration: Globalization and the Politics of belonging. New York: Palgrave.
- Castles, S. & Miller J. M. 1993, The Age of Migration: International Population Movements in the Modern World, Third Edition. London: Palgrave.
- Chakravartty, Paula and Sarikakis, Katharine. 2006, Media Policy and Globalization. Edinburgh: Edinburgh University Press Ltd.
- Chalaby, Jean. (ed.) 2005a, Transnational Television Worldwide Towards A New Media Order. London: I.B. Tauris & Co. Ltd.

- Chalaby, Jean. 2000, "New Media, New Freedoms, New Threats" in <u>Gazette: The International Journal for Communication Studies</u>. London: Sage Publications. Vol. 62. No 1. Pages 19-29
- Chalaby, Jean. 2003, "Television for a New Global Order: Transnational Television Networks and the Formation of Global Systems", in <u>Gazette: The International Journal for Communication Studies</u>. Vol. 65, No. 6. Pages 457-472.
- Chalaby, Jean. 2005b, "From internationalization to transnationalisation", in <u>Global Media and Communication 2005</u>. Vol. 1, No. 28, DOI: 1177/1742766650500100107. Accessed at <u>http.sagepub.com.</u> on 12/02/2008
- Chalaby, Jean. 2005c, "Deconstructing the transnational: a typology of cross-border television channels in Europe" in <u>New Media and Society</u>. London: Sage Publications. Vol. 7. No. 2. Pages 155-175.
- Chalaby, Jean. 2007, "Global news TV networks in Europe: a post-national perspective" Abstract and Handout, accessed at: www.wmin.ac.uk/mad/docs/CAMRI_Seminar_10_Oct_2007_Jean_Chalaby.doc on 24/03/2008
- Christian, M. (ed.) 2002, <u>Black Identity in the 20th Century, Expressions of the US and UK African Diaspora</u>. London: Hansib Publications Limited.
- Clancy, Roger, E. 2002, <u>A nation online: how Americans are expanding their use of the Internet.</u> New York: Novinka Books.
- Clarke, Kamari. 2004, <u>Mapping Yoruba Networks: Power and Agency in the Making of Transnational Communities</u>. Durham: Duke University Press.
- Clifford, James. 1997, <u>Routes: Travel and Translation in the late 20th Century.</u> Cambridge, Massachusetts: Harvard University Press.
- Clifford, James. 1999, "Diasporas", in Vertovec S. and Cohen R. <u>Migration, Diasporas and Transnationalism</u>. Cheltenham: Edward Elgar.
- Clifford, James. 2000, "Taking Identity Politics Seriously: 'The Contradictory, Stony Ground" in Gilroy, Paul. Grossberg, Lawrence. McRobbie, Angela. (eds.) 2000, <u>Without Guarantees in Honour of Stuart Hall</u>. London: Verso. Pages 94-112.
- Cohen, Anthony, P. 1985, <u>The Symbolic Construction of Community</u>. London: Routledge.
- Cohen, Robin. 1997, <u>Global Diasporas: An Introduction</u>. London: UCL Press.
- Connor, Walker. 2001, "Homelands in a World of States", in Gurberau and Hutchinson. (eds.) 2001, <u>Understanding Nationalism</u>. Cambridge: Polity Press.

- Conversi, Daniele. 2004, "Conceptualizing nationalism", in Daniele Conversi, (ed.) Ethnonationalism in the Contemporary World: Walker Connor and the Theory of Nationalism. London. New York: Routledge.
- Cottle, Simon. (ed.) 2000, Ethnic Minorities and the Media. Buckingham, Philadelphia: Open University Press.
- Couldry, Nick. 2004, "Actor network theory and media: do they connect and on what terms?" in Hepps, et al, (eds.) Cultures of Connectivity, accessed online on 18/06/2007.
- Cox, Cromwell Oliver. 2000, Race: A study in social dynamics. 50th anniversary edition of caste, class, and race. New York: Monthly Review Press.
- Creswell, J.W. 1997, Qualitative inquiry and research design: Choosing amongst five traditions. Thousand Oaks, CA: Sage Publications.
- Cunningham, Stuart and Sinclair, John. 2001, Floating Lives: The Media and Asian Diasporas. Lanham, Maryland: Rowman & Littlefield.
- Curran, James and Gurevitch. 1991, Mass Media and Society. London: Arnold.
- Curran, James. 2002, Media and Power. London: Routledge.
- D'Aguiar, Fred. 2000, 'Home is always elsewhere: Individual and communal regenerative capacities of loss", in Owusu, Kwesi. (ed.) 2000, Black British Culture and Society. London and New York: Routledge.
- Davidson, B. 1992, The Black Man's Burden; Africa and the course of the Nation-State. Ibadan: Spectrum Books Limited.
- Dayan, Daniel. 1999, "Media and diasporas" in Gripsrud, Jostein. 1999, Television and Common Knowledge. London: Routledge.
- Dayan, Joan. 2004, "Paul Gilroy's Slaves, Ships, and Routes: The Middle Passage as Metaphor". Accessed at http://iupjoournals.org/ral/ral27-4.html on 22/10/2004.
- De Certeau, Luce Giard, and Pierre Mayol. 1998, The Practise of Everyday Life. Volume 2. Minnesota: University of Minnesota Press.
- De Vaus, David. 2002, Surveys in Social Research, 5th Edition. London: Routledge.
- Dehartaigh, Niall. O. 2002, The Internet Research Handbook, A practical Guide for Students and Researchers in the Social Sciences. London: Sage Publications.
- Denscombe, Martyn. 1998, The Good Research Guide for Small-Scale Research Projects. Maidenhead, Philadelphia: Open University Press.
- Denzin, K. Norman. 1997, Interpretative Ethnography Ethnographic Practices for the 21st Century. London: Sage Publications.
- Denzin, N.K. & Y.S. Lincoln. 1998, The Landscape of qualitative research. London: Sage Publications.

- Deutsch, K. 1969, <u>Nationalism and Social Communication. An Inquiry into the foundation of Nationality</u>. Cambridge: Massachusetts.
- Diedrich, M., Gates, Henry., Perdersen, C. (eds.) 1999, <u>Black Imagination and the Middle Passage</u>. Oxford: Oxford University Press.
- Dochartaigh, Niall, O. 2002, <u>The Internet Research Handbook A Practical Guide for students and Researchers in the Social Sciences</u>. London: Sage Publications.
- Donath, Judith, S. 1999, "Identity and deception in the virtual community" in Smith, A. Marc and Kollock, Peter. 1999, <u>Communities in Cyberspace</u>. London: Routledge.
- Douglas, M. 1991, "The Idea of Home: A kind of Space", in <u>Social Research</u>, Vol. 58, No. 1. Pages 287-307.
- Drake, St. Clair. 1971, <u>Black Religion and the Redemption of Africa</u>. Chicago: Third World Press.
- Drake, St. Clair. 1978 & 1990, <u>Black Folk Here and There (2 vols)</u>. Los Angeles: Canter for Afro-American Studies.
- Du bois, W.E.B. 1970 (1915), <u>The Negro</u>. London: Oxford University Press.
- Du Gay, Paul. Evans, Jessica and Redman, Peter. 2000, <u>Identity: a reader.</u> London: Sage Publications.
- Dudrah, Rajinder. 2004, "Diasporicity in the City of Portsmouth (UK); local and Global Connections of Black Britishness" in Sociological <u>Research Online</u>, Vol. 9, No.2, accessed at http://www.socresonline.org.uk/9/2/dudrah.html on 10/10/2006.
- Ebeling, M.F.E. 2003, "The New Dawn: Black Agency in Cyberspace", in <u>Radical History Review</u>, Issue 87 (Fall 2003). Pages 96-108.
- Edgar, Andrew and Sedgwick, Peter. 2002, <u>Cultural Theory: The Key Thinkers</u>. London: Routledge.
- Elmer-Dewitt, P. 1996, "The Information Highway: An Overview" in Cozic, 1996, <u>The Information Highway</u>. San Diego: Greenhaven Press.
- Engel, Christopher. 2007, "Internet and the Nation-state". Accessed at www.colleges.de/engel/engel1.pdf on 27/05/2007.
- Equiano, Olaudah. 1789, <u>The African, The Interesting Narrative of the Life of Olaudah Equino.</u> London: The X Press.
- Eribo, Festus and Jong-Ebot. 1997, <u>Press Freedom and Communication in Africa.</u> Lawrenceville, New Jersey: Africa World Press.
- Eric, louw. 2001, <u>The Media and Cultural Production</u>. London: Sage publications.
- Everard, Jerry. 1999, <u>Virtual States: The Internet and the boundaries of the nation-state</u>. London: Routledge.

- Evereth, Anna. 2002, "The Revolution will be digitized: Afrocentricity and the digital public sphere", in <u>Social Tort, 71</u>, Vol. 20, No 2, Summer 2002.
- Falola, Toyin and Childs D, Matt. 2005, "The Yoruba Diaspora in the Atlantic World". Accessed at http://www.indiana.edu/~iupress/books/0-253-34458-1.shtml on 11/09/2006.
- Fanon, Frantz. 1967, <u>Black Skin, White masks.</u> New York: Grove Press.
- Faringer, Gunilla. 1991, <u>Press Freedom in Africa</u>. West port, Connecticut: Greenwood Publishing Group.
- Fearon, D. James. 1999, "What is Identity (as we now use the word)". Accessed at <u>http://www.standford.edu/-jfearon/papers/iden1v2.pdf on 07/03/2007</u>.
- Fernback, J. and Thompson, B. 2004, "Virtual Communities: Abort, Retry, Failure?" Accessed at <u>http:</u> www.well.com/user/hlr/texts/Vccivil.html on 15/11/2004.
- Fetterman, David. 1998, <u>Ethnography: Step by Step</u>. London: Sage Publications.
- Finlay, L. 2003b, "Through the looking glass: intersubjectivity and hermeneutic reflection", in O. Finlay & B. Gough. (eds.) 2003, <u>Reflexivity: a practical guide for researchers in health and social sciences.</u> Pages 105–119. London: Blackwell Publishing.
- Finlay, Linda and Gough, Brendan. 2008, "Doing reflexivity: A critical guide for qualitative researchers in health and social science". Accessed at http: www.ucl.ac.uk/pcps/research/qua/res/documents/doingreflexivity.pdf on 12/03/2008.
- Fiske, J. 1987, <u>Television culture</u>. London: Routledge.
- Flichy, Patrice. 1995, <u>Dynamics of Modern Communication, The shaping and Impact of New Communication Technologies</u>. London: Sage Publications.
- Fowler, J. Floyd. 2002, <u>Survey Research Methods</u>. London: Sage Publications.
- Frank, Gunder Andre. 1971, <u>Capitalism and Underdevelopment in Latin America</u>. London: Penguin Books.
- Frank, Gunder Andre. 1975, <u>On Capitalist Underdevelopment.</u> Bombay: Oxford University Press.
- Frank, Gunder Andre. 1978, <u>Dependent Accumulation and Underdevelopment.</u> London: Macmillan Press.
- Frankfort-Nachmias, C and David Nachmias. 1996, <u>Research Methods in the Social Sciences.</u> London: Arnold.

- Fredrickson, G. 2002, <u>Racism: A Short History</u>. Princeton: Princeton University Press.
- Friere, P. 1972, <u>Pedagogy of the oppressed</u>. Penguin: Harmondsworth.
- Garvey, Marcus. 1968, <u>Philosophy and Opinion</u>. New York: Arno Press.
- Gates Jr, Henry Louis and William L. Andrews, 1998, <u>Pioneers of the Black Atlantic: Five Slave Narratives from the enlightenment 1772-1815.</u> Washington, D.C: Wilsted and Taylor Publishing Services.
- Gates Jr, Henry Louis. 2000, ''A reporter at large: Black London'' in kwesi-Owusu. (ed.) 2000. <u>Black British Culture and Society</u>. London: Routledge.
- Gauntlett David and Annette Hill. 1999<u>, Television, Culture and Everyday life.</u> London: Routledge.
- Gellner Ernest. 1983, <u>Nations and Nationalism.</u> Oxford: Blackwell.
- Gellner, Ernest and Anthony D. Smith. 1996, "The nation: real or imagined?: The Warwick Debates on Nationalism", in <u>Nations and Nationalism.</u> Vol. 2, No. 3, 1996. Pages 357-370.
- George, McKenzie and Others, 1997, <u>Understanding Social Research: Perspectives on Methodology and Practise,</u> London and Washington: The Farmers' Press.
- Georgiou, Myria and Silverstone, Roger. 2007, "Diasporas and Contra-Flows beyond nation-centrism" in Thussu, Daya Kishan. (ed.) 2007, <u>Media on the Move Global flow and Contra flow.</u> London: Routledge.
- Georgiou, Myria. 2000, "Beyond the Domestic: Constructing Ethnic Identities and Media Consumption in the <u>Public Ethnic Space-The case of the Cypriot Community Centre in North London.</u> Accessed online on 12/04/2006.
- Georgiou, Myria. 2000, "Mapping Minorities and their Media: The National Context-Greece". Accessed online on 12/04/2006.
- Georgiou, Myria. 2000-2003, "Mapping Diasporic Media across the EU: Addressing Cultural Exclusion." <u>Key Deliverable: The European Media and Technology in Everyday Life Network</u>. 2000-2003. Accessed online at www.cestim.it/08media.htm on 12/02/2006.
- Georgiou, Myria. 2001, <u>"Negotiated Uses, contested meanings, changing identities: Greek Cypriot Media Consumption and Ethnic Identity Formation in North London"</u>. PhD Thesis, London School of Economics.
- Georgiou, Myria. 2006a, <u>Diaspora, Identity and the Media: Diasporic transnationalism and Mediated Spatialities</u>. Cresskill, New Jersey: Hampton Press, INC.

- Georgiou, Myria. 2006b, "Diasporic Communities On-line: A Bottom up Experience of Transnationalism", in Sarikakis, K., and Thussu, D. K. (eds.) 2006, <u>Ideologies of the Internet</u>. Cresskill NJ: Hampton Press. Pages 131-146.
- Georgiou, Myria. 2006c, "Cities of difference: Cultural juxtapositions and urban politics of representation", in <u>International Journal of Media and Cultural Politics.</u> Vol. 2, No. 3. Pages 283-298.
- Gibson, William. 1984, <u>Neuromancer</u>. New York: Ace.
- Giddens, Anthony. 1982, <u>Sociology, A brief but critical introduction</u>, London: Macmillan.
- Giddens, Anthony. 1990, <u>The Consequences of Modernity.</u> Cambridge: Polity.
- Giddens, Anthony. 1991, <u>Modernity and Self-Identity: Self and society in the late modern Age.</u> Cambridge: Polity.
- Giddens, Anthony. 1999, "Globalization…" BBC Lord Reith Lecture series. Accessed at http://www.bbc.co.uk/radio4/reith1999/_on 20/02/2004.
- Giddens, Anthony. 2000, "The trajectory of the self", in Du Gay, Paul. Evans, Jessica, and Redman, Peter. (eds.) 2000, <u>Identity: a reader.</u> London: Sage Publications. Pages 248-66.
- Gillespie, Marie. 1995, <u>Television, Ethnicity and Cultural Change</u>. New York: Routledge.
- Gillespie, Marie. 2000, "Transnational Communication and Diaspora Communities", in Cottle, Simon. (ed.) 2000, <u>Ethnic Minorities and the Media.</u> Maidenhead: Open University Press.
- Gilroy, Paul. 1987, <u>There ain't no black in the Union Jack.</u> London: Routledge.
- Gilroy, Paul. 1993, <u>The Black Atlantic; Modernity and Double Consciousness.</u> London. New York: VERSO.
- Gilroy, Paul. 1997, "Diaspora and the Detours of Identity", in Woodward Kathryn. (ed.) 1997, <u>Identity and Difference</u>. London: Sage Publications.
- Gilroy, Paul. 1999, "It Aint Where you're From, It's Where you're at…. The Dialectics of Diasporic Identification", in Vertovec S. and Cohen R. (eds.) 1999, <u>Migration, Diasporas and Transnationalism.</u> Cheltenham: Edward Elgar.
- Gilroy, Paul. 2000, "The Dialectics of Diaspora Identification", in Les Back and John Solomon. (eds.) 2000, <u>Theories of Race and Racism; a Reader</u>. London: Routledge.
- Gilroy, Paul. 2000, "The Sugar You Stir…" in Gilroy, Paul. Grossberg, Lawrence., McRobbie, Angela. (eds.) 2000, <u>Without Guarantees in Honour of Stuart Hall</u>. London: Verso. Pages 126-133.

- Gilroy, Paul. 2000a, <u>Against Race: Imagining Political Culture Beyond the Colour Line.</u> Cambridge, Massachusetts: Harvard University Press.
- Gilroy, Paul. 2000b, <u>Between Camps nations, cultures, and the allure of race</u>. London: Routledge.
- Gilroy, Paul. 2004, <u>After Empire: Melancholia or Convivial Culture?</u> Oxfordshire: Routledge.
- Gilroy, Paul. Grossberg, Lawrence. McRobbie, Angela. (eds.) 2000, <u>Without Guarantees in Honour of Stuart Hall</u>. London: VERSO.
- Gleason, Philip. 1995, "Identifying Identity", in Ashcroft, Bill. Griffiths, Gareth. Tiffin, Helen. (eds.) 1995, <u>The Post Colonial Studies Reader</u> London and New York: Routledge. Pages 194-5.
- Goffman, Erving. 2004, "The Presentation of Self in Everyday Life". Accessed at http://www.cfmc.com/adamb/writings/goffman.htm on 05/05/2007.
- Goldbart, Juliet and Hustler. 2005, "Ethnography" in Bridget, Somekh and Lewin, Cathy, (eds.) 2005, <u>Research Methods in the Social Sciences</u>. London: Sage Publications. Pages 16-23.
- Goldberg, David. 2006, Transnational Communication and Defamatory Speech: A case for establishing norms for the twenty-first century. Accessed at http://ics.leeds.ac.uk/papers/index.cfm?outfit=pmt on 20/06/2007.
- Gomm, Roger. 2004, <u>Social Research Methodology, A critical Introduction.</u> Palgrave: Macmillan.
- Gordon, T.E., and Anderson, M. 1999, "The African Diaspora: Toward an Ethnography of Diasporic Identification". <u>The Journal of American Folklore</u>. Vol. 112, No. 445, *Theorizing the Hybrid*. Summer, 1999. Pages 282-296.
- Graham, Gordon. 1999, <u>The Internet: A Philosophical Inquiry</u>: London and New York: Routledge.
- Graham, Mark and Khosravi, Shahram. 1997, "Home is where you make it: Repatriation and diaspora culture among Iranians in Sweden", in <u>Journal of Refugee Studies</u> Vol.10, No.2. Oxford University Press.
- Greenfeld, Liah. 1995, "Nationalism in Western and Eastern Europe Compared," in Stephen E. Hanson and Willfried Spohn. (eds.) 1995, <u>Can Europe Work? Germany & the Reconstruction of Postcommunist Societies.</u> Seattle & London: University of Washington Press.
- Greenfield, Iiah. 1992, <u>Nationalism: five roads to modernity</u>. Cambridge: Harvard University Press.
- Grosby, Steven. 2005, <u>Nationalism: A very short introduction</u>. Oxford: Oxford University Press.
- Guest, Robert. 2004, <u>The Shackled Continent: Africa's Past, Present, and Future.</u> London: Macmillan.

- Guibernau, M. and Hutchinson. (eds.) 2001, <u>Understanding Nationalism</u>. Cambridge: Polity Press.
- Guibernau, Montserrat. 1999, <u>Nations without States</u>. Cambridge: Polity Press.
- Guimaraes, Jr. Mario, J.L. 2005, "Doing Anthropology in Cyberspace: Fieldwork Boundaries and Social Environments", in Hine, Christian. (ed.) 2005, <u>Virtual Methods Issues in Social Research on the Internet.</u> Oxford: Berg. Pages 141-156.
- Guion, Lisa. 2007, "Conducting an in-depth Interview". Accessed online at http://edis.ifas.ufl.edu on 26/01/2007.
- Gunaratne, Shelton. 2007, "A system view of 'international' communication, its scope and limitations", in <u>Global Media and Communication 2000.</u> Vol. 3, No. 267. Accessed online on 12/20/2007.
- Gunter, Barrie. 2000, <u>Media Research Methods Measuring Audiences, Reactions and Impact</u>. London: Sage Publications.
- Hall, Stuart and Paul Du Gay. (eds.) 1996, <u>Questions of Cultural Identity</u>. London: Sage Publications.
- Hall, Stuart. 1989, "Ethnicity: Identity and Difference", in <u>Radical America.</u> Vol. 23. Pages 9-20.
- Hall, Stuart. 1990, "Cultural Identity and Diaspora" in J. Rutherford. (ed.) <u>Identity: Community, Culture, Difference</u>. London: Lawrence and Wishart.
- Hall, Stuart. 1995, "New Ethnicities", in Ashcroft, Bill. Griffiths, Gareth. Tiffin, Helen. (eds.) 1995, <u>The Post Colonial Studies Reader</u> London and New York: Routledge. Pages 199- 202.
- Hall, Stuart. 1997, <u>Representation: Cultural Representations and Signifying Practices.</u> London, CA: Thousand Oaks; New Delhi: Sage.
- Hall, Stuart. David Held and Tony McGrew. (eds.) 1992, <u>Modernity and its futures</u>. Cambridge: Polity.
- Halloran, James. 1997, "International Communication Research: Opportunities and Obstacles", in Ali Mohammadi. (ed.) 1997, <u>International Communication and Globalization</u>. London: Sage Publications.
- Hammer, Julianne. 2006, "Palestinians Born in exile: diaspora and the search for a homeland", in <u>An interdisciplinary Journal of Jewish Studies.</u> Vol. 24, No. 3. Pages 194-196.
- Hammersley, Martyn and Atkinson, Paul. 1983, <u>Ethnography.</u> London: Routledge.
- Hanafi, Sari. 2005. "Reshaping Geography: Palestinian Community Networks in Europe and the New Media", in <u>Journal of ethnic and migration studies.</u> Vol. 31, No. 3. Pages 581 – 598.

- Handler, Richard. 1988, "Nationalism and the Politics of Culture in Quebec", in Canadian Journal of Political Science. Vol. 21, No. 4. Pages 842-843.
- Harris, E. Joseph. (ed.) 1993, <u>Global Dimensions of the African Diaspora, Second Edition.</u> Washington D.C.: Howard University Press.
- Harvey, David. 1990, <u>The Condition of Postmodernity: An Enquiry into the Origins of Cultural Change.</u> Oxford: Basil Blackwell.
- Hastings, Adrian. 1997, <u>The Construction of Nationhood: Ethnicity, Religion and Nationalism.</u> Cambridge and New York: Cambridge University Press.
- Hechter, Michael. 2000, Containing Nationalism. Oxford and New York: Oxford University Press.
- Hechter, Micheal. 1975, <u>Internal Colonialism.</u> London: Routledge.
- Herman, S. Edward and McChesney W. Robert. 1997, <u>The Global Media: The New Missionaries of Corporate Capitalism.</u> London: Continuum.
- Hernandez-Coss, Raul and Egwuagu Bun, Chinyere. 2007, "The UK-Nigeria Remittance Corridor Challenges of Embracing Formal Transfer Systems in a dual financial Environment". Washington D.C.:World Bank Working Paper No. 2.
- Herskovits, Melville J. 1990 (1941), <u>The Myth of the Negro Past</u>. Boston: Beacon Press.
- Hesmondhalgh, David. 2002, <u>The Cultural Industries.</u> London: Sage Publications.
- Hewitt-Taylor, Jaquelina. 2006, "Use of Constant Comparative Analysis in qualitative research", in <u>Nursing Standard</u>. Vol. 15, No. 42. Pages 39-42.
- Hewson, Claire. Yule, Peter. Laurent, Dianna and Vogel, Carl. 2003, <u>Internet Research Methods: A Practical Guide for the Social and Behavioural Sciences.</u> London: Sage Publications.
- Hiller, H. Harry and Franz, M. Tara. 2004, "New ties, old ties and lost ties: the use of the internet in diaspora", in <u>New Media and Society</u>. London. Sage Publications. Vol. 6. Pages 731-752. Downloaded from http://nma.sagepub.com, on 19/02/2008.
- Hine, C. 2000, <u>Virtual Ethnography</u>. London: Sage publications.
- Hine, Christian. (ed.) 2005, <u>Virtual Methods Issues in Social Research on the Internet.</u> Oxford: Berg.
- Hine, Christian. 2000, <u>Virtual Ethnography</u>. London: Sage Publications.
- Hobsbawm, E.J., 1990, <u>Nations and Nationalism since 1780: Programme, Myth and Reality.</u> Cambridge: Cambridge University Press.

- Hoffmann-Axthelm, Dieter. 1992, "Identity and reality: the end of the philosophical immigration officer", in Lash, Scott and Friedman, Jonathan. (eds.) 1992, Modernity and Identity Oxford: Blackwell Publishing. Pages 196-217.
- Hogg, Micheal and Dominic Abrams. 1988, Social Identifications: A social psychology of intergroup relations and group processes. London: Routledge.
- Hroch, Miroslav. 1996, "From National Movement to the Fully-formed Nation: The Nation-building Process in Europe," in Balakrishnan, Gopal, (ed.) Mapping the Nation. New York and London: VERSO. Pages 78-97.
- Huntington, Samuel P. 1997, The Clash of Civilizations and the Remaking of the World Order. New York: Simon and Schuster.
- Ignacio, Emily Noelle. 2003, "Laughter in the Rain: Jokes as membership and resistance" in C. Lee, Sau-Ling Cynthia Wong, 2003, Asian America.Net: Ethnicity, Nationalism, and Cyberspace. London: Routledge. Pages 158-176.
- Ignacio, Emily Noelle. 2005, Building diaspora: Filipino community formation on the Internet New Brunswick, NJ: Rutgers University Press.
- Innis, Harold. 2007, Empire and Communication.Lanham, MD: Rowman & Littlefield.
- Ite, U.E. 2002, "Turning Brain Drain into Brain Gain: Personal Reflections on Using the Diaspora Option", in African Issues, Vol.30, No.1. Pages 76-80.
- Jaffrelot, Christopher. 2007, "For a theory of nationalism", in Questions de Recherche/Research in Question. Accessed online at http:www.ceri-sciences-po.org/publica/question/qdr10.pdf, on 18/06/2007.
- Jap, van Dijk. 1999, The Network Society. London: Sage Publications.
- Jick, Todd D. 1979, "Mixing Qualitative and Quantitative methods: Triangulation in action", in Administrative Science Quarterly. Volume 24, Pages 602-611. 1979.
- Jones, Liz and Somekh, Bridget. 2005, "Observation", in Bridget, Somekh and Lewin, Cathy, (eds.) 2005, Research Methods in the Social Sciences. London: Sage Publications. Pages 138-145.
- Jones, Steven. (ed.) 1998, Cybersociety 2.0 Revising Computer-Mediated Communication and Community. London: Sage Publications.
- Jones, Steven. 1997, Virtual culture: identity and communication in Cybersociety. London: Sage publications.

- Jones, Steven. 1998, "Information, Internet, and Community: Notes toward an Understanding of Community in the Information Age", in Jones, Steven. (ed.) 1998, <u>Cybersociety 2.0 Revising Computer-Mediated Communication and Community.</u> London: Sage Publications. Page 1-34.
- Jordan, Tim. 1999, <u>Cyberpower: The Culture and politics of cyberspace and the Internet.</u> London and New York: Routledge.
- Jorgensen, L. Danny. 1989, <u>Participant Observation: A Methodology for Human Studies.</u> London: Sage Publications.
- Kadende-Kaiser, R. 2007, "Interpreting language and cultural discourse: Internet communication among Burundians in the diaspora". Accessed at http://muse.jhu.edu/journals/africa_today/v047/47.2kadende.html, on 18/06/2007.
- Kalra, S. Virinder. Kaur, Raminder, and Hutnyk, John. 2005, <u>Diaspora and Hybridity</u>. London: Routledge.
- Karim, H. Karim. (ed.) 2003, <u>The Media of Diaspora</u>, London: Routledge.
- Karim, H. Karim. 1998, "From Ethnic Media to Global Media: Transnational Communication Network Among Diasporic Communities" <u>International Comparative Research Group, Strategic Research and Analysis Canadian Heritage</u>, June, 1998. Accessed online at www.transcomm.ox.ac.uk/working%20papers/karim.pdf on 16/06/2007.
- Kearney, M. 1999, "THE LOCAL AND THE GLOBAL: The Anthropology of Globalization and Transnationalism", in Vertovec, S. and Cohen R. (eds.) 1999, <u>Migration, Diaspora and Transnationalism,</u> Cheltenham: Edward Elgar Publishing Limited. Pages 547-538.
- Keats, M. Daphne. 2000, <u>Interviewing a practical guide for students and professionals</u>. Milton Keynes: Open University Press.
- Kedourie, Elie. 1960, <u>Nationalism</u>. London: Hutchinson.
- Kirshenblatt-Gimblett, Barbara. 1994, "Spaces of Dispersal" in <u>Cultural Anthropology.</u> Vol. 9, No 3. Pages 339-344.
- Kleinsasser, Audrey, M. 2000, "Researchers, Reflexivity, and Good Data: Writing to Unlearn", in <u>Theory into Practice</u>: Vol. 39, No.3. Accessed at http://www.jstor.org/view/00405841/ap05174/05a00070/0 on 22.02.2008.
- Komolafe, J. 2007, "Searching for fortune: the geographical process of Nigerian migration to Dublin, Ireland." Accessed online at www.africamigration.com/archive on 02/02/2007.

- Lankshear, Colin and Leander, M. Kevin. 2005, "Social Research in Virtual Realities", in Bridget, Somekh and Lewin, Cathy. (eds.) 2005, <u>Research Methods in the Social Sciences.</u> London: Sage Publications. Pages 326-334.
- Latour, Bruno. 1987, <u>Science in action: How to follow scientists and engineers through society.</u> Milton Keynes: Open University Press.
- Laughlin, Jim Mac. 2001, <u>Reimagining the nation-state: the contested terrains of nation-building.</u> London: Pluto Press.
- Law, John and Hassard, John. (eds.) 1999, <u>Actor Network Theory and After.</u> London: Blackwell Publishing.
- Lax, S. 1999, <u>Beyond the Horizon: Communication Technologies: Past, Present and Future.</u> Luton: University of Luton Press.
- Lax, Steven. 2001, <u>Access denied in the Information age.</u> Basingstoke: Palgrave.
- Lemelle, S.J. 1994, <u>Imagining Home: Class, Culture and Nationalism in the African Diaspora.</u> London: VERSO.
- Ley, David and Kobayashi, Audrey. 2004, Back to Hong Kong: Return migration or transnational sojourn? in <u>Global Networks A journal of transnational affairs.</u> Vol. 5. No. 2. Pages 111-127.
- Ley. David, 2004, "Transnational spaces and everyday lives "in <u>Royal Geographical Society</u> (with The Institute of British Geographers). NS 29. Pages 151-164.
- Loomba, Ania. 1998, <u>Colonialism/Post Colonialism.</u> London: Routledge.
- Maier, Karl. 2000, <u>This House has Fallen Nigeria in crisis.</u> London: Penguin Books.
- Mallapragada, M. 2000, "The Indian Diaspora in the USA and Around the Web", in David Gauntlett. (ed.) <u>Rewiring media studies for the digital age.</u> London: Arnold.
- Mallet, Shelley. 2004, "Understanding home: a critical review of the literature", in <u>The Sociological Review.</u> Volume 52, No. 1. Pages 62-89.
- Mannur, Anita. 2003, "Postscript: Cyberspaces and the Interfacing of Diasporas", in Braziel, J.E. and Mannur, A. (eds.) 2003. <u>Theorizing Diaspora,</u> USA, UK: Blackwell Publishing.
- Manzrui, Ali. 2006, "Seven pillars of media wisdom". Accessed online at www.ngrguardiannews.com on 24/11/2006.
- Marienstras, Richard.1999, "On the notion of diaspora", in Vertovec, S and Cohen, R. (eds.) 1999, <u>Migration, Diasporas and Transnationalism.</u> Cheltenham: Edward Elgar Publishing Limited. Pages 357-63.
- Markham, Annette N. 1998, <u>Life Online: researching real experience in Virtual Space.</u> Atlanta, London, N. Delhi: Walnut Creek.

- Marshall, McLuhan. 2001, <u>Understanding Media: The Extension of Man.</u> London: Routledge.
- Marthoz, Jean Paul. 1999, "Freedom of the media", in Tawfik, M., Bartagnon, G., and Courrier, Y. (eds) 1999, <u>World Communication and Information Report, 1999-2000</u>. Paris: United Nations Educational, Scientific and Cultural Organisation's publication.
- Massey, Doreen. 1995, Spatial divisions of labour: Social structures and the geography of production. 2nd edition. New York: Routledge.
- Maykut, P. 1994, <u>Beginning Qualitative Research: a Philosophic Guide</u>. London: Routledge.
- Mckenzie George, Powell, Jackie and Usher, Robin. (eds.) 1997, <u>Understanding Social Research: Perspectives on Methodology and Practice.</u> London and Washington: The farmers' press.
- McLeod, John. 2004, <u>Postcolonial London: Reworking the metropolis</u>. USA: Routledge.
- McQuail, Denis. 2000, <u>McQuail's Mass Communication Theory 4th Edition.</u> London: Sage Publications.
- McRobbie, Angela. 2005, <u>The Uses of Cultural Studies.</u> London: Sage Publications.
- Mercer, Kobena. 2000, "A Sociography of Diaspora" in Gilroy, Paul., Grossberg, Lawrence., McRobbie, Angela. (eds.) 2000, <u>Without Guarantees in Honour of Stuart Hall</u>. London: VERSO. Pages 233-44.
- Miller, C. Delbert and Salkind, J. Neil. 2002, <u>Handbook of Research Design and Social Measurement.</u> 6th Edition. London: Sage Publications.
- Miller, D. and Slater, D. 2000, <u>The Internet: An ethnographic approach.</u> Oxford: Oxford University Press.
- Mintz, Sidney, and Richard Price. 1976, <u>An Anthropological Approach to the Afro-American Past</u>. Philadelphia: Institute for the Study of Human Issues.
- Mitzen, J. 2004, "Ontological security in world politics, and Implications for the study of European security", prepared for the <u>CIDEL Workshop, Oslo, October 22-23, 2004</u>, "from Civilian to Military Power: The European Union at a Crossroads?" Accessed online on 23/03/2006.
- Mohammadi, Ali. 1997, <u>International Communication and Globalization, A Critical Introduction.</u> London: Sage Publications.
- Moore, B. 1984, <u>Privacy: studies in social and cultural history.</u> New York: Sharpe.
- Moores, S. 1993, <u>Interpreting audiences: the ethnography of media consumption.</u> London: Sage Publications.
- Morley, D. & Robbins, K. 1995, <u>Global Media, electronic landscape and cultural boundaries.</u> London: Routledge.

- Morley, David. 1886, <u>Family Television: Cultural Power and Domestic Television.</u> London: Comedia.
- Morley, David. 2000, <u>Home Territories, media, mobility and identity.</u> London and New York: Routledge.
- Moser C.A., and G. Kalton. 1998, <u>Survey Methods in Social Investigations</u>. London: Heinemann Educational Books.
- Naficy, Hamid. 1999, <u>Home, Exile, Homeland film, media and the politics of place</u>. New York and London: Routledge.
- Nairn, Tom. 1977, <u>The Break-up of Britain</u>. London: New left Books.
- Naughton, J. 1999, <u>A brief history of the future.</u> London: Weidenfeld and Nicholson.
- Negroponte, Nicholas. 1995, <u>being digital</u>. London: Coronet Books.
- Nesbitt, Njubi. 2002, "African Intellectuals in the Belly of the Beast: Migration, Identity, and the Politics of Exile" in <u>African Issues</u>. African Studies Association. Vol. 30. No. Pages 70-75.
- Newman, L.W. 2003, <u>Social Research Methods, Qualitative and Quantitative Approaches.</u> Boston: Pearson Education, INC.
- Nkrumah, K. 1964, <u>Concientism: Philosophy and Ideology for decolonisation</u>. London: Panaf Books.
- Norris, Pipa. 2002, <u>Digital Divide: Civic Engagement, Information Poverty, and the Internet Worldwide.</u> USA: CUP.
- Nwolise, O.B.C. 1992, "Blacks in the Diaspora: A case of neglected catalyst in the achievement of Nigeria's foreign policy goals", in <u>Journal of Black Studies</u>, Vol. 23, No. 1. Pages 117-134.
- Odi, Amusu. 1999, "The Igbo in Diaspora: The Binding Force of Information" in <u>Libraries and Culture.</u> Vol. 34, No 1, Winter 1999, University of Texas Press.
- Okafor, Chike. 2004, "Nigerians in the Diaspora: Cracking under pressure or adopting the culture of their host country". Accessed at http://www.nigerdeltacongress.com/narticles/nigerians on 28/04/2006.
- Okome, O. Mojubaolu. 2004, "African Migration to the United States: Dimensions of Migration, immigration, and exile". Accessed at http: www.africaresource.com/scholar/globa.htm on 22/03/2004.
- Okome, O. Mojubaolu. 2004, "Africans on the Move: Transnational, Intranational, and Metaphorical Migrations", accessed online at http://www.africanmigration.com/articles/editorial/.htm on 05/06/2005.
- Okome, O. Mojubaolu. 2006, "Immigrant Voices in Cyberspace: spinning continental and Diaspora Africa into the World Wide Web". Accessed online on 11/12/2006.
- Okpewho, I., Davies, B.C., and Manzrui, A.A. 1999, <u>The African diaspora: African origins and New World identities</u>. Bloomington: Indiana University Press.

- Olaniyan, Tejumola. 2005, "African Writers, Exile and the Politics of a Global Diaspora", in <u>West Africa Review</u> (2003) ISSN: 1094-2254. Accessed at http://www/westafrica-review.com/vol4.1/olaniyan.htm/ on 10/06/2005.
- Ong, A. 1999, <u>Flexible Citizenship: the cultural logics of transnationality</u>. Durham NC: Duke University Press.
- Ong, A. and Nonini, D. (eds) 1997, <u>Ungrounded empires: the cultural politics of modern Chinese transnationalism</u>. New York: Routledge.
- Ong, Aihwa. 1999, "Cultural Citizenship as Subject-Making: immigrants Negotiate Racial and Cultural Boundaries in the United States", in Vertovec, S. and Cohen R., (eds.) 1999, <u>Migration, Diaspora and Transnationalism.</u> Cheltenham: Edward Elgar Publishing Limited. Page 112-137.
- Owusu, Kwesi. (ed.) 2000, <u>Black British Culture and Society: A Text Reader</u>. London: Routledge.
- Özkirimlii, U. 2000, <u>Theories of Nationalism: A critical Introduction</u>. London: Macmillan Press Limited.
- Padmore, George. 1956, <u>Pan-Africanism or Communism</u>. London: Dennis Dobson.
- Palmer, A Colin. 1981, <u>Human Cargoes: The British Slave Trade in Spanish America, 1700-1739.</u> Illinois: University of Illinois Press.
- Papastegiadis Nikos. 2000, <u>The Turbulence of Migration.</u> Cambridge: Polity Press.
- Papastegiadis, Nikos. 1998, <u>Dialogues in the Diasporas, Essays and Conversations on Cultural Identity.</u> London: Rivers Oram Press.
- Parham, A. 2007, "Diaspora, community and communication: Internet use in transnational Haiti". Accessed online at http://www.blackwell-synergy.com/links/doi/10.1111%2Fj.1471-0374.2004.00087.x on 18/06/2007.
- Parnwell, Mike. 1993, <u>Population Movements and the Third World</u>. London: Routledge.
- Pattie, P. Susan. 2001, "Longing and belonging: issues of homeland in the Armenian diaspora". Accessed online on 08/03/2007.
- Peel, Michael. 2006, <u>Nigeria-Related Financial Crime And Its Links With Britain.</u> London: Chatham House report.
- Polit, D. F. and Hungler, B.P. 1999, <u>Nursing Research, Principles and Methods. 6th Edition.</u> Philadelphia: Lippincott.
- Portes, Alejandro and Rumbaut, Ruben C. 1996, <u>Immigrant America: A Portrait</u>. California: University of California Press.

- Portes, Alejandro. 1997, "Globalization from Below: The Rise of Transnational Communities" WPTC-98-01. Princeton University, September 1997. An earlier version of this essay was published in W.P. Smith and R.P. 1996, Korczenwicz, <u>Latin America in the World Economy</u>. Westport, CN: Greenwood Press. Pages 151-168.
- Portes, Alejandro. 1997, "Immigration theory in the new century: Some problems and opportunities" in <u>International Migration Review</u>, Vol. 31, No. 4. Pages 799-825.
- Preece, Jenny. 2000, <u>Online Communities Designing Usability, Supporting Sociability</u> Chichester: John Wiley and Sons, Ltd.
- Radhakrishnan, R. 2003, "Ethnicity in an Age of Diaspora", in Braziel, J.E. and Mannur, A. (eds.) 2003. <u>Theorizing Diaspora.</u> USA, UK: Blackwell publishing.
- Rapport Nigel and Andrew Dawson. 1998, <u>Migrants of Identity: Perceptions of Home in a world of movement</u>. Oxford: Berg.
- Renan, Ernest. 1996, "What is a Nation?" in Eley, Geoff and Suny, Ronald Grigor. (eds.) 1996. Becoming National: A Reader. New York and Oxford: Oxford University Press.
- Rheingold, Howard. 1993, <u>The virtual community: homesteading on the electronic frontier.</u> Cambridge, MA: MIT Press.
- Rheingold, Howard. 2000, "Community development in the Cybersociety of the Future" in Gauntlett, David. (ed.) <u>Rewiring media studies for the digital age.</u> London: Arnold. Pages 170-8.
- Riggs, Fred. 2005, "Diasporas and Ethnic Nations, Causes and Consequences of Globalization", at http://www2.hawaii.edu/~fredr/diaglo on 25/04/2006.
- Robert, Markley. (ed.) 1996, <u>Virtual Realities and their Discontents</u>. Baltimore and London: John Hopkins University Press.
- Robin, K. and Webster, F. 1999, <u>Times of Technoculture from the Virtual life</u>. London and New York: Routledge.
- Robins, Kevin and Aksoy Asu, 2005, "Whoever Looks Always Finds: Transnational Viewing and Knowledge-Experience", in Chalaby, Jean. (ed.) 2005, <u>Transnational Television Worldwide Towards A New Media Order.</u> London. I.B. Tauris & Co. Ltd. Pages 14-42.
- Robins, Kevin and Aksoy, Asu. 2001, "From spaces of identity to mental spaces: lessons from Turkish-Cypriot cultural experience in Britain", in <u>Journal of Ethnic and Migration Studies.</u> Vol. 27, No. 4. Pages 685-711.
- Robins, Kevin. 2000, "Cyberspace and the world we live in", in Bell, D. and Kennedy, B.M. (eds.) 2000, <u>The Cyberculture Reader</u>. London: Routledge.

- Rodney, Walter. 1972, <u>How Europe Underdeveloped Africa.</u> Tanzania: Tanzania Publishing House.
- Rojek, Chris. 2003, <u>Stuart Hall</u>. Cambridge: Polity.
- Rosenberg, Richard, S. 1997, <u>The Social Impact of Computers</u>. London, New York: Academic Press.
- Safran, W. 1991, "Diasporas in Modern Societies: Myths of *Homeland* and Return" in <u>Diaspora</u>. Vol. 1, No. 1. Pages 83–99.
- Sarikakis, Katharine and Chakravarty, Paula. 2006, <u>Media Policy and Globalization: History, Culture, Politics.</u> New York: Palgrave Macmillan.
- Sarikakis, Katharine and Leslie, Regan Shade. 2008, <u>Feminist Intervention in International Communication. Minding the Gap</u>. Maryland: Rowman and Littlefield.
- Sarikakis, Katharine, and Thussu, D. K. (eds.) 2006, <u>Ideologies of the Internet</u>. Cresskill, NJ: Hampton Press.
- Sartre, Jean-Paul; translated by Hazel E. Barnes. 1958, 2003, <u>Being and Nothingness</u>. London: Routledge.
- Saunders, P. and Williams, P. 1988, "The constitution of the home: towards a research agenda", in <u>Housing Studies</u>. Vol. 3, No. 2. Pages 81-93.
- Sayyid, S. 2004, "Beyond Westphalia: Nations and Diasporas. The Case of the Muslim Umma". Accessed at http://www.jamaat-e-islami.org/rr/nationsdiasporas-sayyid.html on 22/10/2004.
- Schiller, Nina Glick, Basch, L., and Blanc-Szanton. (eds.) 1992, <u>Towards a Transnational Perspective on Migration: Race, Class, Ethnicity and Nationalism Reconsidered</u>. New York: The New York Academy of Sciences.
- Schneider, Steven, M. and Foot, A. Kirsten. 2005, "Web Sphere Analysis: An Approach to Studying Online Action", in Hine, Christian. (ed.) 2005, <u>Virtual Methods Issues in Social Research on the Internet.</u> Oxford: Berg. Pages 157-170.
- Scholte, Jan Aart. 1996, "The Geography of Collective Identities in a Globalizing World", in <u>Review of International Political Economy</u>. Vol. 3, No. 4. Pages 565-607.
- Schulz, H and Hammer, J. 2003, <u>The Palestinian Diaspora, Formation of identities and politics of homeland.</u> London: Routledge.
- Schwandt, T.A. 1997, <u>Qualitative inquiry: A dictionary of terms</u>. Thousand Oaks, CA: Sage Publications.
- Seabrook, Jeremy. 2003, <u>The No-nonsense guide to World Poverty.</u> London: New Internationalist Publications ltd.
- Segal, Ronald. 1998, "Globalization and the Black Diaspora", WPTC-98-15, November 1998. Accessed online on 17/09/2007.

- Servon, Lisa J. 2002, <u>Bridging the digital divide: technology, community and public policy</u>. Oxford: Blackwell Publishing Ltd.
- Sheffer, Gabriel. 2003, <u>Diaspora Politics: At home abroad</u>. Cambridge: Cambridge University Press.
- Shepperson, George and Price, T. 1958, <u>Independent African.</u> Edinburgh: Edinburgh University Press.
- Shepperson, George. 1993, "African Diaspora: Concept and Context". In Harris, Joseph. (ed.) <u>Global Dimensions of the African Diaspora</u>. Washington, D.C.: Howard University Press. Page 46.
- Shields, Rob. (ed.) 1996, <u>Cultures of Internet virtual spaces, real histories, living bodies</u>. London: Sage Publications.
- Shields, Rob. 1996, "Introduction: Virtual Spaces, Real Histories and Living bodies" in Shields, Rob. (ed.) <u>Cultures of Internet virtual spaces, real histories, living bodies</u>. London: Sage Publications. Pages 1-10.
- Shuval, Judith. 2000, "Diaspora Migration: Definitional Ambiguities and a Theoretical Paradigm", in <u>International Migration.</u> Vol. 38, No. 5. Pages 41-57.
- Shyllon, Folarin. 1974, <u>Black Slaves in Britain.</u> London: Oxford University Press.
- Shyllon, Folarin. 1977, <u>Black People in Britain 1555-1833.</u> London: Oxford University Press.
- Silverman, David. 2005, <u>Doing Qualitative Research, Second Edition</u>. London: Sage Publications.
- Silverstone, Roger. 1994, <u>Television and Everyday life</u>. London: Routledge.
- Silverstone, Roger. 2005, <u>Media, Technology And Everyday Life In Europe: From Information to Communication.</u> London: Ashgate Publishing, Ltd.
- Simola, R. 2000, "Time and Identity: the Legacy of Biafra to the Igbo in diaspora" in <u>Nordic Journal of African Studies.</u> Vol. 9, No. 1. Pages 98-117.
- Sinclair, John and Cunningham. 2000, "Go with the flow: Diasporas and the Media", <u>Television and New Media.</u> Vol.1 No.1. Pages 11-31.
- Skinner, Elliot, P. 1982, "The Dialectic between Diasporas and Homeland", in Harris, Joseph. 1982, <u>Global Dimensions of the African Diaspora</u>. Second Edition. Washington, D.C.: Howard University Press.
- Sklair, Leslie. 1998, "Transnational practices and the analysis of the global system", Seminar delivered for the Transnational Communities Programme Seminar Series, Oxford University. 22/05/1998
- Slevein, James. 2000, <u>The Internet and Society</u>. Cambridge: Polity Press.

- Smith, A. Marc and Kollock, Peter. 1999, <u>Communities in Cyberspace</u>. London: Routledge.
- Smith, Andrew. 2006, "'If I have no money for travel, I have no need' Migration and Imagination'', in <u>European Journal of Cultural Studies.</u> London: Sage Publications. Vol. 9, No. 1. Pages 47-62.
- Smith, Anthony. 1991, <u>National Identity</u>. London: Penguin Books.
- Smith, Anthony. 1994, "Gastronomy or geology? The role of nationalism in the reconstruction of nations." <u>Nations and Nationalism.</u> Vol. 1, No. 1. Pages 3-23.
- Smith, Anthony. 1995, <u>Nations and Nationalism in a Global Era</u>. Cambridge: Polity Press.
- Smith, Anthony. 1998, Nationalism and Modernism: A Critical Survey of Recent Theories of Nations and Nationalism. London: Routledge.
- Smith, Anthony. 1999, <u>Myths and Memories of the Nation</u>. Oxford: Oxford University Press.
- Smith, Anthony. 2002, "Dating the nation", in Daniele, Conversi. (ed.) 2002, Ethnonationalism in the Contemporary World. London. New York: Routledge.
- Smith, Micheal Peter and Guarnizo, Luis Eduardo. (eds.) 1998, <u>Transnationalism From Below</u>. New Jersey: Transaction Publishers.
- Smith, Micheal Peter and Guarnizo, Luis Eduardo. 1998, "Transnationalism from below", in <u>Comparative Urban and Community Research</u>. New Brunswick: Transaction Publishers.
- Smith, Robert. 2004, "Actual and Possible uses of cyberspace by and among states, diasporas and migrants". Accessed at http://www.nautilus.org/gps/vitual.diasporas/papers/smithpaper.html on 21/04/2007.
- Smith, T.M., 1983, "On the validity of Inferences from Non-random Samples", Journal of the Royal Statistical Society, Vol. 146. Pages 394-403.
- Somerville, P. 1989, "Home sweet home: A critical comment in Sounders and Williams" in <u>Housing Studies</u>. Vol. 4, No. 2. Pages 113-118.
- Sreberny, Annabelle. 1991, "The Global and the Local in International Communication", in Curran, J., and Gurevitch. 1991, <u>Mass Media and Society</u>. London: Arnold. Pages 93-119.
- Stalder, Felix. 2006, <u>Manuel Castells The Theory of the Network Society.</u> Cambridge: Polity.
- Stalker, Peter. 2001, <u>The No-Nonsense Guide to International Migration</u>. Oxford: New Internationalist Publications Ltd.

- Stamatopoulou-Robbins, Sophia Chloe, 2005, "Palestine online: An emerging virtual homeland?" <u>Refuge Studies Centre, Working Paper Series</u> Department of International Development, Queen Elizabeth House, University of Oxford.
- Stige, Brynjulf. 2002, "General Criteria for the evaluation of qualitative research articles". Accessed at http://www.njmt.no/forumqualart_1.html on 25/02/2008.
- Suasek, Maruska. 2002, "Narratives of 'Home' and 'Homeland': The symbolic construction and appropriation of the Sudeten German Heimat", in <u>Identities: Global Studies, Culture and Power</u>. Vol. 9. Pages 495-518.
- Takourang, Joseph. 2004, "Contemporary African Immigrants to the United States". Accessed at http://www.africanmigration.com/articles/j_takourang.htm. on 17/03/2004.
- Tapper, Richard. 2001, "Anthropology and (the) Crisis: Responding to the Crisis in Afghanistan", in <u>The Journal of the Royal Anthropological Institute</u>. Vol. 17, No. 6. Pages 13-15.
- Taylor, Philip. 1997, <u>Global Communication, International Affairs and the Media since 1945</u>. London and New York: Routledge.
- Tehranian, Majid and Tehranian Katherine Kia. 1997, "Taming Modernity: Towards a New Paradigm" in Mohammadi, Ali. (ed.) <u>International Communication and Globalization.</u> London: Sage Publications. Page 119-167.
- Thornton, John. 1992, <u>Africa and Africans in the making of the Atlantic World, 1400-1800 (Second Edition).</u> Cambridge: Cambridge University Press.
- Thussu, Daya Kishan. (ed.) 2007, <u>Media on the Move Global flow and contra-flow</u>. London: Routledge.
- Thussu, Daya Kishan. 2000, <u>International Communication: Continuity and Change.</u> London: Arnold.
- Tololyan, Khachig. 1996, "Rethinking Diaspora(s): Stateless Power in the Transnational Movement" in <u>Diasporas</u>. Vol. 5. No. 1. Pages 3-36.
- Tomlinson, John. 1999, <u>Globalization and Culture.</u> Cambridge: Polity Press.
- Tsagarousianou, Roza. 2004, "Rethinking the Concept of Diaspora: Mobility, Connectivity and Communication in a Globalised World" in <u>Westminster Papers in Communication and Culture,</u> 2004, (University of Westminster, London). Vol.1 No. 1. Pages 52-65.
- Tsaliki, L. 2003, "Globalization and hybridity: The construction of Greekness on the Internet", in Karim, H. 2003, <u>The Media of Diaspora</u>. London: Routledge.

- Tunstall, Kate. (ed.) 2006, <u>Displacement, Asylum, Migration</u>. The Oxford Amnesty lectures, 2004: Oxford University Press
- Turkle, Sherry. 1995, <u>Life on the Screen: Identity in the age of the Internet</u>. New York: Simon and Schuster.
- Uya, Okon Edet. 1971, <u>Black Brotherhood: Afro-Americans and Africa.</u> Lexington: Lexington, MA: D.C. Heath.
- Van Der Zon, Marian. 2008, "'Aliens go Home': A Critical Media Analysis of the Chinese Migrants". Accessed online at http://www.islandnet.com/~vipirg/publications/pubs/student_papers/00_chinese_migrant_media_analysis.pdf on 25/03/2008.
- Van Dijk, Jap. 1999, <u>The Network Society.</u> London: Sage Publications.
- Van Hear, 1998. <u>New Diasporas: Dispersal and Regrouping of migrant communities</u>. Seattle: University of Washington Press.
- Vertovec, S. 2000, "Religion and Diaspora". Paper presented at the conference on "New Landscapes of Religion in the West", School of Geography and the Environment, University of Oxford. Accessed online on 22/11/2007.
- Vertovec, S. 1999, "Conceiving and researching transnationalism", in <u>Ethnic and Racial Studies</u>. Vol.22, No. 2. Accessed online at http://www.transcomm.ox.ac.uk/working%20papers/conceiving.PDF on 19/02/2007.
- Vertovec, S. 2005, "The Political Importance of Diasporas", in <u>Centre on Migration, Policy and Society.</u> Working paper No13, University of Oxford. Accessed online on 20/12/2007.
- Vertovec, S. 2006, "The Emergence of Super-Diversity in Britain", in <u>Centre on Migration, Policy and Society</u>. Working paper No 25, University of Oxford. Accessed online on 20/12/2007.
- Vertovec, S. and Cohen R. (eds.) 1999, <u>Migration, Diaspora and Transnationalism,</u> Cheltenham: Edward Elgar Publishing Limited.
- Vertovec, Steven. 2001, "Transnationalism and identity" in <u>Journal of Ethnic and Migration Studies.</u> Vol. 27, No. 4. Pages 573-582.
- Wa Thiongo'o, Ngugi. 1981, <u>Decolonising the Mind: The Politics of Language in Africa Literature.</u> London: John Currey Ltd.
- Walliman, N. 2001, <u>Your Research Project, A Step-by-Step Guide for the First-Time Researcher</u>. London: Sage Publications.
- Wang, J. 2006, "The Politics of Goods: A case study of consumer nationalism and media discourse in contemporary China", in <u>Asian Journal of Communication</u>.Vol.16, No. 2. Pages 187-2006.
- Ward, K. 2005, "Internet Consumption in Ireland-Towards a 'connected' domestic life", in Silverstone, R. (ed.) 2005, <u>Media Technology and Everyday life in Europe</u>. London: Ashgate Publishing Limited.
- Waters, Malcolm. 1995, <u>Globalization.</u> London: Routledge.

- Webster, Frank. 2002, <u>Theories of the Information Society 2nd Edition</u>, London: Routledge.
- Wellman, Barry. Janet, Salaff. Dimitrina, Dimitrova. Laura, Garton. Milena, Gulia and Caroline, Haythornthwaite. 1996, "Computer Networks as Social Networks", in <u>Annual Review of Sociology.</u> Vol. 22. Pages 211-238.
- Westwood, S. and Phizacklea, A. 2000, <u>Trans-nationalism and the politics of Belonging.</u> London and New York: Routledge.
- Willis, Paul. 2000, <u>The Ethnographic Imagination</u>. Cambridge: Polity.
- Wilmot, Patrick. 2006, "Murtala Mohammed". Paper delivered in Kano, Nigeria, 13/02/2006 at a symposium on General Murtala Mohammed, assassinated former Nigeria's military ruler.
- Wilmot, Patrick. 2006, "To them that hath: corruption and the destruction of Africa", Paper delivered in Kano, Nigeria, 13/02/2006 at a symposium on General Murtala Mohammed, assassinated former Nigeria's military ruler.
- Wilson, Carlton. 1997, "Conceptualizing the African Diaspora", <u>Comparative Studies of South Asia, Africa and the Middle East</u>. (Formerly South Asia Bulletin), Vol.XVII No 2. Accessed online on 12/04/2006.
- Winston, Brian. 1998, <u>Media Technology and Society. A history: From the Telegraph to the Internet</u>. London: Routledge.
- Wood, A.F. et al, 2001, <u>Online Communication: Linking technology, identity and culture</u>. Philadelphia, PA: Lawrence Erlbaum Associates.
- Woodward, Kath. 2000, <u>Questioning identity: gender, class, nation</u> London and New York: Routledge.
- Woodward, Kathryn. (ed.) 1997, <u>Identity and difference</u>. London: Sage Publications.
- Woolgar, Steve. (ed.) 2002, <u>Virtual Society? Technology, Cyberpole, Reality.</u> Oxford: Oxford University Press.
- Yanow, Dvora. 2006, "Dear Reviewer, Dear Author: Looking for Reflexivity and Other Hallmarks of Interpretative Research". Prepared for delivery at the 2006 Annual Meeting of the American Political Science Association, August 30th -September 3, 2006.
- Young, Micheal. 2001, "Time, Habit and Repetition in Day-to-Day life" in Giddens, Anthony. (ed.) 2001: <u>Sociology: Introductory Readings</u>. Revised edition, Cambridge: Polity Press.
- Zachary, G. Pascal. 2005, "Diaspora, Capitalism and Exile as a way of life: Some observations on the political and economic mobilization of dispersed peoples". Accessed at http://www.nautilus.org/archives/virtual-diasporas/paper/zachary.html on 11/02/2005.

- Zack-Williams, A.B. 1997, "Africa Diaspora Conditioning: The case of Liverpool" in <u>Journal of Black Studies</u>. Vol. 27, No.4. Pages 523-542.
- Zuelow, Eric. 2006, The National Project, National studies information clearing house. Accessed at http://www.nationalismproject.org /about.htm on 01/08/2006.

Official Reports/Special Studies

- "Against Race-A Review" Cambridge: Harvard University Press, 2000. http://www.asante.net/articles/Gilroy-Review.html
- Diasporas, Migration and Identities: Report on AHRB Seminar, Bristol, 19, November 2004. <u>Breakout sessions</u> Terminology (facilitator: Robin Cohen, University of Warwick).
- <u>Irregular migration in the UK</u> an ippr fact file, April 2006. Institute of Public Policy Research. www.ippr.org
- Migration and Co-Development, 2006, <u>Social Remittances of the African Diasporas in Europe. Case studies: Netherlands and Portugal</u>. North-South Centre of the Council of Europe
- <u>Nigeria: People, Environment and Development, 2003,</u> Publication of Community Conservation and Development Initiatives, Lagos
- Report on the high level Committee on the Indian Diaspora, August 2000 in <u>Other Diasporas: A Global Perspective</u> http://indiandiaspora.nic.in /contents.htm
- <u>World Migration 2003, Managing Migration, Challenges and Responses for People on the Move</u>, IOM International Organisation for Migration, Geneva, Switzerland.
- Heath, Anthony. McMahon, Dorren and Roberts, Jane. 1999, "Ethnic Differences in the Labour Market: a comparison of the SARs and LFS". The Centre for Research into Elections and Social Trends is an ESRC Research Centre based jointly at the National Centre for Social Research (formerly SCPR) and the Department of Sociology, University of Oxford. Accessed at http://www.crest.ox.ac.uk on 20/07/2008.

ABOUT THE AUTHOR

Dr. Abiodun Adeniyi had his first degree from the Ahmadu Bello University (ABU), Zaria, after which he worked at Today Newspapers, Kaduna, as Lagos Correspondent. He soon joined The Guardian Newspapers, Lagos, Nigeria, covering various beats in Lagos and Abuja, for more than a decade. Adeniyi had earlier bagged a Diploma in Journalism at the International Institute of Journalism (IIJ), Abuja, Nigeria. He won the British Chevening Scholarship in 2003 to study International Communications at the University of Leeds, England (being one of 35 selected candidates of over 10,000 applicants) and began his Ph.D. research immediately after his Master's Degree programme at the same University. He was awarded his doctorate degree in Communication Studies in 2008, for his research on Internet and Diasporic Communication: Dispersed Nigerians and the Online Mediation of Distance, Longing and Belonging. The research investigated the intersections between international communication and the construction of identity, the evocation of nationalism, and how transnationalism is played up in the matrix. He used the Nigerian Diaspora as a case. His PhD thesis is one of few African-Centred theses first published by the University of Leeds under the joint Etheses Project. The project ran with the Universities of Sheffield and York.

Adeniyi returned to his native Nigeria in 2009, working as a Communications Consultant on the platform of the World Bank Economic Reform and Governance Project (ERGP) at the Bureau of Public Procurement (BPP), Presidency, Abuja. On expiration of the contract, he became Lead Consultant at Witswords Consults Limited (WCL), Abuja, before joining Baze University, to teach and to resume his extensive works in Diasporic Communication, specifically redefining how the nascent Nigerian Diaspora is imagined and re-imagined, against the background of changing technologies of communication; and how they appropriate these opportunities for relating with origin, with each other and with host community-a faint triangle in a sometimes fluid exchange of meanings.
He has been visiting professor of Communication and Multi-Media Design at the American University of Nigeria (AUN), Yola, a visiting professor of research methods for doctoral students at the University of Abuja and an external examiner to many universities, including the National Open University, Abuja. He is also an occasional consultant for a range of organisations including DFID, World Bank, European Union (EU), USAID, and the IOM/OIM, amongst others. Adeniyi has facilitated training in several Ministries, Departments and Agencies (MDAs), and for private organisations, in the fields of communication, enterprise promotion, efficiency and productivity improvement. He is sometimes engaged as an

individual consultant to senior private and public officials on speech writing, public policy, research, documentation, biography, strategy, issues, perception and impressions handling, or on various knowledge management affairs. He is regular at several Newspapers, TV and Radio Station, commenting on public issues, besides invitations to deliver public lectures, or as discussant in seminars, workshops and public conferences. Widely published, his other research interest aside Diasporic Communication are in the fields of strategic communication, and media and governance.